Look Back
With Gratitude

By DODIE SMITH

Novels

I Capture the Castle
The New Moon with the Old
The Town in Bloom
It Ends with Revelations
A Tale of Two Families
The Girl From the Candle-lit Bath

For Children

The Hundred and One Dalmatians
The Starlight Barking
The Midnight Kittens

Plays

Autumn Crocus
Service
Touch Wood
Call it a Day
Bonnet Over the Windmill
Dear Octopus
Lovers and Friends
Letter from Paris
I Capture the Castle
These People: Those Books
Amateur Means Lover

Autobiography

Volume I	*Look Back With Love*
Volume II	*Look Back With Mixed Feelings*
Volume III	*Look Back With Astonishment*
Volume IV	*Look Back With Gratitude*

Look Back With Gratitude

Dodie Smith

MULLER, BLOND & WHITE

First published in Great Britain in 1985 by
Muller, Blond & White Limited
55 Great Ormond Street
London WC1N 3HZ.

Reprinted 1986

British Library Cataloguing in Publication Data

Smith, Dodie
    Look back with gratitude: volume four of an
    autobiography.
    1. Smith, Dodie——Biography   2. Authors, English
    ——20th century——Biography
    I. Title
    828'.91209   PR6037.M38Z/

ISBN 0 584 11124 X
Typeset by D. P. Press Ltd, Sevenoaks, Kent
Printed and bound in Great Britain by
Redwood Burn Limited, Trowbridge, Wiltshire

TO

my husband, Alec Beesley, with gratitude as always – and to
Christopher Isherwood with many happy memories.

CONTENTS

ILLUSTRATIONS

I

To New York, 1939

On my voyage to America in January 1939 I began a Journal in a beautiful coral, leather bound, gilt-edged book, large and inspiring. It had been a present from my manager, Alec Beesley, whom I was soon to marry after seven years of all but legal marriage, following five years of devoted friendship, begun at Heal's where he was Advertising Manager and I was a Buyer. He was with me on the S.S. Manhattan, as was our much loved Dalmatian, Pongo, and our ex-actress housekeeper, Eileen Potter, whom we very much liked. This was to be no brief trip to New York (as my three previous ones had been) to help cast one of my plays and to go to theatres. This time we intended to see far more of America, certainly drive to California and then, possibly, go round the world.

I planned to write in the Journal every day and so, for many weeks, I did. Eventually the entries became less frequent, but much longer. Reading through the early pages I find the journal writer a stranger to me, not only to myself as I am now, but also to my remembered self. Could she have been quite sincere? Did I really like the S.S. Manhattan quite so much and enjoy the crossing more than any of my six previous Atlantic crossings? I now suspect I was out to sell myself happiness.

Someone who did, surprisingly, enjoy the voyage was Pongo. He was given a large double kennel from which he could see other dogs and swiftly started a flirtation with a brown lady spaniel. Alec exercised him round the decks every morning and, though always pleased to see Alec, he was also pleased to go back to his bed where he had churned his blankets into a nest. I spent much time with him and was encouraged to scratch his stomach but never permitted to tidy his bed. Sitting in his pen I learned to know owners who visited their dogs by their feet and legs.

We had told Eileen Potter to treat the voyage as a holiday and feel free to make friends – which we seldom wanted to do. She said firmly that she would help exercise Pongo but, on the first morning, sent a message that she was too seasick. I went to see her. Surprised to hear we hadn't been sick, she said gloomily, 'We're *all sick* DOWN HERE,' managing to convey that Deck B (first class) was lower than the hold. But she recovered quickly and became the life and soul of a large party.

As for Alec, any boat was a joy to him and he was greatly looking forward to seeing more of the world. I kept telling myself I was, too.

We arrived in New York thirty hours late in bitter weather and were thankful to have no trouble with the customs beyond paying duty on Pongo. He was said to look a very valuable dog (he wasn't, except to us) and we willingly settled for twenty-five dollars. Then someone from the John C. Wilson office escorted us to our hotel.

Jack Wilson, whose production of my play *Dear Octopus* was running on Broadway, had booked us a housekeeping apartment at Essex House – not, to me, a glamorous hotel but it was comfortable and overlooked Central Park, ideal for Pongo. He showed his approval by a prolonged rolling on our wine-coloured carpet; later we were moved to a suite with an off-white carpet which didn't show his hairs. He was well-liked by the staff. A lift attendant once remarked, with obvious approval, 'Spoilt rotten, isn't he'?

We already knew that *Dear Octopus* in New York was unlikely to be as successful as *Dear Octopus* now was in London, or as my *Call It A Day* had been in New York. The notices had not been bad, but rather tepid, and it was in a very large theatre with a very expensive cast. The direction, by my co-director in London, Glen Byam Shaw, was intended to be an exact copy of London but nothing came out the same. Much of the comedy had gone. Lucille Watson, in the Marie Tempest part, seemed to me competent but charmless. Lillian Gish was certainly charming but as Lillian Gish, not as the character I had created. Even Jack Hawkins, never less than excellent, was too extrovert for the part created by John Gielgud. Still audiences were mildly enthusiastic, business was said to be 'building' and Jack Wilson planned to transfer to a smaller theatre. There was plenty of optimism.

We were extremely busy. I gave various interviews, hoping to help the play. We went to many theatres, were entertained by many people, did much entertaining ourselves. A dinner party I particularly remember was given for us by Elmer Rice and his wife, in their apartment which looked along Broadway. Kurt Weill, the composer, and his wife were there, also that brilliant playwright,

Sydney Howard, and his wife. I had a long talk with Sydney Howard, who knew I planned to go to Hollywood but not work there. He earnestly advised me not to, adding, 'If you ever do, remember that working for movies can kill a playwright's capacity for self-criticism.'

We also talked about his farm, which he dearly loved. Six months later he was killed there. He had cranked his tractor; it had been left in gear, it leapt forward crushing him against a wall. To this day, I harrow myself by thinking of his agony and his realisation that there could be no escape.

Jack Wilson transferred *Dear Octopus* from the Broadhurst Theatre to the Morosco Theatre, where both my earlier plays *Autumn Crocus* and *Call It A Day* had run successfully. Now, I had taken no royalties in New York and I offered to share a little in the losses, if there were any. In the second week of the *Dear Octopus* transfer, business did go up slightly, but not enough and Jack felt that we must close. Every member of the company then offered to play for fifty dollars a week but neither Jack nor I felt we could accept this most generous offer, as there was little booking. So the run ended. I was sorry for Jack, who had tided the play through seven losing weeks, and sorry for the loyal company; and I had come to see that miscasting was not the only reason for failure. The play was too typically English to please New York at that time. England was thought to be effete, complacent, lazy. We should go to war with Germany and they would cheer us on. I remember writing to Sir Ambrose Heal. 'There is a lot of vicarious belligerence over here.'

On February 21st, towards the end of the run of *Dear Octopus*, Alec and I got up early and, leaving Pongo with his devoted Mrs Potter, went off to Philadelphia where we were to be married by a judge. This had been arranged for us by Maurice Speiser, an excellent attorney to whom Jack Hawkins and his wife, Jessica Tandy, had introduced us. (They had first met in my *Autumn Crocus*.) There were various advantages to being married in Pennsylvania rather than in New York, one of which was that we should avoid publicity. I did not want the news to reach certain friends in England until I felt sure my letters about it to them had arrived. I had imagined that being married by a judge would be similar to an English registry office marriage and was not pleased when we were treated to a long, fully religious ceremony, but at least the judge did not lecture us. Maurice gave us a wedding breakfast at his beautiful old Philadelphia house, and we then went back to New York and did not say one word about the wedding to anyone.

But we were not able to avoid publicity. Astoundingly soon New York papers were telephoning to say the news was already in the English papers and how it got there I never did discover. I didn't mind American publicity. But I winced when I heard that an English Sunday paper was quoting me as saying, 'I, who have given romance to so many others, now find it for myself.' Seeing that Alec and I had been married for seven years in every way but legally, I found this embarrassing.

We were now ready to drive to California but first had to settle Mrs Potter in a hotel where she could wait for us. We chose the one where Mrs Patrick Campbell lived with her Pekingese dog, Moonbeam, which she would not put through England's quarantine. I felt much sympathy for her – even if she had nearly knocked me backwards down the stairs of the Everyman Theatre in London when I was a struggling actress.

We set out on March 10th, with a driver to get us through New York's heavy traffic. Strange to remember now that our much-loved Rolls-Royce, brought from England, my greatest extravagance, had cost new just under £2,000. It was a pale grey, custom-built, Sedanca-de-Ville. Once we were on our own Alec opened up the front; Pongo, warm behind his electrically-operated glass division, as usual sat arrogantly with his elbow on the armrest.

Not long after the driver left us, when we were on an almost empty road, I saw to my horror a car coming straight at us. Mercifully, the driver swerved sharply and passed us without accident. Alec has always said that the shock of that moment cured him forever of driving on what was, for America, the wrong side of the road. In all the thousands and thousands of miles we drove in America, including six long coast-to-coast journeys, it was the nearest he ever came to having an accident.

The fact that we were now married lent that journey a honeymoon quality and it was certainly more convenient at hotels; though whenever practical we have continued to prefer separate bedrooms. I am quite sure this has contributed to the long happiness of our marriage. We spend so much more time together than the average married couple, sharing so many of our waking hours. We are always so happy in each other's company and yet we both of us like a certain amount of privacy. The nights are a good time for it.

Possibly we are freaks, though perfectly normal regarding sexual matters. And as we have now been happily married for over forty-five years, I sometimes think many marriages might benefit from our kind of freakishness.

It was to take me ninety-five pages of my Journal to get us to Beverly Hills. Through Pennsylvania, Maryland, Virginia, the Carolinas, Georgia, Florida, Mississippi, Louisiana, Texas, New Mexico, Arizona . . . through thousands of miles of high roads often spoilt by advertisements, but also through some beautiful country; and it was a particular pleasure to drive south from New York's winter into spring and then into summer. Towns – I especially liked Charleston, Savannah and other old towns of the South with their surviving great houses – New Orleans, Houston, San Antonio, El Paso on the Mexican border, Phoenix . . . I dutifully filled in my Journal every night, but I find it reminds me of little I have forgotten. I wrote appreciatively and cheerfully, but I also wrote of the worsening situation in Europe. And of course I was homesick. Lunching with me in New York, Lucille Watson had said, 'Beware of homesickness; it can take the blue out of the skies.' I was trying not to let it, so I remember it now more than I wrote about it then.

It took us a leisurely twenty-four days and over three thousand miles to reach Beverly Hills, by which time the coral leather Journal was nearing its end. I eventually had sections of journal-paper stapled and ready for binding. They never have been bound.

Of the whole trip I liked least the day we drove into California; I was bitterly disappointed in the arid countryside, and I never did come to like Los Angeles. But Beverly Hills was charming with its Drives planted with trees, many of them flowering, and its beautifully kept houses; I never saw two alike. We stayed at the Beverly Hills Hotel, already considered old-fashioned but there were newly-built houses in the grounds and we were the first tenants of the upper part of one of these. It was more luxurious than any New York hotel I had ever stayed in. We had a dining-room, a drawing-room, two bedrooms, a fully appointed kitchen and two bathrooms with huge square baths in which it was impossible to lie down without skidding. Our meals were brought hot from the hotel in far less time that it took to get room service in New York.

The evening we arrived Pongo scared us by refusing food but recovered when offered 'Breast of Chicken Marie Tempest, sous Cloche'. Presumably that dated from one of her long ago visits to

America. We thought of her, still playing *Dear Octopus* to capacity in London, a comforting thought after its New York fate.

After dinner Ned Brown of the Frank Vincent agency (a tie-up with my London agents) called on us. Poor young man he couldn't believe I didn't want to work in movies. Surely I would just *see* the Studios? He had already made appointments for me.

So next day, having engaged a young secretary to clear off a shoal of unanswered letters and to take care of Pongo, we went with Ned to Metro-Goldwyn Mayer and lunched with a pleasant man named Kenneth McKenna who already had a 'project' lined up for me. It was to make a screen-play out of several plays included in Noel Coward's *To-night at 8.30*; Metro thought the characters needed 'a little humanising'. I felt strongly that Coward characters were best left as Coward characters. But surely I could just *think* about it and come in one day and meet the producer, Sidney Franklin? Mr McKenna was very persuasive. I agreed.

From then on I was firmly taken to a different studio every day. Universal, United Artists, Warners, Fox . . . Everyone was pleasant. At the Selznick Studios it was suggested that I might tackle the film of *Intermezzo*, for Leslie Howard. We had tea with him and liked him. I was given a script by John van Druten, the English playwright, made from the Swedish version. There was nothing wrong with it, the dialogue was admirable, I didn't fancy rewriting good work. Meanwhile, Metro were being more and more persuasive. I met Sidney Franklin, an important producer I gathered, and liked him. Wouldn't I try the job just for a month?

We were liking Beverly Hills more and more. We had taken Pongo to the Pacific and let him run on the beaches. We had driven him up to the hills, where, after the rains the wild flowers were beginning. We knew many English players; I had actually enjoyed a few parties. (Never have I been a party girl.) True I was still homesick. Often in the evenings when we sat by our log fire (genuine eucalyptus logs, even if they were assisted by a gas flame) I would tell myself it would now be dawn in our Essex cottage. I would remember the yew tree swaying at my bedroom window, a faint mist over the fields, the pond palely reflecting the first light . . . But I might as well be homesick in Beverly Hills as anywhere else and Metro were willing (if not exactly exuberant about it) to pay me $2,500 a week. *Dear Octopus* in London was still making plenty of money but we were spending plenty. Was it wise to sneeze at making $10,000 for four weeks' work? I agreed to try

Metro – subject, of course, to a satisfactory contract.

That contract! Arguments with my agents went on and on. The worst trouble was in connection with my trial month during which, it now seemed, *I* was to be the one on trial. I shouldn't be free to leave at the end of the month. And though they did eventually agree to this, they insisted that, if I did decide to stay, I must sign on for three months or as long as they needed me, while they could get rid of me at the end of any week. None of this fitted with what had been said to me by Kenneth McKenna and by Sidney Franklin, who assured me it was all the fault of 'the boys in the front office', but as the boys remained adamant I bowed out, though remaining on good terms with McKenna and Franklin who said they still hoped we could work together one day.

I now regretted I had ever considered working in Hollywood, after all the years I had said I never would. My job was the theatre. Anyway, we would now move on, especially as life in Beverly Hills seemed a bit expensive when I had just kissed goodbye to $10,000. We would go and see San Francisco.

Most of our journey was within sight of the sea, often almost on the edge of golden beaches. On the other side of the road were high hills on which there were frequent notices of 'Danger. Rocks falling' and sometimes 'Dangerous but Passable', which struck me as a good title for a play. We broke the journey by staying the night at San Luis Obispo and then just outside Carmel, a small town with a nursery-rhyme charm and a stretch of coast line where sea lions disported themselves close to the shore. We stayed there a day and explored the inland country and, in the beautiful Carmel valley, we found a little place named Robles del Rio. There was a small hotel run by a Canadian mother and son. Everything was simple and charming. There was a good swimming pool and, as yet, very few guests. Pongo was welcomed in the dining room. There were bungalows with large picture windows looking towards a vast stretch of green hills. We decided to stay a few days and stayed for seven weeks.

One reason for this was that I at last had an idea for a new play and, working on a large table at my picture window, I never had a more peaceful workroom or a more beautiful view, which I never tired of looking at; indeed, I looked at it more often than at my work. I seemed to have got out of the habit of writing. But it would come back . . . given a little time. Meanwhile, we decided to do some serious reading.

There was a good bookshop in Carmel where we bought around a dozen Tolstoys in the Oxford University Pocket Edition and started on a course of chain-reading. I loved *Anna Karenina* and some of the shorter books, but my progress with *War and Peace* was slow. It was to Alec whom Tolstoy really meant most. He said he felt as if he had found a friend, and *The Kingdom Of God Is Within You* was the nearest he ever got to a religion. The only Tolstoy I ever disliked is *What Is Art?* which I continue to think is a very wrong-headed book. Looking back, I see that the habit of really serious reading was the first of the blessings that came to me through living in America.

Sometime after we settled down I was tempted to go back to Hollywood to work on the film of *Rebecca*. Alfred Hitchcock, who was to direct, had asked for me. I had known Hitchcock in London and liked him; I liked him even better after we now had two long telephone talks. The job was simply to supply dialogue; he was already working on the story-line with someone else and I doubted if I could turn out good dialogue for a story and characters so very unlike my own work and there was absolutely no scope for humour. Also I had not particularly liked the novel. I put all this to Hitchcock and asked him to think it over. He rang me next day to say I had given him a sleepless night but he still wanted me. He eventually persuaded me to agree but I regretted it afterwards, feeling sure I should let him down. I need not have worried. The terms of the contract were quite impossible. I should have had to remain for just as long as the studio wanted me. I bowed out with relief but regretted, and still regret, that I wasn't able to work with Hitchcock.

We settled down into our peaceful routine and I got on better with my play; I neared the end of the first act. Then disaster struck. Pongo bit a five-year-old child.

It happened by the swimming pool when Alec and Pongo were alone there. I was writing in my room. Pongo was safely tethered to a tree with his dinner dish beside him, in which he had left a few biscuits. Alec dived, swam under water, and came up to find Pongo barking and a child screaming. Alec had barely picked the child up before the bathing-pool attendant, who liked Pongo, rushed out of the hotel to say that he had seen the incident through a window and the child had both pulled Pongo's tail and attempted to steal Pongo's dinner. (Simultaneously?) The proprietors of the hotel then came out and were solidly on Pongo's side. The child was not a guest, but the son of people who lived nearby and who had been warned again and again not to let him come to the pool on his own.

But he was both screaming and bleeding and a doctor had to be sent for, all the more so as the child's parents had now arrived and were most belligerent.

The doctor said it was a very small bite and Pongo, now at his affectionate best, was obviously a healthy dog, but as in America there was always a fear of rabies, the health authorities would have to be notified. We drove into Carmel and got Pongo an attorney.

The attorney couldn't have been kinder, nor could the health authorities who came next day to inspect Pongo and the child. We got the impression that they liked Pongo best. All that was asked of us was that we would stay in the locality for three weeks. Then another inspection took place, Pongo and the child were pronounced in perfect health. We gave the child a handsome present and Pongo's attorney refused to be paid for holding a watching brief. All was well – except that for me the peace of Robles had been shattered and my work on the play had dried up. So, too, had the Californian hills and though their uniform gold was almost more beautiful than their uniform green had been, for me they were now arid.

So on to San Francisco which we knew was considered an impressive town. We spent a dutiful week being impressed by it. What I remember best are the steep hills where the cable cars looked as if they were going to slide down backwards. Then we both decided we wanted to get back to the East Coast. Neither of us any longer wished to go round the world. Alec felt sure there would be a crisis in Europe by the late summer. New York would now be too hot so we would drive to New England. Another three thousand miles lay ahead of us, but by a northerly route different from our earlier coast to coast drive.

It had been cool, even cold in San Francisco with a wind blowing the sea mist into the bay. Nothing had prepared us for the fierce onslaught of heat we soon ran into. We usually drove with the front of the Rolls open and Alec still preferred this, even in the blazing sun. But I have never been able to stand much direct sunlight. I cowered in the back and took my mind off my own discomfort by trying to help Pongo. He was near collapse, then I managed to get some ice cubes which I rubbed on his head. When they melted I slopped the remaining ice-water over him and myself. In the early evening we stopped at a small hotel. It had a weedy pond which was most uninviting, but it invited us all right and the three of us hurried into it to cool off.

After another almost unbearably hot day we decided to sleep during the days and drive by night. Some of the dawns were beautiful, but Pongo could not get the hang of sleeping all day and would demand to be taken out. In Spokane, at midday, he showed clearly that the pavement was scorching his paws and, after barely sketching a leg lift, pulled on his leash back into the hotel. I was glad when, having driven up into the cooler Rockies, we were able to stop trying to turn day into night.

Whenever we pulled up in a town the Rolls created a sensation. In Bismarck, North Dakota near the Canadian border, while Alec was studying a map, I heard a cry of, 'Oh, look! There's a funny old car!' and within seconds we were surrounded by a crowd of well over fifty people. One old man, after giving our two-year-old Rolls a long, silent look, said, 'Well, I don't want it.'

However, someone called at our hotel and invited us to be shown over Bismarck's civic buildings, which we found most impressive.

By the time we eventually reached New England the weather was perfect and we greatly liked the countryside. We stayed for a peaceful week at a small hotel in Dorset, Vermont from which we drove around exploring, and going over several houses which could be rented by the month. The proprietor of the hotel took great trouble to please us and was particularly nice to Pongo. Then he staggered us by assuring us we should never meet a Jew in his hotel. No one with a Jewish name or face was ever admitted knowingly; and if he did, after a day or so become suspicious, he would ring up the guest and ask for a subscription to a Jewish charity and any guest who agreed to send one was instantly got rid of. This story so shocked us that we were thankful when we found a house we wanted to rent.

It was on the outskirts of Manchester, Vermont, a beautiful village with a wide, tree-lined street of large white houses, all beautifully kept. Everywhere there was a feeling of antiquity. Our white weatherboard house was old, frail looking and filled with delicate early American furniture. It was surrounded by stony green fields and there was a stream in which I bathed – once only; it was the coldest water I ever got myself into. For the first time since I reached America I felt I was in a place where I could be happy – if only war didn't happen.

Eileen Potter then joined us from New York. She had occupied herself happily in reading and exploring the city, but she admitted that she had been a little lonely – until recently. With a beautiful,

actress-like gesture of the arms, she announced: 'Mrs Beesley, I'm
in love.' It seemed sad to take her away from New York at such a
moment, but we learned that there was a little matter of her new
friend's divorce to be settled and she would be happy to be with us
for at least six months. We all of us enjoyed settling in, exploring the
neighbourhood and talking, talking, mainly about England.

Alas, almost at once the war crisis in Europe began to loom. It
loomed larger and larger though the three of us assured each other
that war couldn't happen. We hired a radio, a very inadequate one,
and sat by it for hours. During those darkening days I found myself
comforted by the age of the house. It had been built long before the
American Revolution and I could almost think of it as an English
house. It was full of elaborate patterns, on the wallpapers, the
tufted rugs, the embroidered chair covers. Hour after hour my eyes
followed those patterns while we waited for news.

Each night I wrote in my Journal, summarising the day's
developments, buoying myself up with optimism. But on September
3rd, that inadequate radio relayed the sound of Mr Chamberlain's
voice declaring that England was at war. It was followed by an air
raid siren.

II

Back to California

Next day, the owner of our house and his wife, a well-to-do middle-aged couple, descended on us. We had met them when taking over the house and liked them, but nothing had prepared us for their enveloping kindness now, which was particularly American. To them, we were strangers in a strange land and in need of help, practical help. They wanted to drive us into New York to consult their attorney. Of course we must become citizens at once, surely we did not want to return to chaos in England? Everything could be arranged. . .

One memory of them has always remained with me. I was looking at the wife and thinking what a pretty woman she would be if she didn't use too much make-up, when she suddenly said, 'You're thinking I'd be quite pretty if I didn't make-up so heavily. The truth is that, without make-up, you'd never notice me.' I liked her greatly.

We never had the slightest intention of becoming American citizens but, as Alec was unfamiliar with traffic regulations, we did let them drive us into New York to find a hotel where we could spend the winter. Our present home, only ever let for the summer months, was not adequately heated. And we felt that New York would be a better centre for us in many ways.

We stayed at the Sherry Netherlands which I liked better than any other New York hotel I had stayed at. I remember thinking it would be my last taste of luxury for a long while as we must now settle at a much cheaper hotel. We could, legally, have got money from England but we were determined not to.

We eventually found a reasonably-priced housekeeping apartment at the Croydon Hotel which was fairly close to Central Park for Pongo's walks, and settled there in late September. Mrs Potter could cook for us here. We bought a small but fairly adequate radio on which I hoped to get news direct from England but never could. What I longed for was the *feel* of England – I longed to be there. Alec said he would go back any time I wished. But he was, and had been since his school-days at Dulwich College, during the 1914–18 war, an absolute conscientious objector and had refused to carry a gun and bayonet in his Officers' Training Corps. He'd been offered a drum, but came to feel it was part of militarism. So they let him resign from the O.T.C. When young, his grandmother taught him the maxim, 'Do unto others as you would be done by' (which he has tried to live up to). He considered that this, plus the terrible slaughter of the First World War, were the basis of his conscientious objection. It now seemed pointless to cross the Atlantic and say, 'We're here, but we won't do anything to help the war effort'. And the thought of quarantine for Pongo in wartime was unbearable.

So I lived from day to day, listening to the radio, reading and even painting; the view from our windows was dreary, but dreariness can be paintable. Later, I found an ink drawing I did of a Dalmatian in a London basement area, near the dustbin; I remembered he was to have been the hero of a story about Pongo, the famous dog detective. It was 17 years later that Pongo, then dead, became the hero of my children's book, *The Hundred and One Dalmatians*.

The only writing I did was in my Journal or in letters to England. Oh, the countless letters I wrote and received while in America.

In memory our period of marking time seems to go on and on, but in reality it was little over three weeks before Kenneth McKenna rang up from Hollywood with another offer from Metro. This was to work with Sidney Franklin on an old play, *Waterloo Bridge*, set in England during the First World War. I asked about salary. Oh, that would be the same as we had previously agreed. I should be free to leave at the end of a month and after that it would be a matter for discussion. Anyway, my agent would set it all out for me. All Mr McKenna wanted to know now was that I was willing to come. He was pleasant and persuasive and the play, by Robert Sherwood, sounded interesting. A month's salary would keep us for many months. I felt I'd do better to earn it than to sit in New York doing nothing. I agreed.

Alec and I plunged into plans and preparations and within hours we got a long telegram from my Hollywood agent setting out the whole offer. It now appeared Metro only intended to pay $2,000 a week, not $2,500. More telephone talks and telegrams followed. Kenneth McKenna insisted he had thought the earlier offer was for only $2,000 and he hadn't actually mentioned a figure on the telephone. Well, there just might have been some misunderstanding (I never quite believed this), anyway, the boys in the front office were now dead set on not paying more. Again I agreed, not realising I was doing myself a serious disservice for the future, for eventually the salaries of Hollywood writers were frozen at the highest one they had received before America entered the war and I was never able to earn more than $2,000 weekly.

Now everything was rush, rush. Metro were peeved because I wouldn't come at once, by train, because of Pongo. He would have had to travel in a 'suitable container' and no container in the world would have suited him. Metro finally agreed we should drive provided we kept in touch with them by telephone and telegrams. It must have been a gruelling drive for Alec, though he loved driving. I find I have only one memory of that over three-thousand-mile trip. We stayed at a motel in Phoenix where we were told of an English couple who had stayed there the previous week and the husband had, quite unexpectedly, died. I had been feeling depressed, more and more longing for England. I suddenly pulled myself up and counted my blessings.

Mrs Potter, escorting all our luggage by train, was at the Beverly Hills Hotel to welcome us. We had been given the pleasant apartment we had occupied in the Spring, but at once decided we must get a furnished house, which would be far cheaper. Alec found one and moved us into it in less than a week while I worked at Metro.

I had now read *Waterloo Bridge*. It was the story of a Canadian soldier who, in 1917, meets an American prostitute on Waterloo Bridge in a blackout. Believing her to be a respectable chorus girl he falls in love with her and wants to marry her. She runs away from him and he then learns the life she has been leading but he still wants to marry her. He searches for her and eventually finds her again on Waterloo Bridge. She begs him to leave her and go back to France – his leave is ended. Coerced by a Military Policeman, he goes. By then an air raid is in progress. She stands on Waterloo Bridge, holds up a lighted match and shouts: 'Here I am, Heinie! I'm right down here!'

Even the writing of a most distinguished American dramatist did not make this convincing to me. (Someone said of the proposed film, 'It's about the First War which nobody will like; it's about prostitution which the Censor won't like; and it's about the old

Waterloo Bridge which is no longer there.') So I was not outraged by the alterations Sidney Franklin proposed to make. He was already working on a new story line, assisted by two Germans one of whom, George Froeschel, I soon came to like and admire. The Canadian soldier was to become an officer in a famous English regiment. The girl (a part for Vivien Leigh) was to be a highly respectable ballet dancer watched over by a dragon of a ballet mistress (a part for Madame Ouspenskaya). They were to meet, have one gloriously romantic day and then the officer was to be whisked back to the trenches. Soon his death is (erroneously) announced. The girl, dismissed from the ballet and desperately poor, becomes a prostitute. The young officer returns, has no idea she is a prostitute, takes her to his home, intends to marry her. But all is discovered and she ends by throwing herself under an army lorry on Waterloo Bridge.

My job was to invent romantic details for this now preposterous story – and disabuse my German collaborators of a few ideas that were just a bit *too* romantic. (No, they couldn't, during the First World War, travel about England by stage coach). How should they spend their romantic day? I suggested an idyllic village and had to describe it pretty well house by house and shop by shop. What would there be in the window of the butcher's shop – something really unusual? I suggested a large, sleeping black cat. Sidney liked that. The village school children should be heard singing *John Peel*. Then there should be a ruined castle with a moat and swans. Fine – and then Sidney's interest flagged. Nothing was unusual enough. We must start again.

I was in despair. We had spent hours and hours on that village. Suddenly George Froeschel said, 'Let's make it a pouring wet day instead of a fine one.' I helped him to sell that one to Sidney Franklin, but the weather had to cheer up before we reached the ruined castle.

By the end of the first week we had come nowhere near hammering out the whole story-line, let alone clothing it with detail. One reason for our slow progress was that Sidney (not that I then called him by his Christian name) was constantly interrupting to tell some funny story, gossip about other movies and plays and, above all, talk of ailments, his own and those of friends whom he frequently telephoned for news.One friend appeared to be at death's door. I gathered that there had been nothing whatever wrong with him so he had felt he ought to have a check-up and they had found a GERM. Mr Franklin's manner became grave, then dramatic, finally he shook his head gloomily and told his secretary to remind him to telephone the hospital next day.

However, I was never less than impressed by his talents and he taught me something I was never to forget. I had been trying to cover up what he thought to be a deficiency in the story-line by saying I could make it convincing by characterisation, dialogue and humour. (Humour? In that story?) He said patiently that he loved my plays, he loved good characterisation, dialogue and humour. But he could seldom get any of them from any writer, so he had to count on the story-line alone to carry a movie through. And once again we went back to work on the story-line.

After two week's work in Sidney's office, the four of us had only reached the half-way house of the story, when the hero was called back to the trenches and the heroine was driven to prostitution. I then said that if Metro wanted any actual writing from me by the end of my trial month I must go home and start it. (I had insisted that I should write at home, not at the studio; most writers worked in offices and were expected to hand in five pages a day.) So I was hurried off, with everyone's good wishes.

The house Alec had moved us into was in Cove Way, Beverly Hills. It was meant to be an old English manor and even had bricks sticking out of the walls to indicate that there had been ruins. But it was a skilful fake and very pretty, built on a little hill and looking down on a garden and a kidney-shaped swimming pool. There were many beautiful trees, eucalyptus, the blue-flowered jacaranda, and mimosa. One mimosa tree was taller than the house. Our view, just across the road, was a stretch of wild hillside, belonging to Mary Pickford whose house, Pickfair, was a little way along the road. (Once when I was walking past it a police car drew up beside me. Unaware that walkers in Beverly Hills were regarded with suspicion, I thought I was being offered a lift and said sweetly, 'No, thank you. I'm just out walking my dog,' at which the police officers exploded with laughter and drove on.)

I had a particularly pleasant bedroom looking down on the swimming pool and up to the wild hill. Here I settled down to work and was getting on surprisingly well when, three days later, Sidney Franklin rang up to say he wanted to come and see me. No, he didn't expect to see any work but he had a few suggestions. I persuaded him to tell them to me on the telephone, saying I needed all my time to get the work done – and made it clear I needed to be left alone. But two days later he was back on the telephone again. The boys in the front office now insisted that he should come and see, well not actually the work, but they wanted to make sure I *was* working. Some writers who worked at home did not. So I let Mr Franklin come and he was much comforted by the piles of handwritten pages on my desk. He was also impressed by the house and the pool and the Rolls and the general set-up. He now suggested we should be on Christian name terms and said he hoped I would one day work with him on a film about Hans Christian Andersen. It would be a job we could take our time over, perhaps work at Palm Springs for a change. Meanwhile, the present job was most urgently needed.

So I worked all the weekend and by Monday night had achieved seventy pages of manuscript and reached as far as we had got to in the story-line. I then sent for a Metro secretary and dictated my work to her. It was hard to get the job done by the Friday night.

My trial month was now up so I had to decide if I would continue – provided Metro wanted me to. I enclosed a note with the script saying I was willing to, but adding that I did not feel I could continue working at quite such high pressure.

On Monday morning Sidney Franklin's secretary rang asking me to come to the studio. I asked to speak to him personally and he came on the line only long enough to say he had no time to talk, but could tell me definitely that Metro wanted me to continue. Not one word did he say about my work; still, I felt reasonably cheerful. But from the moment I entered his office I was engulfed in gloom. He began by saying he was sorry he'd asked me to come down as he now had a lunch engagement and could only spare a few minutes. He then said he and I must press on with the story-line while he had my work rewritten.

Distinctly taken aback, I asked why it needed rewriting. Oh, all scripts had to be rewritten. In my case there were technical faults and he thought some of my dialogue needed 'emotional heightening.' I hated the idea of anyone changing my dialogue so I asked if I couldn't do the work myself. He said no, I must stick to the story-line and he'd better warn me that, when I went back to writing dialogue, I'd have to work just as fast as I had been working. He was sorry but that was that.

His whole manner was so discouraging that I asked him point blank if he hadn't liked my work. He said he had and the prospective director of the picture had liked it and that Mr Mannix –

a very top boy in the front office, I gathered – had said that nobody else had ever offered them seventy pages of usable script in two weeks. But all this information was given to me in the most grudging offhand manner. There was no trace of the purring bonhomie he had doled out when he visited me only a few days earlier. What could have happened?

I had a flash of intuition. Again and again, I had seen him treat the two Germans, who had worked with us, in a manner on the edge of rudeness. It had often annoyed me, all the more as they accepted it humbly and treated him with great respect. I had always treated him as an equal and often argued with him – and sometimes suspected this annoyed him. Was he, now that I was signing on to stay for as long as he needed me, simply trying to establish supremacy? Much later, when I knew Hollywood better, I came to believe my intuitive judgement had been right.

During the conversation he threw in that, in spite of the rush, the whole job would take a considerable time as I might have to do one final rewrite of the whole script. I said quietly that I didn't think I could stay the course. I should get too tired to turn out good work. It would be better if I left *now*.

He looked annoyed, rather than distressed; said it would be difficult for him. I then said I would be happy to go on helping with the story-line, but I didn't feel I could write more dialogue. He said he would think it over and now he must go to lunch.

In the afternoon he rang up to say he would let me go. He was pleasant, almost apologetic and still said he hoped we should work together one day. But I think he knew, as I did, that the trouble between us was really a clash of personalities. He wanted a subservient writer and I should never be one. In some ways I quite liked him, but his typical Hollywood producer's Napoleonism was anathema to me.

My agents quickly brought me offers of more work but nothing that attracted me, even if I had now felt willing to try another film job. But we did not, for the moment, consider leaving Hollywood as we particularly liked our Beverly Hills house. It was mainly furnished with antiques bought in Europe by its owner, Marion Balderston, wife of John Balderston, part-author of a play I had greatly liked, *Berkeley Square*. It was at their house that I first met Charles Brackett, a very successful writer-producer of films. I liked him but nothing told me that he would later become one of the great friends of my lifetime, one of the most important blessings for which I can thank America.

The English colony in Hollywood had been officially told by the Consul to stay where it was and to try to enlist American sympathy for England's war effort. I can't feel that Alec and I ever did that, but it was a relief to feel there was no onus on us to return – for the moment; it was still a case of marking time. Meanwhile I must work on something, but what? Not a play; I couldn't let it be produced in London unless I was there. Could I learn to write a novel?

I read E.M. Forster's *Some Aspects of the Novel*, Percy Lubbock's *The Craft of Fiction* and then, by happy chance, found Henry James's *The Art of the Novel* in a Beverly Hills bookshop. The only book by James I had ever read was *The Turn of the Screw* which I hadn't much liked, and I knew he was supposed to be a difficult author. But soon after I began reading those prefaces to his own novels, I had the extraordinary experience of falling in love with the mind of a writer. I have always disapproved of underlining or marking books in any way, but I marked dozens of passages in *The Art of the Novel*, determined to be able to find them again. Then I started reading his novels but not many of them were easily available and, though I admired them, I was not, as yet, as fanatical about them as I was about the prefaces. Around this time we went to dinner with the novelist A.J. Cronin and his wife and I asked him the secret of writing a bestseller. He said, 'First, intensity. And in your case, stop reading Henry James.' I never did, but I did one day write a bestseller.

It was that evening that I met a director of Cronin's Boston publishers, Little, Brown & Co and he asked me, if I ever did write a novel, to send it to him. Possibly that encouraged me, as I did at last start work. My novel was to be called *A Queen in the Family* and was to be about a young Lancashire girl who, in the early nineteen-hundreds, married a minor Balkan royalty. Her adventures in the Ruritania which I intended to create in detail – uncomfortable, dangerous and far from romantic – were to cover forty years. But she never got as far as Ruritania as it took me over twenty thousand words to cover a fortnight on the Lancashire moors and I decided that no one with my passion for detail could be let loose in a novel covering forty years. Besides, another project was beckoning.

The editor of an English Sunday paper had again and again asked me to write an autobiography he could serialise. (Unbelievably, the title he suggested for this was *My Seven Tremendous Years*.) I certainly wouldn't write for his Sunday paper, but I would like to write a short autobiography. I particularly wanted to write about my family and my childhood. I would touch on my failures as an actress,

my years as a business woman and then as a playwright. I didn't
think it would take long.

It didn't. Never had I worked so fast. I had now taught myself to
touch-type and could create on the typewriter. With the greatest
ease I got myself to the age of twenty and then found I had typed a
hundred and fifty thousand words. The whole book would need to
be longer than *War and Peace*. And who would want to read it with
a war on and me out of England? Regretfully, because I liked what I
had written about my family, I packed it away and did not open the
packet for thirty years (when it eventually became *Look Back With
Love*, the first volume of my autobiography).

That year in Cove Way, Beverly Hills, from the autumn of 1939 to
the autumn of 1940, I considered myself unhappy, always homesick
for the English countryside and the London theatre world, always
anxious about the war and our own future. Yet I remember happy
interludes in that pleasant house and garden. We usually had lunch
by the pool, but we had the portable radio with us, listened to the
news every hour even if we were swimming. Always, always I hoped
for good news of the war and always, always, it got worse.

We had a good many friends, including John van Druten, whom
we met again at one of the John Balderstons' parties. I had seen
little of him since we had crossed the Atlantic together in 1932, after
which we had never become really friendly owing to a little
mischief-making on the part of a shared friend. He was still wary,
but he did ask us to dinner and we asked him back; and gradually,
like stiff-legged dogs beginning to wag their tails at each other, we
became at ease, all the more because, like Alec, John was a pacifist
and, like me, he was interested in Christian Science. But our real
friendship, another of the blessings I owe to America, came later.

By late summer, Eileen Potter, who had stayed with us far longer
than her stipulated six months, wanted to return to New York and
her elderly lover. (She had been a good friend and we kept in touch
with her until she died, back in England, thirty years later.) We
despaired of getting a reasonable replacement for her; also, as I was
still determined not to work on movies, we felt we ought to live in a
smaller house and a less expensive place than Beverly Hills. We
remembered little Carmel, near which we had stayed the previous
year, drove there and found a most unusual bungalow at less than a
third of the rent we were now paying. It had one very large, high,
raftered room with three tall, domed windows, a small dining room
almost surrounded by windows, three bedrooms, and a maid's

bedroom off the good kitchen. At the front there was a charming walled garden. But what attracted us most was that all the back windows looked across less than a hundred yards of rough grass to the Pacific, and bang in front of those three tall domed windows, was the rock where the sea lions disported themselves. We had been sad to think of leaving our pleasant house and pool but, with the thought of that view ahead of us, we finally drove off from Beverly Hills in high spirits.

III

Carmel Idyll

We were in the Seventeen Mile Drive, a large private residential area with an hotel, a Country Club and the beautiful Pebble Beach golf course. Few of the houses were close together and I remember no eyesores. There were woods and wooded hills. One could wander for miles along the narrow roads rarely meeting traffic or people. Deer grazed freely and often at night gazed at us through our tall, uncurtained windows their eyes reflecting the light. Pongo never chased the deer and was popular with the game wardens. There were no shops but Carmel was only a short drive away. One collected one's letters from the Country Club.

After some disasters with daily help we got a resident housekeeper, Miss Hickson, who was a New Zealander and more English than the English. When I asked her if she could make a steak-and-kidney pudding she said, 'My grandmother would have been mortified if I couldn't. She taught me.' Miss Hickson was widely travelled, having had to take to the boats in *two* separate shipwrecks, but remained an ultra respectable maiden lady, speaking the most exquisite English. Like all our help she adored Pongo and was, in every way, a pleasant person to share a small house with.

Soon after we settled, Gerald Savory, the playwright, and his pretty wife came to see us on their way to San Francisco. They brought with them a portable electric gramophone which changed its own records. I had never known such things existed and we hastened to get one and then, just as I had acquired an interest in serious reading during our earlier stay near Carmel, I now acquired an interest in classical music. I had, in a haphazard way, listened to it on the radio while in Beverly Hills and I knew just what records I wanted to start with. They were Brahms's First Symphony, Prokofiev's Classical Symphony and Cesar Franck's Symphonic Variations. I found a shop that would let me borrow all the records I wanted to try and we listened pretty well seven evenings a week, swiftly amassing a collection. Very early music, madrigals, Purcell, Scarlatti, Bach – but not the choral works: Beethoven – but not the symphonies (strange this, as I find Beethoven chamber music exquisite; the difficult late quartets, which came later, were never difficult to me). Handel but not The Messiah – Schubert, Brahms, Debussy, Ravel, Franck and, most particularly, Fauré. I am puzzled by the blind spots in my taste. Try as I might I could rarely enjoy Mozart, surely a terrible loss. And I like few symphonies or operas. My taste in modern music never got beyond Vaughan Williams though I worked hard on Hindemith and Bartok. Of course I added to my knowledge of music over the coming years but the basis of it, one of the great solaces of my lifetime, was found in Carmel, California.

Of popular music we mainly enjoyed Mexican records and West Indian calypsos, which I now find almost painfully nostalgic. For me, classical music is exempt from nostalgia; I seldom associate it with places or happenings. But a Mexican record will instantly take me back to Carmel where our life, in spite of devastating war news and perpetual homesickness, came to have an idyllic quality. We shared music and reading, we walked on the shore gathering exquisite sea shells and driftwood for our open fire some of it too beautiful to burn; one piece, known as 'Igdrasyl' trailed around with us for years. One day Alec met a small sealion stranded on a road a little way from the sea. He managed to carry it into our garage and sent for a game warden who said he knew that sealion pup and it was always coming out of the sea, and when sealions started doing that they really ought to be put down – unless one could find them a home in a tank. Alec heard of one through the local vet, at a hotel a few miles along the coast. And there, after bottle-feeding during the night, our sealion was installed with another. Alec had delivered it in the Rolls, handling it with considerable caution, having been told it had badly savaged two wardens. It had not previously occurred to him it might bite and he had carried it like a baby.

I don't remember any wintry weather but during the late autumn there was often a thick sea mist; once Pongo, out with us before going to bed, dashed off into the woods and came back smelling horrible after an encounter with a skunk. We rubbed him with some of the scented maquis-like herbs that grew all around hoping they might lessen the smell. They removed it entirely and the skunk discharge must have acted as a fixative for the herb scents, for

Pongo smelt heavenly for days.

Every morning Alec drove to the Country Club for letters, taking the coast road past Seal Rock. I would watch for him, seeing Pongo who, for this short trip, was allowed to travel at the front of the Rolls with his fore feet up on top of the windscreen, his ears blown back by the wind. We had so many letters from England that keeping up with them made it hard to find time for work. Most of Alec's time was spent on packing parcels for English friends. He turned our spare room into a work room and it came to resemble a grocer's shop. We gradually came to be sending parcels to forty people and had also to employ New York parcel-sending firms. But all the best parcels of clothes and food were packed by Alec. It was a comfort to send those parcels. My old Auntie Blanche had a letter returned to her by the Censor because she asked for some parrot seed; but as she told us about the Censor we knew what she wanted and the parrot got his seed. (It died the same day she did.)

In the spring there was a carpet of wild flowers between us and the Pacific. I counted twenty-two different kinds, some of them so small that we had to buy miniature vases to hold them. The spring made me long for our Essex cottage and it was partly to assuage that longing that I began a novel about a house built onto the ruins of a Suffolk castle which I had seen back in the nineteen-thirties. I invented an eccentric family who lived there and the work went well. I *knew* those people, I *lived* in that castle. I completed five long chapters and then – Rudolph Hess descended onto Scotland. In my foolishness – the wish being father to the thought – I imagined this meant that Germany would capitulate, the war would soon end. And by the time the excitement had blown over my zest for writing that novel had blown over, too. And then Pongo got ill.

Though he had never been a really strong dog since the kidney trouble that so nearly killed him in his youth, he had kept wonderfully well in America and now, at seven years old, was still puppyish enough to chew the heels of my slippers. Alec always took him for a morning walk and then, at six in the evening, there would be a very peremptory scratch on my door to tell me to stop work and to go for an evening walk. One evening, not long after we started out, Pongo stopped dead and hung his head. I noticed that he was breathing heavily. He was so unwilling to walk that I had difficulty in getting him slowly home. Next morning, he was coughing badly. The local vet said the trouble was now his heart.

There was nothing to be done but to cut down on his exercise –

which he no longer wanted to take – be careful with his diet and give him certain tablets. He improved and, for some weeks, was almost himself. Then the cough came back, unfortunately just when John van Druten was due to stay with us – or rather, we were putting him up at the Country Club, our spare room now being given over to parcel-packing.

John had written to me soon after we left Beverly Hills. I had answered and soon type-written letters were flying between us. He was capable of writing two long letters in one day and he wrote the kind of letters one wanted to answer instantly, even if only to disagree with him. It was through letters that we at last became real friends. The correspondence, which must amount to well over a million words, continued till his death in 1957; his last letter to me was written only the day before he died. As we both kept carbon copies, we both had a complete set of the letters and both sets survive.

We were determined that Pongo's illness shouldn't spoil John's visit for him and for several days I don't think it did. He was most sympathetic and, knowing that I was now out of touch with the Christian Science practitioner who had helped Pongo in England, he suggested I should ring up his Hollywood practitioner. This lady expressed supreme confidence and, unaccountably, laughed at everything I said. Such waves of unfaith in her flowed from me that I wonder she didn't dematerialize.

As Pongo was now worse, our local vet suggested we should take him to a celebrated vet at San Jose, half a day's drive away. Alec did so and was advised to leave him for treatment. We then concentrated on entertaining John, but we were miserable in case our poor dog was missing us and when John left a few days later we were on our way to San Jose almost before his car was out of sight. We found Pongo weaker but, according to the vet, not suffering and there was still hope. So we stayed at an hotel, seeing him twice a day trying to get him to eat. He always managed a flicker of his tail on sight of us, but the flickers got weaker and weaker and by the third day he would not even drink, though he would lick an ice cube if we held it to him. We remembered how, during his earlier illness in England, he had recovered when at death's door, but the vet at last said there was no hope whatever and that Pongo was now suffering. So we felt we must let him go.

I had never felt such grief since my mother died when I was eighteen. The only thing which helped me at all was writing in my

Journal, page after page about Pongo's life and death. At last I seemed to have written my worst grief out of my system, only to find it replaced by a frightening neurosis. I feared I had been responsible for Pongo's death.

One of the reasons we did not return to England was that we could not let him face the six month's quarantine. Had I, therefore, subconsciously wished him dead? If so, might I not now subconsciously wish Alec dead – because it was his attitude to war that was causing me to remain in America? To my conscious mind, he mattered more than anything in the world to me, but how did I know what my subconscious mind was up to? I had adored Pongo.

My subconscious mind must be firmly put in place. I would get another dog. I would get *two* dogs; that would be a double barrier against death wishes.

Of course I didn't let Alec know about my neurosis. I knew he was longing for another dog and we believed we should never get over Pongo's loss until we had one. I pointed out that *two* dogs might prevent our becoming so obsessed as we had been over Pongo. We must be sensible about these dogs.

There were no good Dalmatian puppies to be had anywhere near Carmel, but there were several well-known Dalmatian breeders near Beverly Hills. And the Rolls needed servicing. This would put it out of action for several days, but John van Druten at once offered us the use of his new car and chauffeur for the great Dalmatian hunt. So back to Beverly Hills.

We particularly wanted one of the puppies to be liver-spotted, not easy to find but we got one, a male aged two months, from a little-known kennels. And from Leo Meeker's famous 'Four-in-Hand' Kennels we were able to get a beautiful six months old black-and-white bitch. We eventually registered her as 'Four-in-Hand' Folly, and as the liver-spotted pup had no kennel name we registered him as 'Freckles of Finchingfield', hoping he would one day see our English village (which he did). He never learned to answer to 'Freckles' or any other name until we tried saying 'Buzz' very loudly. He took to that,

We boarded the pups with the Hollywood vet, who had once been Pongo's, until the Rolls was ready to take us back to Carmel. That return journey began disastrously; Folly was terribly car-sick. Fortunately, the car seats were protected by tough loose covers, but still we had to turn back; Alec had a theory that she might travel better by night. This proved to be the case. From darkness to dawn she was troubled by nothing but hunger; she had to be fed almost continuously. It took her six months to grow out of car sickness if she travelled by day. Hunger she never did grow out of. For her fourteen years of life she was the hungriest dog I ever knew.

So we came back at first light to the little house overlooking Seal Rock and at last the aching sense of loss for Pongo was assuaged. There is an old superstition that a good dog cannot enter heaven until his master has a new dog to guard him. I hoped that Pongo, now free even of his love for us, would find a shore as beautiful as Carmel's to gallop on and all his old desire to gallop.

Not that our two pups could be said to guard us. We, and practically everything in the house, needed guarding from *them*. I remember writing to John van Druten, 'I'd like to take them to the shore but I'm so afraid they might damage the sea.' It was then I decided that, whereas one dog is a pet, two dogs are a pack and our pack was too large for our small house. They were never still and there was no place where they could safely be shut up. They would have wrecked the little walled garden in a few minutes. Buzz was the worst. Though he adored Folly – and she him – he plagued her so much that she frequently took refuge under chairs. We could only get our meals in peace if we shut him in a wicker dog-house and covered it with a rug like covering a canary, turning his day into night.

We found a larger house, a little way inland, isolated and almost surrounded by woods. It had various advantages. The huge main living room, a Californian idea of a mediaeval Great Hall, was filled with heavy furniture that didn't look damageable. (We were wrong about that; Buzz had a knack for chewing the corners of upholstered furniture). There were six large bedrooms. We turned a downstairs one into a dogs' playroom, removing carpet, curtains and all furniture. Nothing remained but a built-in wooden window seat. Both pups chewed that.

Our dear Miss Hickson gave the vast kitchen a slightly wan look, but said the house would be 'an adventure'. (Well, she'd survived two shipwrecks). The pups, after a disastrous day, decided they were now house-trained (well, almost) and we were happy to give them access to a walled garden where there was nothing but grass and empty beds. (None of us yet knew there were bulbs in those beds.) There was something mournful about this many windowed but tree darkened house, but at least humans and canines could get away from each other sometimes and I was able to write.

I did research for a play to be set in 1910, in the London I first came to live in. I felt that, as I wasn't capable of writing about wartime England, I must take refuge in the past. The nearby Monterey Library was most helpful and I enjoyed the research, but couldn't get going on the play. I then made twenty-eight pages of research notes for a play to be set in Manchester in the year 1900. Not a line of this was written, but twenty-eight years later I used the title, *A Tale of Two Families*, for a novel set in Essex in the nineteen-sixties. I wrote dozens of letters, dozens of pages of my Journal but nothing that could conceivably make any money and not one penny had I earned since working at Metro two years earlier. We cut down expenditure – the house was surprisingly inexpensive – but I was now demonstrating a rule that has operated throughout my life; if I cut expenditure, I cut earnings. It seems I must trustfully launch out on expenditure and then the necessary earnings will come in – touch wood.

At last I got an idea I was enthusiastic about. It was to be mainly set in the 'thirties, with a prologue during the First World War and an epilogue during the present war, both set in Regent's Park. I got on well, sure that at last I was on the right track – and then, in December, Pearl Harbour happened and America was suddenly at war. That night a great many panic-stricken people in Monterey, and adjacent Pacific Grove, jumped into their cars and drove wildly inland, having seen a massed Japanese invasion approaching by sea. It proved to be the Monterey sardine fleet returning to harbour as it had for many, many years.

A local black-out was instantly imposed, with no black-out materials available. We decided to paste black roofing-paper over our huge hall windows, spend our days by artificial light and crawl into bed in the dark. We had barely finished blacking-out the hall when Chicago radio informed us that there were enemy aircraft over San Francisco. Washington radio immediately said there were not. San Francisco said there had been. The argument went on for days; then Washington won.

Very soon the black-out was called off – just as well as it was practically non-existent. But an atmosphere of panic remained, particularly as regards the Japanese residents of California. Most of them were American citizens, many had been born in America, but they were nearly all hurriedly shut up in camps in very difficult conditions. We visited some of them and took them things they needed. They were gentle and uncomplaining with their hardworking lives in ruins, their businesses grabbed at knock-down prices.

Working at great speed I wrote a screen-play about a Californian family at the outbreak of war which unwittingly harbours a spy. I called it *Fifth Column at the Fosters*. Metro offered my agents $20,000, a good price for this, and they planned to make it instantly. Then they failed to get the star they wanted and after six weeks cancelled the deal. Already the story's topicality was fading and I never managed to sell it. But by then we were well into the spring and I had worse things to worry about. Alec, as a resident alien, was now involved in the American draft.

The position of conscientious objectors was far worse in America than in England. Only religious reasons were accepted and objectors needed the full backing of a church such as the Quakers. Alec had no such backing and the local Draft Board announced its intention of being just as tough as possible and roping into the Army all the men it could. Fortunately, as it grimly admitted, it only had the haziest idea of the draft law and Alec could appeal on several grounds. And we were given to understand that appeals took a long time. We could only get advice about the draft law and then wait and hope for the best – which was not a very good best. If his appeal was allowed, he would be shut up in the mountains to fight forest fires. If it failed, he was likely to be shut up in prison. But I would not let myself believe that a married man of thirty-nine would be called up very soon and, meanwhile, we had to find somewhere else to live. The big, gloomy house had become impossible for us. Miss Hickson had left to do some teaching job, we'd had a disaster with a dishonest Philippino boy and we were now managing with an occasional cleaning woman. Fortunately, we rented the house on a monthly basis.

We found a small, pretty house high up in the hills, with a wonderful view of the coast, and a large fenced garden. It had charming modern furniture – I remember a white grand piano – and its whole atmosphere was cheerful. But my memories of it are painful as we lived in perpetual suspense.

If Alec *was* shut up – in a camp or in a prison – what could I do? I could not leave him and go back to England: obviously I must stay as close to him as possible. Could I stand being on my own? This hit me particularly one day when he had driven to San Francisco to get in touch with some pacifist organisation. I was all alone except for the dogs who were restless without him. A thick sea mist was rising all around. I felt the house would drown in it. I wandered about the pretty, rather movie-like rooms, played the white grand piano, got lonelier and lonelier, thinking of facing the night ahead. I passed some hours writing to John van Druten who replied that he was seriously worried about my state of mind – and he probably had cause.

But I cheered up when Alec got back and I heard he had found people who would advise and help him. And we went on living from day to day, eating our lunch in the little courtyard – Alec was a much better cook than I was – and our suppers on trays in front of the open fire. And I went back to work on the play set between two wars. I had almost finished it when the situation changed drastically.

We were listening to the radio one morning when we heard that England, reversing an earlier decision, was now calling its Hollywood nationals home. There was no question of compulsion, but we both felt we must accept this ruling. And though Alec was still resolutely pacifist, he now felt he could undertake fire-fighting, which seemed to us both immensely valuable work.

My relief at the thought of returning to England was only tempered by anxiety about our two dearly-loved dogs; even if we could accept quarantine for them, we were far from sure it could be arranged during wartime. We must find them ideal conditions in America and come back for them when the war was over. But first we needed to find out how we could get home.

We boarded the dogs at a vet's and drove to San Francisco to see the British Consul. It was, I think, the Vice-Consul who saw us and he couldn't have been more charming – or more stone-walling. If Alec would agree to fight, he could instantly be extricated from the American draft and sent home; otherwise he did not rate ship-room across the Atlantic. No, fire-fighting would not do, nor any form of civilian work; it must be the armed forces. *I* could go home whenever I could get a passage; the Vice-Consul intimated almost apologetically that I was just a little too old to be conscripted for anything. But nothing could be done about Alec.

We found this hard to believe as we knew of several conscientious objectors who had returned to England and gone on conscientiously objecting. In Beverly Hills we had known the Los Angeles Consul quite well. We would see if he could do better for us. So a few days later we took the long drive down along the coast and stayed again at the Beverly Hills Hotel. And while waiting for our appointment with the Consul, we found what seemed an ideal place in which to leave the dogs if we should have to; it was high in the hills and only a few dogs were boarded and they seemed to live on happy family terms with the kennel owners. It would be a wrench but if Folly and Buzz were well looked after . . . And to me, being back in England would compensate for much. If only the Consul could help us!

He was as charming as the San Francisco Vice-Consul but just as adamant. Alec must be willing to join the fighting forces, or stay in America. Well, it was some comfort that we shouldn't have to leave the dogs.

But if we had to stay with Alec's future so uncertain, we now felt we must come back to Beverly Hills. I should need to earn money by film work – if I still could. And we had some good friends there. We had never felt the lack of friends in Carmel, being happy in each other's company, but if I should be left alone. . .

We had our Carmel house on our hands but on the day we returned the owners informed us that they wanted it back if we could possibly give it up. So the move was on.

On our last day we drove round saying goodbye to the shopkeepers who had come to seem like friends. Books, records, charming fancy goods, exquisite cashmere rugs . . . so many Carmel treasures have now been with us ever since. And Alec paid a last visit to the local Draft Board. Most of its members had now got to like him and were interested in all the information he had collected from peace organisations and from our New York attorney. It really was the American chaotic draft law that was to blame. Our Board couldn't make head nor tail of it and admitted that fifty per cent of the appeals against its judgements were accepted. Actually it had done us a good turn for if they had classified Alec as a conscientious objector, he might already have been sent to a fire-fighting camp. As things were, he could go on appealing. But we still lived in perpetual suspense.

At twilight we drove round the quiet roads of the Seventeen Mile Drive and took a last look at our first little house, overlooking Seal Rock. Already I felt nostalgic about that house. I had thought of myself as unhappy there, but I now had many happy memories of it. They were to grow happier. Indeed, in retrospect, the whole of our two years in Carmel, in spite of our anxieties, have become for us a shared idyll of companionship which we would willingly live again.

IV

John, Charlie, Christopher

The dogs behaved beautifully on the long drive to Beverly Hills, Buzz usually travelling on top of our steamer trunks which stood, end upwards, at the back of our heads. It was a good thing he liked this position as Folly, much as she loved him, frequently kicked him off the back seat of the Rolls. We had already booked accommodation at the Beverly Hills Hotel; no luxury apartment this time but a fairly large bedroom with a balcony where the dogs could sit in the sun.

Furnished houses were now in short supply and sky-high in rent. It took us a week to find one that was possible for us. It was in North Palm Drive and, though reasonably comfortable, did not compare well with the house in Cove Way we had previously lived in. We now had no swimming pool and the fairly large back garden looked neglected. And it was nearly three times as much as we had been paying in Carmel. I should need to get work quickly.

There had been changes at the Frank Vincent Agency which represented me. Richard Halliday was now looking after writers. He had taken the trouble to visit us in Carmel with his most charming wife, the actress Mary Martin, and suggested all sorts of plans for me. Not wishing to have anything more to do with movies I had stone-walled the lot, so I was hardly surprised when I now went to see him, to find him pleasant but not optimistic about my chances. He said jobs were scarce; and I knew that now I was a writer in need of work, I was less likely to be sought after than in the days when I constantly refused it.

I was about to leave when I felt I had better mention Alec's C.O. troubles – for all I knew Dick might be the patriotic type who would wish to have no more to do with us. His manner changed instantly. He said he had enormous sympathy with Alec's point of view and he would do everything he could to help. He got me an offer from Paramount within two days.

It was to work with Charles Brackett whom I had met while living in Beverly Hills: an ex-novelist, once the New Yorker dramatic critic, and now – after great success as a film writer with Billy Wilder – a film producer. He was an Easterner (his wife, after years in Hollywood, said she still hadn't unpacked), a Mayflower American, utterly unlike the movie world. I can perhaps give a shorthand impression of him by saying that when, having engaged me, he heard that I was moving house, he suggested I should take at least two weeks (on full pay) to read the book I was to adapt and 'give an occasional thought to it' while I got on with the move. Once I was comfortably settled we would meet again and talk.

I was thankful for that kindness as the day I first saw him was the day we moved into the North Palm Drive house. And also on that day, Alan Barr, of the pacifist organisation in San Francisco which had been so helpful to Alec, came to see us and we had to give him dinner and put him up for the night. The kind owner of the house, Mrs Belzer, lent me someone to help make up the beds and prepare a meal, but everything was pretty chaotic. Fortunately Alan Barr did not mind at all and I was glad to realise Alec could count on him. The next day they went off to drive to some pacifist camp and I began the job of getting straight. There was so much to do that, for the next week, thinking about the film became a blissful recreation.

The novel I had to adapt was *The Uninvited* by Dorothy Macardle, a ghost story set in a lonely house on a North Devon cliff top. It had great possibilities as a film and I enjoyed working on it. Alec (he had been glad to meet other conscientious objectors at the camp and had plans for helping them) did far more work on the house than I did and, though it was two weeks before we could get a maid, I was soon busy making notes for a story-line and ready to see Charles Brackett again.

We then talked for two weeks in Charlie's pleasant offices at Paramount. But we never talked for very long at a time. He would suddenly say, 'You're tired. Let's go and get ice-cream sodas', or he would take me round the studios, look in on the shooting of a picture or on a movie being shown in a projection room; or he would simply stop talking about *The Uninvited* and gossip about life. He encouraged me to tell him stories of my childhood, rarely – and only heavily encouraged by me – slipping in a few of his own. Sometimes we discussed the problems of writers. He had a theory that they must always be kept happy, continually praised. He said, 'If I'm hard put to it I praise their punctuation. "What a witty comma that is."'

Eventually I was sent home to write the script as far as we had discussed it, 'But don't work yourself too hard. No writer should put in too long a day.' But I got on fast and soon handed in my work for his verdict. His first words to me on the telephone were, 'Has anyone ever told you that you write like an angel?'

Knowing his theories about praising writers I discounted this, which was just as well as I eventually managed to dig out of his compliments that he wanted most of my work changed. I at once tried to bow out of the job but he wouldn't hear of it. We must go on discussing the story-line while another writer – 'He admires you enormously' – made 'a few technical changes'. This was just what had happened to me at Metro, to my fury, but now the circumstances were very different. I admired and liked Charlie and wanted to please him and I found myself agreeing with his main criticism. He said, 'You despise movie audiences. You write down to them as you never would to theatre audiences.' He also found some of my writing too sentimental – and so it was. But the sentimentality had been put in to please him; throughout all our discussions I had found him far more sentimental than I was. I had yet to learn that there is a vast difference between English and American sentimentality.

So I was coaxed back for some more weeks of conversations which were very enjoyable; and life at home had become enjoyable, too. We now had a good maid, a Mrs Passmore, given to saying, 'Since Mr Passmore passed away.' And John van Druten was in Hollywood, back from opening his successful play in New York, *The Damask Cheek*. We saw much of him and he rang up, without fail, every morning while I was having breakfast in bed, to tell me about his previous day's miseries at Metro, where he was doing highly paid work. And one Sunday in early December John brought Christopher Isherwood to see us.

My first impression of him was that he radiated goodness. Perhaps this was partly because I knew of his interest in religion. Later I discovered that, though he was undoubtedly good in many ways, what he really radiated was a sunniness of temperament which enabled him to like and be liked by almost everyone. Certainly Alec and I liked him from that first meeting and presumably he liked us as he came again the next Sunday and from then the Sunday meetings went on for years and years. John once remarked, 'Well, I thought you'd like each other but not *quite* so much.'

Owing to his work with the Quakers, Chris's plea of conscientious objection had been accepted and he was expecting to be called up for forest fire-fighting. Alec was now doing valuable work as a Counsellor to conscientious objectors – not encouraging them to be CO's, but telling them just what the Draft law allowed which, in many cases, their draft boards purposely (or sometimes through sheer ignorance) failed to do. He particularly admired Jehovah's Witnesses for their courage. Young boys of 18 were stood up in court and sentenced to any period from a year and a day to 5 years in jail for refusing the draft on sincerely held religious grounds, which their draft boards and most courts refused even to contemplate. All over America there was no consistency by judges in such sentencing (religious or otherwise) and this made for confusion and hardship.

Alec was still battling with *his* draft board. But early in December there was a ruling that men over thirty-eight would not be drafted which let both Chris and Alec out. Chris then began plans to live at the Vedanta Temple in Hollywood in preparation for one day becoming a monk, which depressed me as I feared it would deprive us of his company.

What with Charlie, Christopher and John our life was a whirl of sociability compared with what it had been at Carmel. And a few weeks after we first met Chris, he brought Aldous Huxley to see us. I had admired him since my twenties and was almost too much in awe of him to talk naturally – whereas Alec got on with him wonderfully well. Actually, one did not have to do very much talking; it would have been a waste with Aldous Huxley there. Never had I heard anyone talk so brilliantly (though modestly) on any subject that was mentioned. We met him a number of times but I never felt at ease with him; this was partly because I did not now like the mixture of religion with slight pornography in his work. But I continued to feel he was a most admirable man. I have one endearing memory of him. We stopped the car to talk to him on the Hollywood Sunset Strip. He was wearing a pale pink woollen jacket known as a 'loafer coat'. The sleeves had shrunk almost up to his elbows and when the jacket blew open I noticed a label saying 'Do not wash.'

By Christmas, which Chris spent with us, I was still working with Charlie, either talking or writing. I no longer resented alterations to my work. I had come to realise that Charlie's films were *Charlie's* films and that, though he liked having the dialogue mapped out, he would almost always change it beyond recognition. Busy all day, he would do this in bed in the small hours, scrawling on a block of yellow paper in writing which only he and his secretary, Helen Hernandez, could read. He loved this work. He once quoted to me, 'I'd rather re-write than be President.' He could cut dialogue skilfully but his additions, usually jokes or very melodramatic lines, embarrassed me so much that I once wanted to take my name off *The Uninvited*. He disarmed me by saying, 'Will you let me keep your name if I add "Bad taste by Charles Brackett?"'

I believe he was unique among Hollywood producers because he never resented criticism. He said honesty was of untold value and virtually unobtainable in the movie world. All the same I think he may sometimes have found me a bit too frank. Two years later, when I had worked with him several times, I criticised a character he had invented called Lord Desham. No English lord, I told him, could be so insultingly superior. He looked me in the eyes and said, 'Woman, you *are* Lord Desham.'

I must have worked on *The Uninvited* for over three months and later I was recalled to help with casting and the sets and, later still, to watch some of the shooting and the daily rushes of scenes shot. Charlie tried to interest me in every detail. He had a theory that I could end up as a movie producer – not that I wanted to. I should mention that, in the Hollywood hierarchy, producers are tops and writers, however highly paid, are very low. Of course the boys in the front office are the highest tops of all. Charlie kept me away from these as much as possible in case I didn't bow low enough – he was none too keen on bowing low himself. But when I did meet some of them I found them as pleasant as everyone else at Paramount.

Still, much as I had enjoyed the job, I was thankful when at last I finished work on the script. Alec and I celebrated our freedom by taking the dogs on an afternoon walk along the wide alleys that separated the back gardens of houses on the Drives, where we could safely let the dogs run free. It was early January, warm and sunny. Cascades of semi-tropical flowers overflowed the white walls and, below them, were the recently turned-out Christmas trees, some of them still trailing their tinsel. I was thankful to feel I could now concentrate on work of my own, with no anxiety about money. Paramount had only paid me $1,250 a week to start with – I had been too anxious for work to haggle about salary – but this rose to $1,500 after a month (later, they paid me $2,000 a week at which, as it was my highest salary before the war broke out, I was legally 'frozen'). On that sunny New Year walk I must have had the pleasant consciousness of having earned around $20,000 in a comparatively painless way. I had stopped minding changes to my script because I had realised how inefficient as a movie writer I was. Charlie had once told John (they were old friends) that I persistently undersold myself. John had replied, 'It may sound like that, but she really knows just how good she is.' I certainly didn't consider myself good at writing *movies*.

By mid-January we were getting sad at the thought of losing Christopher. I have a vivid memory of him, sitting cross-legged on our sofa, saying he was getting into practice for life at the Vedanta Temple. He was of medium build, neatly – almost meekly – dressed with fair hair which was unruly, though short. He wore thick white woollen socks and sturdy black shoes. The socks and shoes were particularly noticeable when he sat cross-legged. He had a habit of beaming on me for long periods. I, of course, beamed back and if I turned away, say, to pour coffee, I would turn back to find him still beaming. I began to feel he really was in training for some kind of sunny sainthood. He could talk of anything – books, music, religion, people he had known, and in a most stimulating way; but he never monopolised the conversation. He had a pleasing habit of starting some quite erudite subject by saying, 'As, of course, you know. . .' I didn't . . . but I soon did.

One day not long before he was due to go 'In', he arrived unexpectedly just as I was due to go out to fit a dress. He was apt to be impatient about such feminine foibles as fittings and particularly intolerant about my visits to hairdressers. 'Why can't you just shove your head under a tap?' However he and Alec accompanied me to the fitting and then we all went home to dinner. I think that was the day when he gleefully told us that he had secured a number of envelopes advertising a film called *Kiss The Boys Goodbye*, which had a large pink mouth printed on them. He had used these for farewell notes to various men friends. His last words to us after his last Sunday lunch were, 'Well, see you next Sunday, perhaps', but we didn't believe it. Surely if he was training to become a monk. . .?

However, towards the end of next week, he telephoned to say that he could come 'out' if we could come and get him (he had sold his car, in the process of getting rid of worldly goods) and I can't recall that while at the Temple he ever missed a Sunday with us. From now on we had full details of his life – fascinating, even though I could make little of Vedanta and could not bear the thought of a writer as brilliant as Christopher spending three or more hours a day worshipping the goddess in the Temple, bringing her flowers and lots of little meals, including butter. (We never discovered if anyone actually ate the meals.) Chris said he felt the need of discipline and his much-loved Swami Prabhavananda thought he would progress faster if he accepted the path of ritual. We were often to visit Chris at the Temple and to like some of his associates, including Swami whom Alec particularly admired. But I never could feel happy that Chris was there. However, he eventually managed to do some of his own work every day, even if it was only for ten minutes or so, late at night. And at long last his novel, *Prater Violet*, was to get written.

I was slow to start work myself after finishing, temporarily, at Paramount. I had so many unanswered letters to cope with and then I had an orgy of journal writing. I knew I ought to go back to the play I had written at Carmel; Alec, who had liked about ninety per cent of it, was always encouraging me to. But I wasted weeks chasing will-o'-the-wisp new ideas. Then, at the beginning of March, I decided to ask John his opinion of my play as it stood. John and I talked perpetually about plays, but whereas he found it helpful to tell me his ideas – he said I fertilised them – I found it killed my ideas stone-dead to tell anyone, even Alec, about them. But this play was semi-finished and not a tenuous, floating idea. I'd be glad to have John's verdict.

We arranged that he should read the script at our house one morning when Alec and I had to be out. When we got back we found he had gone off to a lunch engagement leaving a note saying this was my best play and needed hardly any changes. He joined us for dinner and then spent the whole of the next day, reading the play aloud to me and continually praising it. He also made a few helpful suggestions, but what mattered most was his assurance that I had not lost my skill in the five years since I had finished *Dear Octopus*.

He then went off to his ranch in the desert south of Palm Springs to work on a play of his own. It was to be about a young American soldier, on leave in New York, meeting a girl and sharing a weekend with her during which they fell in love. The weekend was to be spent in the girl's apartment which was to be seen completely on stage: bedroom, sitting-room and kitchen. John was convinced that audiences would enjoy seeing a few days of shared happiness in war time, the gradual getting to know each other of the two characters, their falling in love and making love. There was no real story, but remembering the charm of his play, *There's Always Juliet*, I thought he might just pull this one off. Still, with only two characters, it would take him all his time. And he was worried because he did not yet feel that he *knew* the girl.

A few days later I got a postcard from him saying that he suddenly felt confident that he could write the play if I would let him use an idea from mine. In my Prologue, set in Regent's Park during the First World War, an Army captain, home after being wounded, waits to meet the girl he is in love with. Instead, he is met by her best friend who has to break the news that his girl has thrown him over. He is bitterly hurt and yet, during the next fifteen minutes, he manages to fall in love with the girl who has brought the bad news, and she with him. I had challenged myself to make this convincing. John swore I had, and Alec agreed with him. John now wanted to add the heroine's best friend to his two-handed play, make both the girls actresses – as my girls were – and make the man switch from girl to girl exactly as I had done. The bare facts sound like sheer plagiarism on John's part, but characters, period, setting would be totally different and the Prologue was only a tiny part of my play, the bulk of which dealt with a marriage which, though happy, is seriously menaced. (Only in the Epilogue does one know if it survives.) I did not think what John wanted to do could possibly damage my play. (And it never did.) And in giving him the go-ahead I was thankful I could a little repay him for his encouragement when I had badly needed it.

John then started off, full-steam-ahead (it took him all of ten days) on *The Voice of The Turtle*, the most successful play he ever wrote. Looking back now and remembering some sad patches our friendship was to run into later, I am glad to remember that time when we were able to help each other.

There must, I think, have been a shortage of writers in the Studios now as I had a great many offers of work – I once had three offers in two days. I refused them firmly, determined to work on final improvements to my play, which I decided to call *Lovers and Friends*. But I did not feel I could refuse Charlie when he recalled me for a month's work at Paramount. I enjoyed it, but by now Alec and I were again worried about the Draft. It was now decreed that men of thirty-nine *might* be called up after all, if they were needed, so once again we lived from day to day. He was all the more anxious not to be hauled off to prison now, as he was working harder and harder on counselling conscientious objectors. Often he was seeing them until late in the evening. The new ruling affected Christopher too, but he had decided that, at worst, he would join a Medical

Corps. He once said – 'Oh, come on, Alec. Let's go and shovel corpses together.'

Free of Paramount, I finished the revision of *Lovers and Friends* and sent it for professional typing. And just about this time Folly came 'into season', to use the delicate phrase favoured in America, and we decided she and Buzz should mate. This was a bit reckless, seeing that Alec was still involved with the Draft, but we wanted it for them and God knows they wanted it for themselves. On Folly's two previous heats, Buzz had been near demented, whether we kept her at home and away from him, or whether she went away. We now sent her to our excellent local vet, who informed us when she was ready for mating and we brought her home for the afternoon. We then let them meet in the largest room in the house, which was my bedroom, and trusted that instinct would tell them what to do. It certainly didn't, as Buzz's only idea, after an ecstatic reunion, was to climb on Folly's head from the front. Obviously knowing there was no future in this she rebuffed him sharply. We then tried to assist, each of us armed with a text book. As the text books didn't quite agree and Buzz remained dead set on a frontal approach, it was a miracle the mating ever took place, after which the dogs remained tied for nearly half-an-hour. By the time we took Folly back to the vet's we were all four of us exhausted.

Around six in the morning we were rung up. Would we please come and catch Folly? She had broken out of her pen, eaten her way through a slatted door, knocked the telephone to the ground (obviously trying to telephone us) and was now racing round menacing the kennel maid and enticing all male dogs to come out of their pens. After we caught her, we were asked to take her home. Fortunately there was a guest room in our garden, never needed as our one spare room was enough for the occasional use of a pacifist friend of Christopher's, Denny Fouts. So we installed Folly there and she seemed peaceful except when Buzz went on troubadour duty outside. We were thankful when she could at last return to us, no longer attractive to poor Buzz. It was some weeks before our vet could tell us that Folly was pregnant. Puppies could be expected in early July.

I had sent *Lovers and Friends* to Jack Wilson in New York and he had already begun trying to cast it; this wasn't going to be easy with such a very English play. There were many letters and telephone calls but for me they now crystalised into the moment when my bedside telephone woke me in the very early morning and a girl's voice, relaying a telegram, said 'Get a load of this, will you? Kit Cornell's going to do your play.'

Soon Jack arrived in Hollywood to discuss casting. He had had to agree that the famous Katherine Cornell and her husband, Guthrie McClintic, should own half the play and that McClintic should direct it, but Jack seemed very much in control. He agreed that the three Motley girls, now in America, should do the sets, just as they had for my *Dear Octopus*. Back in 1932, when I had first met him on an Atlantic crossing, he had told me that if I had one more success I must ask for a royalty of ten per cent of the gross takings on my plays which was unusually high.

I had taken his advice but now, knowing how expensive the whole production was going to be, I offered to accept normal royalties. He wouldn't hear of it. I had been reading a life of Barrie and learned that he and Frohman never had a contract. Jack and I wished we could dispense with one but, as we couldn't, we spent our time trying to make concessions to each other, which usually ended in his making them to me.

As for casting, I now felt I must leave this to him, especially as I had no intention of going to New York for the production. I knew that McClintic would direct the play as a vehicle for his wife (I had never met either of them) and, ignorant as I still was about the American theatre, I should not have felt justified in opposing anything he wished.

I didn't even *want* to be in on the production. I wanted to stay with Alec and the dogs, grateful for every day of our life together and always conscious that it might not continue. I was grateful, too, for Christopher, Charlie and John (who was now back in Hollywood after selling *The Voice of the Turtle*); both our plays would be produced in the autumn. I had made quite a lot of money and seemed likely to make more. I was glad to think I had the summer in which to feel optimistic about my prospects.

V

Of Puppies and Plays

Soon after Jack went back to New York, our vet examined Folly and said we might expect five or six puppies and, though they were not due for ten days or so, we had better settle her somewhere quiet. So back she went into the garden guest room, a large bedroom with a very small bathroom. She seemed quite happy there, but the next morning we found she had destroyed the upholstery of an armchair, ripped a mattress, damaged a rug beyond repair and had retired to the small, dark bathroom to which she returned every time we took her out. So we made up her bed there and tried to keep our minds off what the damage she had done was going to cost us.

A couple of days later, after having some friends to dinner, we went down to say goodnight to her and were astonished to find that three puppies had already been born and another was now arriving. Folly washed it, we dried it and then put it with the other puppies. She was showing no sign of distress and at this rate, if she was only going to have five or six, the whole litter would soon have arrived. But she didn't stop at six and it was when the seventh was being born that we noticed something frightening: the pups were being born *green*. We knew, of course, that Dalmatians have no spots when born, but surely the puppies ought to be white? Then a hideous suspicion struck us. As advised by a text book we had made the basis of Folly's bed a piece of carpet and that carpet was green. Was the dye coming off on the pups?

It was long after midnight but I dashed indoors and telephoned our vet. He said no, it was not the carpet, the pups had every right to be green – something to do with the afterbirth. He was very patient, poor man, but he drew the line at coming to help us. If we and Folly had achieved seven puppies, we were doing very nicely and there probably wouldn't be any more. He was going back to sleep.

I made sure that poor, deserted Buzz was sleeping peacefully in my bedroom, got some warm milk for Folly and returned to find the eighth puppy had arrived. Soon came the ninth. By now Folly was moaning a little and looking pretty exhausted – as well she might, poor girl, seeing this was her first litter. We told her and ourselves that this would be the last pup, but we were wrong. As the night wore on there was a tenth, then an eleventh, then a twelfth. Then the thirteenth pup was born seemingly dead.

We had read in a Dalmatian text book that patched puppies should instantly be put down (patches, unlike spots, show at birth) but we had already treated our one patched pup with the utmost care. Now, however, I felt that in view of this huge litter, I could well be resigned to the death of this last weak and particularly small puppy. Not so Alec. He massaged it and rubbed it with a towel. And then a seeming miracle happened. One moment it was limply motionless – its nose and the skin showing through its hair were a sickly yellow. And then gradually its whole body was suffused with pink, its mouth opened, its little legs wriggled. It was alive! Alec said he felt like God. (Its birth was to be described by me in a book written over twelve years later and eventually recreated in Walt Disney's wonderful cartoon film, *101 Dalmatians*.) The sun was up before Folly delivered her final puppy, making fifteen in all – a staggeringly high number for a first litter. Only then did I get out of my new and expensive, black lace dinner dress.

That morning, a Saturday, a temperamental Danish housekeeper, who had been with us only a few weeks, left without notice. Her main grievance was that we could not supply her with a pound of butter weekly, entirely for herself. In vain did we explain about wartime food shortages. She said everyone knew that all Danes had to have a pound of butter a week and the United States Government would have to make arrangements for it. She then stomped out in a frenzy of butter-deprived rage. We had guessed she wouldn't stay long and had already written to our New Zealand housekeeper in Carmel, asking if she would care to rejoin us. She had accepted in her usual spirit of adventure but couldn't be with us for a couple of weeks. And to add to my immediate problems I was due at Paramount that morning for the first rough cut of *The Uninvited*.

This didn't go well and Charlie asked me to come back on the payroll and advise him on improvements. I said I couldn't spare the time. He then offered as an inducement to cut all his scenes which I hadn't liked, including a horrible comic seasick scene. I said I could advise him to cut that scene without going on the payroll and that, if he would come to Palm Drive, I would give him all the advice I could, for free, but I couldn't tie myself up. Then I hurried back to Alec who was overlaid with puppies. Charlie arrived next day and, it being Sunday, we also had Christopher and John. What any of us had to eat I can't imagine.

Alec spent much of the weekend with Folly, rotating the pups so that fifteen could share accommodation for eight. Obviously she couldn't go on feeding them all and on Monday, after much telephoning, Alec located a dog-pound where they had a stray with some milk to give. He drove off to get her, also bringing back a doll's feeding bottle and an old fashioned fountain pen filler. Astonishingly, the stray was a Dalmatian, too. We installed her in Alec's bathroom and gave her an enormous meal of meat and milk. Though pitifully thin, she had milk to give but would need a lot of feeding up. I stayed with her until she settled down to sleep on the bed we had made up for her; she was timid but very friendly. We now had eighteen Dalmatians in the house.

Alec spent the afternoon with Folly, doing duty as a foster mother; we felt the stray must have a long rest before we tried her on the job. The doll's feeding bottle worked well but took a very long time. The fountain pen filler was quicker, but it was difficult to regulate the flow. Still, Alec did extremely well, though in great discomfort. We had been advised to draw the bathroom curtains and make it resemble a dark cupboard, so Alec, sharing the cramped floor space, was continually bumping his head into the bath, the lavatory basin or the lavatory seat – and he was extremely hot in the California heat. By the time he came out he was tottering – and covered in milk.

The next day we introduced one of the puppies to the foster-mother. There was one frightening moment and then she took to it, fed it and washed it. We brought her two more – thanking heaven Folly couldn't count. All went well. We felt that was enough for one day and Alec again spent the afternoon feeding Folly's puppies. I tried my hand but was no good whatever; the puppies would not keep still. And anyway I had to cope with the house and visits from Charlie. By the Wednesday I felt I must have some help so Alec drove to the Employment Bureau for a cleaner.

The coloured girl he brought back was a wonder, but wasn't free to come again, so next day he went back. There were more would-be employers than cleaners waiting and I doubt if he'd have had any luck if our girl of the previous day, who was waiting to be called for, hadn't stood up and shouted, 'One of your girls go to Mrs Beesley. That poor lady's in bad trouble. She's just had fifteen puppies.'

The foster mother accepted six, but her milk was decreasing so Alec drove her and her contingent to the breeder in the Van Nuys valley from whom we had bought Buzz, who agreed to help out by hand-feeding while the foster mother kept the puppies clean; she was a magnificent puppy-washer. In the end we gave the six to the kind breeder who would sell them advantageously. It was going to take us all our time to find good homes for our remaining nine. We eventually boarded the foster mother at our vet's until she was found a home in a fine house on one of the Drives. She was led away on a new red collar and leash by a proud new owner who was quite unperturbed by the fact that she had two black patches and a feathery tail.

Our domestic troubles were over once Miss Hickson arrived and started making her New Zealand grandmother's steak-and-kidney pudding for us and our guests. Soon our remaining puppies were feeding themselves. Day after day they lay with Folly in the garden, with Buzz in slightly wary attendance. A large poinsettia bush shaded them from the hot sun, the scarlet blooms contrasting most decoratively with all the black and white. By the third week the puppies' spots began to come through. Charlie, Christopher and John came to admire. Incidentally, Folly's enormous family was born on the same day that one of Charlie's daughters gave birth to her first child. We got over the strict wartime embargo on greetings telegrams by sending one saying: 'What only one! Folly Beesley.'

I look back on that summer with pleasure. Not feeling I could start some piece of work until *Lovers and Friends* was produced on Broadway, I spent my time journal writing and letter writing, listening to records and reading. I guiltily remember putting words to one movement of my favourite Beethoven last quartet in B flat major:

> Puppies at play
> What a pretty sight.
> Merry and gay
> But, hell, how they bite.

In reading, it was one of my great Henry James periods, mainly *The Wings of the Dove* and *The Golden Bowl*. Chris shared my love of late Beethoven and Henry James. John did not, yet he drove me round the many Los Angeles bookshops looking for secondhand copies of James; they were scarce. Charlie had no time for music and, though he had read widely, now only enjoyed detective novels. I liked those, too, so we could swap them. Alec, in spite of all his work for pups, pacifism and parcel packing, got through a surprising amount of reading. Inspired by Chris, we both of us read pretty well everything by E.M. Forster.

Our only worries were the still-threatening Draft and the problem of finding good homes for the puppies – and the sadness of letting them go just as they were developing personalities. We kept one for ourselves and called him Dandy. Often during his fourteen happy years I wondered how his brothers and sisters had fared.

Early in September our pleasant landlady, Mrs Belzer, came to tell us that we should have to leave at the end of the month when our lease was up as the house was being sold. We then had to show her the serious damage done by Folly, in the guest room. Mrs Belzer then told us that the house and all the furniture really belonged to her daughter, the film star Loretta Young, who would not dream of letting us pay for damage done in such circumstances. We could only feel grateful that the American reverence for motherhood extended even to mother dogs.

Houses were scarcer than ever but Charlie took a hand. There was a house in Tower Road he had rented during his early years in Hollywood. (He now had his own attractive house in Bel Air.) He felt nostalgic about that house, would like visiting us there. He got permission to show it to us.

We drove for nearly half-a-mile up a private road that wound its way to the top of a wooded hill. Here there was a courtyard from which there was a view of more and more wooded hills. The house, ochre-painted, was vaguely Spanish; it was large, but not impossibly so. The rooms were beautifully proportioned and admirably furnished. There was a feeling of light and space. But the greatest beauty was the unusually large patio, reached through the tiled hall. From here one looked down on a sloping garden, a swimming pool and the wooded hillside to a panoramic view stretching on one side to Los Angeles and on the other to the Pacific. An enormous basement, blasted out of the solid rock, was intended as a bolt-hole from possible Californian earthquakes.

We *loved* that house but surely the rent would be beyond us? It was, Charlie admitted, $800 a month. But he would talk to the owner whom he knew well. She had been a film star, Eleanor

Boardman, once married to King Vidor, now married to a Frenchman, Henri d'Arrast. Still a very beautiful woman, Charlie said, but a very disagreeable one. However, he thought he could cope.

She eventually offered the house to us for $600 a month, she paying for the gardener. This was still more than we felt we ought to pay. But Charlie then asked me for two weeks' work, to help him with a new idea. I shouldn't have to write, just talk; if even so much as a note had to be made Charlie would himself make it. The salary for two weeks would pay the rent of the house for over six months. I stopped worrying.

The only snag was that Charlie wanted me during the time we moved house which put a lot of work on Alec. I felt guilty while I was pleasantly chatting at Paramount, eating ice-cream and reading *East Lynne* (which Charlie's story, dealing with thwarted mother-love, vaguely resembled). But I was allowed two days off for the actual move. I spent much of these going through the inventory with Mrs d'Arrast. Disagreeable was a mild word for her. The inventory was hopelessly wrong and I eventually became as tough as she was – I'd almost forgotten I was capable of this. But what impressed her most was my behaviour when she opened a drawer in the palatial drawing-room and found a mouse, complete with a small pink family. She said, 'I'll get the gardener to kill them'. I screamed, 'Leave them alone!' She looked quite terrified and hastily closed the drawer. After that her manner was far more civil.

(That mouse and her family remained with us for a surprisingly long time. I dropped food into the drawer every day. Lying on two of the three enormous sofas of an evening, Alec and I used to watch the mother mouse come out of the back of the drawer and make her way down a table leg. No doubt she needed exercise. Eventually she and her family disappeared, presumably to the garden as we were never overrun with mice.)

For the last few days of my job Charlie came and worked with me on our patio, very pleased at having settled us just where he wanted us. Soon he established a routine of coming to lunch every Monday.

Miss Hickson made the move with us. She loved the house and we got coloured help to do the cleaning for her, leaving her with only the cooking. She had now become interested in Eastern religions and enjoyed talking to Christopher about them. We no longer fetched him from the Temple in the Rolls, as we had now acquired a secondhand Bantam car (surprisingly made in Minneapolis): the smallest car I ever saw, to help over petrol, now rationed (though there was no law to stop one having as many cars as one liked). To get three humans, two grown Dalmatian dogs and one large puppy into that tiny car was something of an achievement, and must have looked a fine sight in front of a Vedanta temple. Christopher said we were now more conspicuous than in the Rolls.

John had gone to New York to direct his *The Voice of the Turtle*, and I had barely finished working with Charlie when rehearsals for *Lovers and Friends* started. My main worry was that Raymond Massey had been cast as the leading man. Excellent actor though he could be, I did not see how he could be convincing as a young English army officer in the prologue and then, for the rest of the play, a senior member of a long-established firm of London solicitors. But Jack Wilson assured me he would be perfectly acceptable in New York and Kit Cornell particularly wanted him, so I agreed. Raymond Massey (I knew him only slightly) then wrote to ask if I would change the name of the character he played as he had – he said for purely private reasons – a dislike for the name Rodney. Very unwillingly, I offered alternatives but these met with no approval. However, Jack then telephoned to say that Ray had now got to like the name Rodney, so all was well.

But only for the moment. Soon Mr Massey telephoned – a long expensive call – to say Rodney ought to be 'more onto himself'. Nothing he said made sense to me, but I said I would give it the most careful consideration. Mercifully, Guthrie McClintic telephoned next day to tell me not to worry. He said all Ray needed was an occasional 'spangle' on his part, which Mr McClintic had now supplied. I never found out what the spangles were.

What worried me more was a polite letter from Miss Cornell saying there was one scene she felt she could not play. Could it be drastically cut? It was a scene I particularly liked. I wrote back saying of course I would make cuts if she wished me to, but I'd like to tell her first how I had imagined the scene would be directed. I described this in some detail and she shortly wrote to say that her husband had re-directed it on the lines I had suggested and it was now one of her favourite scenes. It was then that it first dawned on me that I ought to be at rehearsals.

The pre-New York opening was in early November, in Detroit. I was rung up after curtain fall. Katherine Cornell spoke first, in her warm, gracious voice. Wonderful house, wonderful reception, far more comedy than they had expected, she must now work hard on that . . . Jack then took over, even more enthusiastic, already they had a $34,000 booking in Detroit– 'That's $3,400 to you, darling.' Kit's performance was unbelievably beautiful, Ray was a bit pompous but that could be coped with. He went on so long that I reminded him how much the call was costing him. He said, 'What the hell do we care, darling, when we're making all this lovely money?' Dear Jack, my favourite of all managements.

He had asked for some cuts, on the score of length. We had been expecting this and Alec, much better at cutting than I was, had them all ready to send. The Detroit notices were fairly good, but they all treated the play as a highly polished, brittle comedy. It was meant to be a serious study of a marriage with only incidental comedy. And I was soon told that Ray Massey was getting all sorts of wrong laughs in serious scenes. Then he and his wife, Dorothy, telephoned one night for fifty minutes, asking me if I couldn't rewrite his whole part to show that he was *meant* to be funny. Even if I could have done this, it would have wrecked the play so all I could do was to explain this gently.

Next time Miss Cornell telephoned, she told me Ray was getting wrong laughs she couldn't have believed any actor *could* get and he'd now written her a long memorandum she couldn't make sense of, so she'd told him to send it to me. When it came it contained nothing he hadn't said on the telephone, but it was followed by fifty handwritten pages of notes from Mrs Massey saying the whole direction of the play had been slanted towards comedy which made things bad for Ray and, rather to my surprise, I found she made out a very good case; but there was nothing I could do now but send the fifty pages on to Jack with some suggestions for cutting the wrong laughs. On the last week of the tour he wrote, from Buffalo, that they'd used all my suggestions and killed every wrong laugh.

On the night the play was due to open in New York, Alec and I sat in our palatial sitting-room, with our sleeping dogs, waiting for the telephone call we had been promised after curtain-fall. We said very little. Alec had been keeping me cheerful for weeks and had nothing new to say. I lay thinking of my London first nights; my various dresses for them, the flowers, the friends, the sea of faces in the audience, the welcome of a friendly house when, at the end, the author walks on amongst the players (as authors usually did in those days). And, along with nostalgia, I now felt guilt towards this present play. I ought to have been there from the first rehearsal, helping it. Yet I knew I could have done very little, with a famous

American director directing his famous American wife in a particularly English play, with only one English player (Henry Daniell).

At last the telephone call came through. Once more Miss Cornell's bright, vital voice: 'Miss Smith? Well, I'm very happy. A wonderful, attentive audience, no false laughs at all, in fact not quite as many laughs as we'd expected. Oh, we haven't exactly lost them, it's just that the audience was quieter. A wonderful reception. . .' Jack took over and said much the same. Neither of them admitted there had been anything wrong, but I suspected the audience hadn't enjoyed the play as much as its out-of-town audiences had.

Very early next morning a long telegram from John was telephoned to me. He had left his *The Voice of the Turtle* which was at Philadelphia, to go to my New York first night. I already knew his own play was doing wonderfully well.

The gist of John's telegram was that Cornell was giving a perfect performance and Henry Daniell was excellent. John hadn't liked anyone else. The play was directed at the usual New York break-neck speed, with no one listening to anyone. Both comedy and reality were missing, but he still loved it and felt sure Katherine Cornell's vast drawing power would carry it to success.

Later in the morning I had a second telegram from John telling me the notices were all bad, except for one critic whose praise was considered the kiss of death. It was a loving sympathetic telegram and concluded, 'Have a nice dinner in the bath and I'll call you from Philadelphia.' I never had had dinner in the bath but I did rather like to eat there, *and* read, *and* listen to the radio.

John's Philadelphia call was mainly to tell me that he knew from Jack that the booking was solid for weeks. John also said he wanted to warn me just how bad the notices were, so they wouldn't be too much of a shock. And when I did eventually receive them they weren't as bad as I expected. But they were pretty bad. Apart from the kiss-of-death gentleman, the best was from Eleanor Roosevelt, a dramatic critic as well as the President's wife. She said she liked the play so much because the people in it behaved like the people she had known in her youth. Alas, it was the good behaviour of the characters which had infuriated several critics. I gathered that, faced with a breaking marriage, it wasn't human to behave so well, certainly not in America. The British, as usual, were showing off their superiority.

Jack said the notices didn't matter. Everyone was happy except at the thought that I might be upset. I must console myself with the certainty of success – which, looking back, it seems to me I did, surprisingly quickly, proud that the play was the leading straight play on Broadway, taking even more money than John's play; but that was because his was in a smaller theatre. *Lovers and Friends* was a success for the season; *The Voice of the Turtle* was to run for nearly a thousand performances.

VI

The Edge of Otherness

It was just as well that royalties were now flowing in, as life in our beautiful hilltop house was proving expensive. Miss Hickson had gone. She disliked having coloured cleaners to help her and I think, too, that having been with us all of three months, slight wanderlust was stirring. She took a job in a progressive school high up in the hills where she was eventually involved in a forest fire and had to rescue children in her little red car. (We kept in touch with her for years.) In her place we had engaged a Swedish married couple, Ruth and Eric Oberg, whose wages seemed to me astronomical, but they were worth every penny we paid them.

Ruth cooked admirably. Eric was a superb butler (not that he resembled an English butler; he was white-coated, slim and fair). They were in their thirties, pleasant to look at, and even more pleasant to live with. After they settled in they said that, if we would tell them our general likes and dislikes, they hoped we would let them run the house for us, order the food, decide on the meals – everything. It was bliss. But rather expensive bliss. . .

Not that they were extravagant on food. It was simply that the equipment of the house wasn't worthy of them. Only the solid furniture had survived from the days when it had been the home of King Vidor and Eleanor Boardman, now my much disliked Mrs d'Arrast. Silver, table linen, glass, bed linen, towels were lacking or in bad repair. We went on a spending spree which did me a power of good. Incidentally, many of the things we bought are with us to this present day.

We also let ourselves go on parcels for England, clothes parcels which could not be sent by New York professional packing firms. Dress materials, stockings, and luxuries such as soaps, lipsticks, toilet waters . . . anything to give friends a bit of a lift. Alec packed madly in any free time he had from his work for conscientious objectors. And we managed to buy a little Bantam station wagon which looked considerably more roadworthy than the first tiny Bantam. There was so much black market petrol about now that it was hard to keep it out of one's tank, but we always felt we ought to, as aliens. Much the same applied to food and one married couple had refused to come to us because we wouldn't let them use their black market connections. Ruth and Eric stuck strictly to rationing and yet managed to supply wonderful meals.

As if to bestow approval on our extravagances, Warner Brothers now bought my first play, *Autumn Crocus*, (the film rights of which had reverted to me) for $20,000. And my agents expected to get a high price for the film rights of *Lovers and Friends*. I had a long and hopeful interview at one Studio where an important executive kept his feet propped on his desk throughout our conversation.

John van Druten returned from New York a week before Christmas, sunnily happy over the success of his *The Voice of the Turtle*. I greeted him with 'Here the Conquering Hero Comes' played by ear on the d'Arrast Steinway grand. He loved that. He had brought us the record album of *Oklahoma*, which for him was tied up with his great success. He said that while on tour he had frequently heard the music and while listening to 'Oh, What a Beautiful Morning' had suddenly felt the words, 'I've Got a Wonderful Feeling, Everything's Going My Way', were going to apply to him. In spite of his many plays, both in England and in America, he felt this was his first smash hit. I was happy for him.

Was I envious? Surely I must have been, but my main memory is of thankfulness that things had turned out as well as they had for me – and I felt this all the more after John had given me an almost line by line report on *Lovers and Friends*. The whole atmosphere was destroyed – Ray Massey had invented comic lines for himself, everything was angled to make a vehicle for Katharine Cornell. But I could hardly feel indignant about this last because John said she was superb, and I knew only too well that it was to her I owed my large earnings.

Chris came for Christmas dinner when Eric staggered me by offering a complete turkey, the breast beautifully sliced, on a dish which he supported by his left hand only. It made me feel nervous but Eric was as steady as a rock. Chris bought me *The Screwtape Letters*, three Merediths – because I'd expressed an interest in Meredith – and a novel by Raymond Chandler, whom Chris much admired. He also brought what he called a horror present, an early record by Frank Sinatra backed by a female choir. After listening to it Chris suggested we might take it out and bury it in the garden. In the end it was pushed in with our pleasant Mexican records, and is still there.

Chris spent the night with us and managed to make it seem like an adventure, almost as if he had run away from school. But he went back next morning because it was Swami's birthday and Chris had to be on duty in the Temple. I resented that Temple, all the more now because he was not doing any writing and even said he just might have to give up writing altogether. But he took the greatest interest in everything John and I wrote, if he didn't exactly hold it in high esteem. When I asked him what he thought of *The Voice of the Turtle* he said, 'Oh, it's really very pleasant, rather like being stroked.' With my work, his attitude resembled a school report that says, 'Could do better if she tried.' Alas, my idea of better was very far from what Chris thought of as better. And both John and I thought Chris knew not one damn thing about the theatre. But none of this prevented us all from being happy together.

Not that I was ever *really* happy, for any waking moment. I had come to accept that I must just put up with an underlying weight of unhappiness at not being in England. Sometimes this welled up in fits of misery, but for the most part I could take a surface pleasure in a very pleasant life. I would wake around eight a.m. in my high, raftered bedroom which had windows on three sides, two with balconies. I would get up, moving quietly not to disturb our brown-spotted father dog asleep on the chaise longue, and go to the largest balcony and look down on the view stretching to Beverly Hills and far beyond and tell myself how beautiful it was and wonder why it didn't mean more to me. I had tried to write a poem about this, my first effort for well over thirty years. It began –

> Nothing in this lovely land
> Seems to make me understand.
> Mountain, ocean, flower, tree,
> Only as through glass I see.
> Nothing enters into me.

Chris said this was beautiful. John said it didn't make sense. I admitted it was no good as a poem, but surely the meaning was clear? John said he simply couldn't understand it – and he could be an angry man when he didn't understand things. He was about to enter an angry period because he couldn't understand Eliot's *Four Quartets*, of which I got occasional flashes of understanding, though

Cove Way

Beverly Hills, California

Carmel, California

Adams House

Orcutt House

Seal Rock

Van Ness House

John van Druten

Adams House

Pongo

Carmel, California

Folly's Milk Bar

Replete

Palm Drive,
Beverly Hills

Bantam Cars

America's smallest

Tower Road

Beverly Hills

Dignity and Impudence

Tower Road,
Beverly Hills

Ruth and Eric
Oberg

Frank Morgan's
Great Dane

'Will it jump?'

'Will it bite?'

The House on the Beach.
Las Tunas

it was only some years later and after I had accomplished the mammoth task of learning them off by heart that I came anywhere near a full understanding.

While breakfasting in bed – Buzz, having been down to salute the morning, always returned to keep me company – I got the war news on the radio and sometimes listened to music, but most of my music came from our record collection which was flourishing during this period of extravagance; at the moment both Alec and I were fascinated by Scarlatti. I then had a bath where only the gold taps reminded me that this had once been a film star's bathroom; then dressed, and went down to join Alec and the dogs for the first walk of the day. I remember the clatter of our dogs' toe-nails on the shining tiles of the hall before we set out.

We would go down the near half-mile twisting drive to the mail box, a walk tinged for me by fear that there might be something unpleasant from Alec's Draft Board. It had, at last, been officially admitted that he was a genuine conscientious objector (in spite of having no church backing) and he had now been classified 4E, which meant that if men of his age *were* called up, he would be sent away to a forest camp. As no bad news came, my walk *up* the hill would be far more spirited. Dandy, already as big as his small father, Buzz, usually found some quite large branch to drag with him, frequently banging our shins; though he sometimes paused to rear up and pull an avocado off a tree, which he then ate. Buzz, though in radiant health, always expected Alec to carry him up hill. Folly went her own way, ignoring her husband and son. She had long ago established ascendancy over them both and, though often affectionate, would sometimes curl her lip in a way which struck such terror in their hearts that they would not go near her without an escort.

In spite of precautions, including a large fenced pen, they would occasionally get loose and go racing up into the hills. We would then beat on an enamel plate with a spoon, indicating that their dinner was being served. If they failed to return, Alec would dash out in the Bantam station wagon hoping to find them on some little road before they got as high as the Mulholland Highway, where there could be traffic. One way or another we always got them back, completely unrepentant and, naturally, expecting dinner whatever the time of day.

After lunch I usually settled down to work, and by work I meant a play. But as I had no idea for one that pleased me I developed a

mania for making notes. As a playwright I had frowned on
note-making feeling that it somehow muzzled one's subconscious
mind. And note-making can be a substitute for creative writing. On
the whole I heartily disapprove of it but, for me, the habit got the bit
between its teeth in the winter and spring of 1944 – not that there
was any real winter in California – I wrote down every idea I could
remember ever having had for a play and I could remember right
back to my childhood. There were twenty pages of these. I made
notes on the technique of play-writing. (Another twenty pages.) I
wrote copiously about all the books I was reading. (Why? I didn't
intend to set up as a critic.) And writing at breakneck speed I turned
out over fifty pages of something called *In Search* . . . the title
meaning that I didn't know what I was in search of. It seems to have
begun as a search for a 'new' kind of play, in which one could
convey one's meaning on some deeper level than realism, but it also
seems a search for some mystical experience – and the odd thing is
that I didn't then really know what a mystical experience was. One
way and another it now strikes me as a fairly crazy piece of writing
by someone I no longer know. All the same, I rather wish I did still
know her.

After a couple of months I firmly began a play, intended to be a
perfectly normal light comedy. I scrapped it in a week and went
back to note-writing – and journal-writing and letters and letters. I
had more of these to answer than normal because John had gone
back to his ranch and wrote nearly every day; he once wrote to me
four times in one day. Many of his letters came by Special Delivery.
The post office cars must have got tired of driving up our private
hill.

In March Raymond Massey left *Lovers and Friends* and Henry
Daniell took over his part, himself being replaced by Arthur
Margetson. Both of them made a success and several critics now
found the play better than they had remembered, but didn't praise it
enough to soothe my pride. And Jack Wilson warned me that it
might not run very much longer as the business was going down
slightly and the McClintics fancied taking it out on tour. What were
my agents doing about the film rights?

What they had already done was, after discussions with Jack, to
ask a quarter-of-a-million dollars for them. I had always felt this was
too much and, though there had been much interest, no studio had
made a definite offer. One reason for this was that, according to
Hollywood standards at that time, the play was censorable as the

wife in it was willing, in order to save her marriage, to condone her husband's infidelity. No doubt that could have been got over had the New York run continued triumphantly but it ended in May. The play then went on tour, for three weeks of enormous business. It was then supposed to open in Chicago for a run which, I was told, might be for months. But something went wrong about the theatre and, suddenly, everything was over. And we never did sell the film.

I had always been determined that the play should not be done in London until I could be there and I felt this all the more after the New York notices. Jack thought I should let Binkie Beaumont do it, but I was dead against this, quite apart from the fact that I wanted to be in London for the production.

Binkie (no one in the theatre world ever referrred to him by his real name of Hugh) was now of even more importance than when he had been responsible for the presentation of my *Dear Octopus*. Indeed, as the head of H.M. Tennent Ltd., he was by far the most important theatrical manager in London. He had also been our close friend and still had our Essex cottage, rent free. But as I had not heard from him for over three years, I took it that he was one (the only) friend who had turned against us and I was determined he shouldn't do my play. He had recently written to me most affectionately, hoping there had been 'no misunderstanding between us,' and wouldn't I send him a script as he felt sure the play would be just right for Diana Wynyard. I replied just as affectionately, but didn't send the script. I had three other enquiries from England, but refused them all. One additional reason for this was that, by the late spring, I had the glimmer of an idea for a play, set in England of this present year of 1944, which I hoped might be a far better play than *Lovers and Friends*.

I went into training for it. We had always had the *Sunday Times* and the *Observer* sent over to us. Now I had two daily papers sent Air Mail as well and steeped myself in them. It wasn't details of wartime life I was after; I wasn't planning the kind of play that needed details. I wanted to get the *feel* of living in wartime England. Later I was to hear that people who read the script found it very difficult to believe it had been written by someone who had not spent the war in England.

It was to take place during a week-end in May, 1944, when the Allied invasion of Europe was imminent – as it was, while I was working. The setting was a decaying country house in Suffolk, where its elderly owner, his American-born heir (now become more

English than the English) and a teenage granddaughter have as housekeeper a governess who had been with the family for thirty years. They are joined for one weekend by the old man's daughter, once a society beauty and now a welfare worker in a factory, a granddaughter now in the Fire Service who brings her touchy working class lover; and a young American great-nephew in England with the USA forces. The play dealt not so much with the present of these characters but with what was going to happen to them when the war ended. I would have liked to use as a title *The Prospect Before Us*, but that had been used for a ballet. So I chose instead *The Sofa And The Window*. A large semi-circular window, looking out over the wide countryside, typified a view of the future; a sprawling old sofa represented a refuge in the past. The scene throughout was the one-time schoolroom of the house, now used as a sitting room.

I looked back on the writing of that play as a time of dreamlike pleasure. Before starting work every afternoon I lay on my bed, looked out of the windows and imagined that the eucalyptus trees visible from two of them were willow trees, below which were English watermeadows. And when I sat down to write I did not feel I was inventing; it was as if the characters, story, dialogue simply unfolded in my mind. But I never wrote fast. The first draft took four months and the revision another three. Daily life continued much as usual. Charlie now came to dinner every Monday as lunch didn't give us enough time to talk. Sometimes Alec and I visited him, but I never got to know his very pleasant wife really well. John was away much, writing two plays. (One, *I Remember Mama* opened in the early autumn with enormous success.) Chris came on Sundays and we spent the afternoons on the patio, gazing down on the view which sometimes seemed to float in a golden haze which made us feel neither it, nor we, were quite real. Alec shared in the conversation but not, I fancy, in the sense of unreality in which Chris and I encouraged each other. We both of us liked to feel we were on . . . perhaps one might describe it as 'the edge of otherness'.

One conversation that comes back to me was about reincarnation – which Chris, officially, believed in. He told me that it was unlikely that Swami Prabhavananda, at the Temple, would come back on earth again. 'And he's not sure I shall have to. He believes that Vivekananda will probably get anyone who has had anything to do with the Temple *in*, after this present life'. Vivekananda, who had founded American Vedanta centres back in 1899, was very much one of the boys in the celestial front office. *In* – as far as I could make out – represented a state of Nirvana, a sort of unknowing bliss which I didn't fancy at all. I had no desire whatever to 'get off the wheel' of this life and, as I couldn't go on living for ever, I'd welcome other lives on *this* earth.

'All the same, you may find yourself *in*,' said Chris. 'You've been to the Temple. Did you have anything to do with the relics?'

'No, I didn't and I don't intend to. And you lay off getting me *in*. By the way, has it ever struck you that it's selfish to want to get in? Ideally, one should stand back and go on reincarnating till the last man's in.'

Chris said that was a very profound thought. I never knew how much of Vedanta he believed, though his whole life attested to the sincerity of his will to believe; his undoubted devotion to Swami Prabhavananda was ever increasing. As for me, I thought of Vedanta as a well-intentioned myth and I doubted if any religion would ever mean more than that to me.

In the small hours of June 6th, 1944, I lay in bed listening to the progress of the Allied invasion of Europe. Alec and I had listened together until long after midnight and then I had suggested we should listen in our own rooms. I knew that our moods would be very different. Alec would be very conscious of the horror, the destruction, the pain and the waste of human life. For me, though basically I agreed with him, the mass spirit of one's country at war would have a moving beauty, not to mention the pleasure of excitement. Never did I know Alec to enjoy the excitement of war. And my own excitement, even my uninvolved interest, shocked me.

I put out the lights, except for the little light from my radio. It was strange, lying there in the Californian moonlight, staring at the leaves of the eucalyptus trees silhouetted against the sky. My mind travelled over the years since I had come to America, back to the days when I made the decision to come. I still felt I had done what seemed nearest right to me, but whether it would prove to have been right in the end I was nowhere near knowing. Never could I have believed that my homesickness would prove so lasting. And, listening to the progress of the invasion, I realised I was homesick for Europe as well as for England. I remember thinking I'd feel more at home in France – or even Germany – than I did here. And then, as so often, I accused myself of gross ingratitude for all America had given me.

At dawn I got up and made some Ovaltine on my electric hot-plate and obliged Buzz by scratching his stomach. He had been the perfect companion for my D-day. There was to be a scene at dawn in *The Sofa And The Window* which I had been working on for a month or so. I wished I could be sharing my D-day with my characters.

I had my revision of the play ready to offer Alec in early October. He was always torn between wanting to praise my work and feeling he must be honest in order to help me. This time, from halfway through the first act, he found himself liking the play more than any of my earlier ones. We did some work on it together then speedily had copies typed.

Chris was so enthusiastic that I wondered if he was letting me off lightly because he approved of my effort to write a more serious play. But he swore he was being honest. I pressed him for criticisms and at last he said, 'When all's said and done, writing stands or falls by diction. If you were a greater writer your characters would say greater things. But are you setting up as Shakespeare yet?'

I asked if he didn't find any dull passages. He said, 'Yes, a few. But good writing must be boring sometimes and the dull passages help to set off the ones that aren't dull.'

I said, 'But there are no dull passages in your work, Chris.'

'That's just my nervousness,' said Chris.

He had at last finished his short novel, *Prater Violet*, which both Alec and I thought magnificent. But he had only finished it with great difficulty and had been ill several times during the past year. I began to think he was no longer happy at the Temple and he had admitted that he was finding the concentration on ritualism difficult. I had an idea he might soon want to leave and, frankly, I hoped he would.

I had never thought my new play could succeed in New York, but Alec felt I ought to let Jack Wilson see it and I wanted John's opinion, so scripts went off.

Jack praised the play, but said it was a study of changing social conditions in wartime England and would not interest New York in a year when audiences only wanted laughter and escapist plays generally. It ought to be on in England *now* and he begged me to send it to Binkie – which I'd already done.

John's reaction staggered me. He obviously really loathed the play, found it dull, depressing, unoriginal. None of the characters came to life. And as I read and re-read his verdict, it suddenly dawned on me that he hadn't even understood the play. He had jumped to wrong conclusions. I tackled him with this when I replied and he cheerfully admitted that he hadn't much liked the first few pages so he had merely skimmed the rest of it. I wondered if such behaviour from one of my dearest friends was forgivable, but as his insults were accompanied by great affection I set about forgiving them.

What mattered far more to me was Binkie's verdict. He cabled at length saying he was absolutely delighted with the script. It was my best work and he would like to present it in the early spring – if kept too long it would lose its topicality. His letter following the cable was even more enthusiastic. I cabled that he could go ahead with plans for casting. And I then came up for air and stopped feeling furious with John.

Around this time Charlie asked me to put in a few weeks talking to him about *To Each His Own*, the film about thwarted mother love which I had helped him with earlier in the year. We weren't hard-up as *Lovers and Friends* had earned more than any play I had ever written; still, money was flowing away like water and there would be the income tax to cope with; also I never felt I could refuse anything Charlie asked of me. So I agreed. Soon after that my agent rang up to say I appeared to be on Paramount's payroll. *Was* I working there?

I explained I had been at home waiting for Charlie to send for me. I now rang him up. No, he hadn't forgotten me. He'd been too busy to work with me, but I could come along to Paramount now. I spent a happy day mainly in looking at rushes of his *The Lost Week End*, but we did in the afternoon put in an hour or so talking. As he looked like being just as busy the next week, I suggested we should postpone the rest of my job until he was less busy. He agreed with relief, all the more so because Paramount was having an economy drive. I went home feeling slightly deflated, particularly as it was a pouring wet day, and when it does rain in California one is inclined to think the end of the world has come.

I found Alec had put violets and narcissi in my bedroom, chocolates, the English mail and a new detective novel on the bedside table, a glass of sherry beside it, and had set out towels and bath oil in the bathroom. (All this, presumably, because the little woman had been out to work on a wet day.) Would I like to have dinner in bed? I would not. But I did very much enjoy relaxing for an hour reflecting on Alec's thoughtfulness and the ludicrous world of Hollywood where I had just earned $2,000 for giving Charlie an hour's advice which he would have been welcome to on any of our Monday dinners for free.

Christopher spent three days with us at Christmas. And John, just back from New York, brought his partner at his ranch, Carter Lodge, for dinner on the eve of Christmas Eve, for lunch on Christmas Eve, and for dinner at night on Christmas Day. Looking back, I wonder Ruth and Eric didn't jib at quite so much entertaining, all the more because they didn't like John. They loved Christopher, liked Charlie but John, no. Eric said Mr van Druten was 'too rich'. He said this without the slightest impertinence. One of the joys of sharing life with the Obergs was that we could discuss anything on terms of perfect equality while, in all their work, they were the perfect servants. And Eric had a great sense of humour. Ruth occasionally had fits of Scandinavian gloom, but she had great charm.

Mr van Druten was certainly rich that Christmas. With his royalties as both author and director of two smash hits, and various side lines, he must have been earning around $7,000 a week. And the film rights for *The Voice of The Turtle* had been sold for half-a-million dollars, his share, for income tax purposes, to be paid over a number of years. But he wasn't as sunnily happy as he had been the previous Christmas over the success of the *Turtle*. And he had become rather grand in his attitude to the theatre, praising little and telling us that he frequently walked out after the first act of other people's plays – to me, unforgivable behaviour on the part of a playwright as well-known as John, as the casts invariably get to know. And he had become astonishingly talkative, almost uninterruptably so. And we did see rather a lot of him that Christmas.

After dinner on Christmas night he told us the kind of plays audiences needed now; they must be given warm, happy plays. John was never a bore and much of what he said was interesting, but he did say it at very great length and the evening developed into a lecture rather than a conversation. So that when, long after midnight, he and Carter accepted one last drink and took themselves off I was, for the first time in my life, relieved to see John go.

Alec and I only drank soft drinks after dinner and Chris had drunk very little alcohol. I said to him, 'Could you fancy some Ovaltine?'

'*Ovaltine?*' gasped Chris. 'Gosh, Ovaltine would be *spectacular.*' His tone managed to combine exhaustion with blissful anticipation.

And then I found we had run out of milk. To this day, over forty years on, I feel apologetic.

VII

The House on the Beach at Las Tunas

We were on our own for New Year's Eve. John had gone back to his ranch and Chris, having lunched with us, was back at the Temple. Alec found sentimental welcomings-in of the New Year embarrassing but he did, this time, oblige by doing the first footing. And Chris rang up soon after midnight to wish us a Happy New Year; he said they had just come out of the Temple and were going to have a little champagne. Alec and I, feeling the New Year had now had enough time to settle down, went out to the patio to look at the lights in the distance below.

In *The World in The Evening* Chris described the nightscape of Hollywood as sparkling like a million cut-price engagement rings. Either this reflected the mood of the narrator, or it is one of Chris's rare descriptive failures for the white lights resembled very big diamonds and the red, green and amber traffic lights, winking on and off, were even larger. The whole effect was most beautiful and it was enhanced tonight by the rockets going up to welcome in the New Year. We felt a little sad to think we should never again see a New Year in from our house on the hill.

We had originally taken it for a year, then extended our lease for six months at a higher rent. When doing so we had agreed to show the house to a possible purchaser provided our lease would not be affected by any sale. We had been out when the 'possible purchaser' called and had returned to find Ruth and Eric much amused because they had been visited by Katharine Hepburn (whom they knew well because they had once worked for her), who had never had the slightest idea of purchasing. She simply wanted to *rent* a house and Mrs d'Arrast had described her as a 'possible purchaser' to us, so that Katharine Hepburn could see all over the house before agreeing to pay a higher rent than we were paying. Our far from delightful landlady pointed out that we could now, if we wished, outbid Katharine Hepburn. But, apart from not wanting to pay an exorbitant rent, we did not wish to have any more to do with Eleanor d'Arrast, who had been unpleasant throughout our tenancy. And we still had the house until March. Anything might happen by then. Perhaps, even, the war might be over.

We stood there on our patio in the first hour of 1945, talking of the future, until the dogs became excited and started to run about with their heads held high like circus horses. We thought there must be a cat up a tree – it was too dark to see – but they soon turned their attention to an outside stone staircase that led to the upper floor of the house. They did not run up, just stood below, heads up, whimpering slightly. Staring upwards, we could just make out a dark mysterious shape. It looked too large to be a dog. Could it be some wild animal, escaped from some private zoo? It made no sound. The dogs were obviously scared; we managed to get them indoors, and then came back with a torch.

The dark shape was still there, dead silent. The torch revealed two glowing yellow eyes. Alec, though with considerable trepidation, went up the stairs; it *was* a dog. He spoke to it, telling it what a good dog it was. Fortunately, it believed him and allowed him to go right up and pat it. Then it followed him down, gently wagging its tail. We now discovered she was a black female Great Dane, by far the largest I ever saw.

I went in, got meat and biscuits and water for her. She wouldn't touch anything, just sat there, perfectly docile and expressing no view on life whatever. What were we to do with her? We remembered there was a little house, near our garage, intended for a chauffeur. Alec took her there on a leash, and I followed with the food. Quite suddenly, she relaxed and ate ravenously. I got more food and some milk, which she loved. Then she settled down for the night and was asleep before we left her.

Alec got up early and let her out, also introduced her to Ruth and Eric who gave her breakfast. She had to be shut up again when our dogs came out, but by now we had discovered she had a dog tag on her collar with a number, so Alec rang the police who reported that the number had been issued to a Pekingese. Was Alec quite sure. . .? After he had convinced them that he did know the difference between a Great Dane and a Pekingese they said there

was nothing they could do to help. He would just have to take the
dog to the dog-pound, which wouldn't be open on New Year's Day.

In mid-morning the milkman informed us he had seen a black
Great Dane at a house in one of the Drives. Alec loaded our visitor
into the little Bantam station wagon, where she looked larger than
ever, and set off. He found the house, but also found its resident
Great Dane on the lawn; so that was that. Two small boys then
approached and one of them said, 'You've got Mr Morgan's dog.
We'll show you where it lives.' They then clambered in on top of the
Great Dane and Alec learned that Mr Morgan was Frank Morgan, a
well-known film actor. A house was eventually reached where the
coloured woman who opened the door accepted the dog as Mr
Morgan's.

'I'd like to see Mr Morgan,' said Alec.

The coloured woman said he was still asleep. It was nearly one
o'clock. 'Then please wake him up,' said Alec firmly.

The woman looked dubious. 'He did have a very late party.' Still,
she did as she was asked. Mr Morgan came down looking half
asleep.

'Why is your Great Dane numbered as a Pekingese?' said Alec.

Mr Morgan wasn't too woozy to get the point. He said he had had
a Pekingese once and it had died. 'I thought I might as well use its
dog tag.' He then turned on some charm and told how he had once
found the Great Dane wandering in the desert 'with bleeding paws'
and had given it a good home. Well, he possibly had – it was in good
condition – but Alec didn't hold with fiddling over dog tags. He said
a few cold words and Mr Morgan promised to get things straight.
The little boys who had followed Alec into the house enjoyed all this
very much.

Some time in January Miss Hepburn called on us to ask if we
could oblige her by leaving our house a short time before our lease
ended, as she then had to get out of her present house. She was most
unlike a film star – no make-up and wildly untidy – and we liked her
so much that we said we'd help if we could. We at once started
house-hunting.

It was far more difficult than we had expected, especially as we
wanted a house high on the hills. We were shown the most unlikely
places, including the famous John Barrymore house. Here, to our
surprise, we found that the caretaker and our dogs were old friends;
it had apparently been to this house that the dogs had come when
they ran away up the hills. All that remained of the gardens were

now parched lawns, empty fishponds, a muddy swimming-pool and thicketries of weeds. The rooms in the house were dirty and sparsely furnished with ludicrous bad taste. When Hollywood luxury becomes decrepit it can be more sinister than any ruined castle.

An even more sinister house was one we had been told about, but to which we had not yet been given the key. Coming across it on one of our house-huntings we pushed our way into the overgrown garden to explore. The house had an unusual basement with a high plate-glass window. Peering in, we saw what appeared to be an elephant charging through a wall. We then saw it was only a third of an elephant, stuffed, fixed to the wall. The rest of the trophy room was occupied by a forest of giraffes, just their heads and necks – about ten feet of their necks. Some months later this house was much in the Los Angeles papers as the home of a woman who had been murdered. She was referred to as 'Fun-loving Mamie Boomhanger'.

After a couple of weeks of searching, we were getting so desperate that we considered taking 'Eagle's Nest', the house that had been Rudolph Valentino's. It had a wonderful view and the furniture, which had been Valentino's, was in good condition, even if it wasn't exactly 'us'. But we heard in time that we should have to let his fans visit the shrine in the garden and it might be hard to keep them out of the house. So that was that.

And then we heard of a beach house, belonging to the film producer, Anatole Litvak, at Las Tunas on the way to Malibu. So we drove down to see it, taking Ruth and Eric with us. From the outside I felt it was hopeless. It backed onto the noisy Roosevelt Highway – there wasn't even a foot of garden. But from the moment we entered the blue-tiled hall, which had a picture-window reaching to the high ceiling, we forgot about the Highway and thought only of the empty sandy beach and the blue Pacific barely a stone's throw away. The staff quarters were ghastly – as so often in the grand houses we saw – but Ruth and Eric could have a be-chintzed guestroom with a mirror-walled bathroom; I could have Anatole Litvak's bed-sitting-room with its vast desk and bookshelves (it was reached by a very modern spiral staircase); and Alec could have the whole of the beach-level floor with a playroom for the dogs, room for his office and the choice of four bunk beds. Once we had worked out how we were to fit into the house, we none of us had any doubts. Ruth remarked, 'Honest, I can't wait to get into it.'

We were able to meet Miss Hepburn's deadline but – though she had already sent many of her belongings ahead of her – she now said she couldn't take the house over until later, which left us with two rents to pay. However, we had liked her so much that we didn't hold a lasting grudge against her. Throughout the ending of our tenancy our landlady, Eleanor d'Arrast, behaved with such characteristic fiendishness that when we finally drove away from the hilltop house it was with far more relief than regret.

19130 Roosevelt Highway was the first really modern house we had seen in America. Every room that faced the sea had a sun-porch or access to a roof top. There was one very large platform built right out over the beach which we were able to fence in by fisherman's netting and ropes so that the dogs could play safely there. They were blissfully happy watching the sea and barking at very occasional human beings. The public had no easy access to the beach and the residents usually stayed on their sunporches unless actually bathing. It was early for bathing yet – cold, and day after day there was a thick sea mist, but I don't remember being depressed by it.

The furniture and decor throughout were modern, simple – and expensive. And there were good original paintings, notably a Utrillo and a Dufy. Colonel Litvak – our movie-producer-landlord now in the Army – was obviously a man of great good taste. I felt grateful to him every time I sat down at my enormous desk; it was the only time in my life I ever had a desk large enough.

Alec's beach-level domain included the usual Hollywood bar. He filled the shelves at the back with flowering plants instead of bottles and fed the dogs from the bar top. Every time they saw their three dishes set out there, they rushed to stand on their hind legs. After eating, they then settled on the large leather sofa to sleep off their food. All the upholstered furniture – except for the be-chintzed bedroom – was of chestnut leather.

Ruth and Eric found the house as stimulating as we did and spent their afternoons on their sun-porch. I was glad to see them happy for, by now, I knew they had one lasting sorrow. Some little while before the war they had sent their baby daughter to Sweden to be looked after by Ruth's mother, their plan being to save enough to start a business in Sweden. Now they waited year after year for the war to end while their child grew older. They longed for her and I think this was the main cause of Ruth's Scandinavian glooms. At her happiest she was a gay creature.

Our three regular friends all approved of our new house. John, after that exhausting Christmas night party, had returned from his ranch a few weeks later completely himself – which meant that he was argumentative, critical and resentful of criticism, but an excellent companion of whom I was deeply fond. He now remarked that it would be pleasant to have friends who had a beach house and I was happy to share the compliment with the house.

Chris had stopped being a Vedanta monk and was now working at Warner Bros but he was still sleeping at the Temple. (He had bought an old car.) His job was to make a film version of *The Woman in White*, by Wilkie Collins, and he planned to make it rather more 'earthy', hoping to start with a D.H. Lawrence scene where 'He grabs her in a stable'. I gathered this was not approved of by Warners. Still, he was having a lovely time. He adored everything to do with film-making. He often reminded me of myself in my stage-struck childhood when the very word 'theatre' was magical for me. I never did understand why, though Chris basically disapproved of the theatre, he found film-making magical.

Charlie came as often as ever, though it meant for him, poor busy man, an hour's drive each way.

By mid-March I had realised that Binkie's plans for an early spring production of *The Sofa and The Window* were not going to materialise. He continued to be enthusiastic about the play and relayed to me much praise from others who had read the script. But he could not cast the leading lady. He insisted she must be a star, and there was no suitable star available who would admit to being forty – which was of the utmost importance to the play. I wanted Valerie Taylor but he said she was not sufficiently a star and, anyway, he could not face a production with her. Having myself faced two, I knew what he meant. She was an exquisite actress, she had no intention of being difficult but her temperament was uncontrollable. Had I been in London I might have fought for her but I could not, as things were, attempt to wish her on Binkie or any director. So I went on waiting and hoping. And I don't remember being worried or depressed. My memories of the Litvak house are happy ones.

This puzzles me. What about my perpetual homesickness? What, above all, about the state of the war? Didn't that harrow me? I find in my Journal:

Saturday March 24th.
    The invasion of Germany is at its ghastly height – the Rhine crossed by the Americans and the British, the Oder crossed by

the Russians. Night after night after night the bombing continues on a far bigger scale than when England was bombed in the Blitz; great towns are devastated. Yet Germany holds on without one chance left. Each day thousands are killed on both sides, soldiers and civilians, because Germany will not give in. One cannot blame the Allies for going on – but one can blame them, I think, for sticking to the parrot cry of 'Unconditional Surrender'. Of course one blames the Nazis, but the German people as a whole have no power to end the war.

I am not taking it in, of course. I doubt if anyone in this comfortable country can. The imagination cannot annihilate space. I believe I suffer worse pangs of pity when I see a bird with a broken wing on the shore. Such a sight will at least distress me for the length of a walk, but does the agony of the world put me off one meal?

In a way, all the foregoing is insincere – just a tribute to the times, on this day of the Rhine crossings. For the truth is I am happier in this house than since we came to America. Of course I have my spasms of homesickness but they are coped with in a few hours. Worse than homesickness is the knowledge that I have really missed the war in England now, that even if some miracle took me home tomorrow, it would be too late.

Sometimes I wake in the night and go through to the bathroom. Through the porthole-type window I can see and hear the traffic still thundering past on the Roosevelt Highway. I think of life in England, women getting up to go to factories. Air raids – though one hopes those days are over now. Always when I come back to bed, the traffic noises now replaced by the thud of the breaking waves, I think of the war. How well could I have stood up to it? I only know that if I had my chance again I would choose to – but only for myself; I would not involve Alec in it – nor choose it even at the cost of losing the dogs.

I suspect those forty thousand words of Journal for 1945 are packed with this kind of writing and it was a method of soothing my conscience so that I could get on with enjoying life. Certainly there is much happiness in the Journal, glorious weather once the sea mists lifted, walks with Alec and the dogs along the sandy shore, bathing – but not for me; Alec and Chris adored it (Chris became lyrical and called the sea his mother), but their combined efforts could not keep me on my feet. The most gentle *looking* waves of the blue Pacific sent me sprawling. I was told to go through them or ride up on them. All I did was to go *down*, with a wall of water on top of me.

In the evenings we lit the fire in the sitting-room half of my bedroom and sat reading. How did I get through all the books I mention in my Journal? Henry James, Joyce, Ivy Compton-Burnett (a recent discovery), Proust – actually, it took me three years to get right through Proust. And music: I had a passion for Verdi's Requiem (never before had I liked Verdi) and I liked it *loud*. But I didn't play that in the evenings because Alec didn't find it music to read by. Neither did I. While I listened I thought of it as an opera – about all power corrupting. I felt that might be one opera I could like.

At midnight we took the dogs out for a last walk – or rather, as we were not now dressed for the shore, sent them out one at a time; had we sent them all together they would have turned into a pack and run for miles. There is a great deal in the Journal about the ever-fascinating behaviour of three deliriously happy dogs. Mention of what I was wearing reminds me that throughout the day I lived in slacks, shirts and beach shoes – or no shoes, only at night changing into what America called a 'hostess gown', usually inexpensive. A dressmaker in Hollywood who had made beautiful clothes for me had figuratively kissed me goodbye when she heard I was going to live on the beach. 'You'll turn into a beachcomber. It always happens.' She was right.

Another reason for happiness was that I was working well. I had gone back to the novel begun at Carmel, to be called *I Capture The Castle*, and was averaging a thousand words a day, a high speed for me – though I could dash off five thousand words of Journal in a few hours, journal-writing not being slowed by my critical sense. Never had I had better conditions to write in: Litvak's huge desk, my tall windows open to the sea and sky. The thud of the waves breaking never disturbed me; indeed, I was often so enclosed with my eccentric family in their Suffolk castle that I was unconscious of my California surroundings.

Alec had discovered he could fish from our living-room sun-porch when the tide was in. Encouraged by a shortage of fish, owing to a strike, he bought a rod and became most professional, catching quite large fish – up to five pounds – and two lobsters. We agreed that, as we weren't vegetarians, we could not be against fishing; still he felt sorry for the fish when he had to kill them (he killed the lobsters instantly; he didn't let Ruth boil them alive). But he came to feel that hauling in fish from one's balcony was a bit like shooting a sitting pheasant. I was sorry when his fishing phase ended as it had provided him with quite a lot of pleasure – not that he needed pleasure; he had a talent for distilling it from the air.

In April President Roosevelt died; I was bitterly sorry that he had died at this stage of the war. It seemed like Moses being forbidden to enter the Promised Land. I noted in my Journal:

> Poor, poor Roosevelt. If there is anything in Aldous Huxley's picture of life immediately after death – with earth still calling – what agony for his spirit. . . But perhaps there is some hidden justice, perhaps the war damaged his character. I cannot feel it has made the slightest difference to Churchill's, except to intensify it and give it scope. I feel he must say to himself, 'For this was I born.'

On May 8th came V.E. Day – Victory in Europe. I treated my Journal to eleven pages of that, after listening to the 6 a.m. broadcast from Europe, on the little radio we bought in 1939, just after the outbreak of war. I had listened to the German invasions of Norway and Holland on it, to the fall of France and the invasion of Europe. I now wrote:

> I didn't think Churchill was quite as impressive as usual. I heard no great phrase which can be remembered; but the indomitable personality was there as always. Truman did quite well, but was a bit like a good understudy keeping the curtain up. Eisenhower spoke beautifully. General Montgomery has the kind of exposed personality which comes out of the radio towards you; one can well understand why he means so much to his men. He brought God into his speech more than the others did, which usually annoys me, but he sounded sincere and, anyway, he felt it only right and proper that God should have a share in V.E. Day.
>
> I turned the radio off after half-an-hour of the Generals and lay thinking. Buzz, who had managed to roll himself up in my yellow cashmere rug, rose and staggered across the bed like a moving mound and collapsed on my chest. In my mind he stood for Alec and the other dogs, all well and happy. Had we left the dogs behind in America when, in 1942, we tried unsuccessfully to go to England, they would now have been without us for nearly three years.

Later in the day I got an impressive broadcast from London, the whole town going mad with joy and relief, the King and Queen and Princesses out on the balcony six times. Piccadilly at midnight (afternoon in California) still packed under the floodlights. I was fated to be out of England on her great days. On Armistice Day in the First World War I had been in France, but then I had felt part of things.

Still, I wasn't indulging in an orgy of nostalgia in that very long Journal entry. Charlie had once said to me 'My poor child, your nose is squashed flat against the glass of that war.' It hadn't been quite so squashed since I had accepted that, as far as my work was concerned, I had now completely missed the War, and the Journal soon deals with my present work – and John's.

He had a new idea for a play and I had praised ninety per cent of what he had told me about it, but that wasn't enough. He became very petulant, picked books up and threw them down, gave me the impression he'd like to kick the furniture. My Journal records that in an effort to smooth him down, I told him how he'd improved as a writer since he came to America (quite untrue; I'd much preferred his English plays). This cheered him up and he told me just how *much* he'd improved. 'Sometimes I'm frightened by my technique. It's so good'. I longed to see a Thurber drawing of a Playwright frightened by his Technique. But his best effort came at the end of a long afternoon when Chris and I had put in some very solid listening (not Alec; he frequently walked out on John); he remarked, '*If* I may talk about myself for *once*. . .'

At the end of May Charlie asked me to work with him for two weeks on *To Each His Own*. He had put this off as long as he could, knowing I was busy with my novel but now he could wait no longer. The film was shortly to go into production. He wanted me to vet all the English scenes and, in particular, the dialogue of the character named Lord Desham for whom an excellent English actor, Roland Culver, had been engaged.

I didn't want to leave my novel. I was over halfway through it and was working with ease. But I should be glad to earn $4,000 and working with Charlie was always more like pleasure than work. However this job wasn't so easy, because Lord Desham's dialogue was truly appalling. Charlie always asked for frankness and never resented it but this time, though he often laughed, I could tell he was disconcerted. I simply could not convince him that no English earl could be so superior. It was then he looked at me and said,

'Woman, you *are* Lord Desham.' I never convinced him. But when, eventually, Roland Culver arrived and objected to every line I had objected to, Charlie, most nobly, at once told him I had already objected, and at last made the changes.

In spite of our – gentle – disagreements I enjoyed my two weeks with Charlie which earned enough to pay our rent for eight months. And our Rolls Royce also got itself a lucrative engagement. It was Alec's habit to deliver me, and the three dogs, to Paramount in it every morning – he would never have allowed me to arrive in a lesser car – and then, as he couldn't get enough petrol to drive back to the beach and then return for me, he had to stay around. Sometimes he joined me to see some film – I remember we saw a rough cut of Charlie's wonderful *The Lost Weekend* – but more often he shopped, exercised the dogs, had the Rolls serviced. One day when he was parking it in Beverly Hills he was approached by someone who asked if it could be hired for a movie. Such a high fee was offered that Alec accepted, stipulating only that he should come with the car and be on the set with it. By coincidence it was Paramount that hired the car. When the great day approached, Alec polished the paint work and chromium until it was quite dazzling; when it moved off one felt pennants should be attached to it.

Unfortunately, it was far too dazzling for the cameras and had to be considerably dulled down. It then appeared as a Vice-Regal car in a film about India and was driven through a bazaar crowded with extras. It had with it *two* uniformed chauffeurs and a monkey. Alec watched over its welfare for a week and then Paramount kindly polished it up again and it returned home having earned a full month's rent of our house.

Charlie suggested that Alec should take a screen test; he would be so right for English officer parts if he could act. (We remembered how the pioneer aviator, Grahame White, once our London landlord, had determinedly called him Major Beesley.) Alec, quite sure he couldn't act, declined. Charlie had once offered me a small but important part in *The Uninvited*; the part of a lunatic, casting which gave Chris and John much pleasure. They were even more pleased, later, when a writer was needed to turn a bestseller about lunatics into a movie; my agents rang me up to say, 'You're Darryl Zanuck's first choice for *The Snake Pit*.'

I had such difficulty in restarting *I Capture The Castle* that I feared I should have to scrap the whole thing. Then, after several days, I managed twenty-four lines – and suddenly I was at work again. I have often looked at Chapter XI remembering how nearly it didn't get written. It gives the impression of having been tossed off with ease.

But I soon ran into domestic difficulties. Our dear Obergs decided to leave. Ruth's delight in our beach house only lasted a short time. Then her glooms broke out again and she seldom seemed well. In May she decided to have all her teeth out. As she had never complained of tooth trouble, I guessed she was determined to have American dentistry before she and Eric returned to Sweden, as they planned to do in a few months. (We, ourselves, had had a good deal of American dental work, but in the interest of keeping our teeth, not getting rid of them; that work has paid dividends ever since.) Ruth now announced she would be in bed for two weeks. I asked if she would like us to send her to a nursing home. She said, 'No, this is my home. I stay here. Eric will nurse me and he won't be able to do *anything* for you.'

The last words were said defiantly but with a touch of hysteria; so I agreed and said we would get in some daily help. 'No, no, no. Eric would not like a stranger in the kitchen.' In the end Eric cooked our breakfasts and we were permitted – just – to employ our doughty New Zealander who was between jobs and drove down every day from Beverly Hills in her little red car.

Ruth got her new teeth and Eric hurried her out to eat a large steak. He was convinced that only steak could restore her vitality. Personally, I found it quite difficult to eat American steaks with my own teeth, but Ruth managed fairly well with her false teeth and seemed cheerful. But one had to handle her tactfully. Part of the trouble was that they hadn't taken their normal holiday, saying they preferred to be paid double instead for it.

Towards the end of July John was at his Hollywood apartment in the Chateau Marmont, making final revisions to a play shortly to be produced in New York. He rang up one morning asking if he could drive down at once for advice. Knowing we had plenty of food in the house I invited him to lunch, then went to tell Ruth.

She threw what Charlie always called a 'ground fit' – as when a child flings itself down and beats the floor in rage. It was too short notice, she was worn out, we had too many guests. Had it been Chris or Charlie all might have been well, but not that rich Mr van Druten. (He had recently told me the enormous amount income tax was taking out of his earnings.) Ruth announced to Eric, 'We leave at once, today!'

I said we would go out to lunch. Eric said, no, he would cook it but he shook his head sadly and added, 'But I think we must go. I have seen this coming. Ruth must rest.'

They stayed on for a few days, giving us time to engage a coloured manservant who was sure he could manage on his own. And in the end we parted friends. But it was sad to part thus with a couple of whom we were genuinely fond. They did return to Sweden, were disappointed, and Eric wrote to Alec asking for financial aid, which was supplied. Some years later we met them in Beverly Hills. They had returned, bringing their daughter and had a good job, I think with Al Jolson. Ruth said all her nervous troubles had been cured by hypnotism.

Our new man, Miller Bridgewater, who was quite young, managed the housework with ease and cooked fairly well. And as he was more than satisfied with the bedroom off the kitchen which the Obergs had spurned, Alec moved up into the be-chintzed bedroom. (Not that he hadn't liked his beach-level room in spite of the fact that, the first night he slept there, the very high spring tide had thundered up against the floor directly beneath his bed and he had woken up terrified, fearing that the whole house was afloat and going out to sea, which has happened on Californian beaches.)

When Roland Culver arrived to play Lord Desham, Charlie asked us to entertain him one Sunday. We found him very pleasant, but Chris took exception to his upper-class manner and accent, and behaved very naughtily. On hearing Mr Culver was staying at the exclusive Bel Air Beach Club he said brightly, 'Oh, my best friend's the cook there.' (The friend was a friend of ours too: Denny Fouts, at present living in Santa Monica, in a very small apartment with a very large and valuable Picasso. He had offered to lend it to us, but we'd never had a wall large enough for it.) Mr Culver seemed quite unperturbed about the cook, so Chris started to talk about venereal disease, asking Mr Culver what treatment was best for it. At last Mr Culver said, in a slightly pained voice, 'I'm afraid I really don't know. You see, I've never had it.' On which Chris said, '*Really?*' somehow conveying surprise.

In August came V.J. Day with its news of the Japanese surrender. Chris telephoned and asked if he could come to dinner, and arrived bringing a bottle of champagne. Miller served the meal and then we sent him off in our little Bantam car, to celebrate with his girl friend in Los Angeles. We sat at the dinner table watching the sun set over the Pacific until it was dark, talking and – in my case – doing some private thinking. God knows I was thankful that the World War was over, but it wasn't going to make all that difference to me, personally. I still couldn't go home, I didn't want to, really. Apart from the fact that I couldn't face quarantine for the dogs, I needed some reason to go, such as a play to present and I now saw that, with the war over, *The Sofa and The Window* would have to be shelved. And Binkie, in spite of continued efforts, was still not within sight of casting it.

While waiting for Chris to arrive I had written in my Journal:

> I wish John would come, too – he's in New York again. Perhaps John and Christopher and Charlie are my chief wartime acquisitions – though I also count my Henry James novels and my record collection. . .
>
> How dulled one's sensibilities are. Life magazine this week has a picture of a Japanese burning to death after being hit by a flame thrower. I was horrified for several minutes, then went back to work and wrote quite easily. And what is one Jap soldier burning to death compared with the dropping of the Atomic Bomb? Thousands have been blown into eternity by it – the lucky ones, that is; probably the others slowly burned or suffocated.
>
> It must be just on seven years since I heard that there was danger of war – in August, 1938, riding in a taxi in Manchester with Alec and Barney Gordon during the pre-London tour of *Dear Octopus*. Nothing has ever seemed quite right for me since and I sometimes wonder if it ever will again. No, I don't wonder. I know it won't – not the natural right for me. It might turn right in a different way. I may yet see the pattern in the carpet. But nothing will give me back those seven years, those seven years of really belonging to England. Non-attachment! What a dreary doctrine, but one that creeps on one in spite of oneself. Another minute and I shall start reliving those seven years. Spare the poor Journal! Surely its million words are enough?

When I broke off there was just time to take the three dogs for their walk before Chris arrived. And, as I watched them playing on the edge of the waves, it was then that I first knew what I so fully realised while we watched the sun set after dinner: that I couldn't quarantine them. I also knew that, though Alec would do just what I wanted, he was very happy here. He always insisted that he was 'not spiritual'; it had become a sort of joke, but he had far more spiritual contact with the sun, the sea and the air than I had. Evening after evening, he would sit watching the lights come on in Santa Monica across the pale twilit sea. And he would be glad to be here a while longer now the world was at peace, which would mean far more to him than it did to me.

When I cabled to Binkie that I thought we should give up all idea of presenting *The Sofa and The Window*, he cabled back with regretful agreement. Then I heard from Firth Shepherd, whose management was well known to me, asking if he could do it, as he had heard such good reports from people who had read it. But apart from the fact that I thought it had dated overnight – over Peace Night – I knew if Binkie couldn't cast it, no one else could. I must just concentrate on getting my novel finished.

Late in August Chris came to live with us, in a room attached to our house intended for a chauffeur. It had its own front door and entrance up a high staircase from the beach and the idea was that he should be entirely on his own. There was a shower, a beautiful view and, by the time Alec had finished carrying extra furniture up that long staircase, it looked charming. Chris asked if we would mind if he had a friend there and we said no, as long as the friend didn't run about the shore brandishing a knife, as some of the jeunesse dorée of Santa Monica were recently alleged to have done. Chris was joined by Billy Caskey who was to be a friend of his – and ours – for years; he showed no signs of being a knife-brandisher.

Chris was determined only to have his Sunday meals with us and would often sit with us while we had dinner and then go out and buy his own meal (maybe with a friend). He was still at Warners and had saved $7,000. I doubted if it would last long at the rate he was spending it, mainly on his friends. And he bought a new car, a convertible, planning to take Caskey for three weeks' holiday in Mexico when he left Warners – which he did, late in September. When they returned they took Denny Fouts' Santa Monica apartment and set up house dominated by the giant Picasso. I got to like it quite well. You just had to accept that it was boss.

It was as well Chris no longer needed to live with us, for by the time he got back from Mexico we knew that Colonel Litvak, back from the war, needed our much-loved house.

VIII

The House on the Beach at Malibu

The move came at a bad time for me. I had recently finished the first draft of my novel and was finding the revision more difficult than I had expected; since beginning the book four years earlier I had become much more self-critical. I hated to break off and house-hunt and the hunt wasn't easy as we both of us wanted to stay within sight and sound of the sea. In the end we took a small, far from satisfactory, house on the fringe of the movie colony at Malibu Beach. This was further up the coast which meant a longer drive for our friends.

One of my last memories of the Litvak house is of waking in the very early morning to find a bat asleep on the pillow beside my head. I almost panicked. Did not bats get into one's hair, were they not covered with vermin? Then I controlled myself and decided that, for the first time in my life, I had the chance to take a good look at a bat. I found it beautiful, fairy-like – perhaps more witch-like, but I had long been attracted by witches. Still, I couldn't go to sleep with it beside me. I slid out of bed quietly, covered it with a handkerchief, then slipped my hand under bat and handkerchief and carried them to the door onto the roof-top accessible from my room. It felt nice to hold, quite dry and faintly warm.

I found it a sheltered place, put it down and removed the handkerchief. It stirred and folded its wings, looking mouse-like. Then it crawled into a crevice. For a while I sat on the parapet of the roof-top, looking at the sea; the sun was already up but the lights of Santa Monica were still twinkling. I felt fond of my bat and sorry to be leaving that very pleasant house.

One advantage to the new house was that it was separated from the Roosevelt Highway by a small plantation of trees and a dank little garden, but the architecture was quite undistinguished. Downstairs there was a kitchen, with a bedroom and shower off it, a dark dining-room, and a fairly large sitting-room, with a wonderful view, but atrocious decor. The walls were dark chocolate, the upholstery peacock blue and orange. There were red chintz curtains with blue, yellow and turquoise flowers and birds on them. The only friend who ever admired that decor was John who had peculiar taste in interior decoration. (At his ranch house he had given instructions that his bedroom should resemble 'the best kind of hotel cocktail lounge.') Still, there were two large sofas, several comfortable chairs and a floor-level cushioned window-seat at the picture window; the dogs monopolised this window seat and spent hours staring at the Pacific and the long lines of sealions which often swam by. And Chris gave us a large Douanier Rousseau colourprint to replace a truly terrible Mexican painting.

Upstairs there were four small bedrooms, with one bath (mine) and one shower (Alec's) between them. Fortunately he liked showers, which were my idea of a wet hell. Alec's room was an unexceptionable brown and there was room for his large desk. My walls were mauve with turquoise paint. I had to buy three bookcases and a desk and had them painted turquoise, too. The desk was barely a third as large as my Litvak desk. But both of us had wonderful views of the Pacific and we were to find in time that the whole house, bad decor and all, had a certain cosiness. It was, incidentally, even closer to the sea than our previous house and the sandy beach was even more deserted, which was good for the dogs and for us.

When we had been there less than a week, Charlie urged me to start on some new work with him. The job this time was to make a screen-play of an old Barrie play, *Alice Sit By The Fire*, originally produced in 1905. He already had a script, but didn't think it would work. Could I make suggestions?

Beyond remembering that my mother had liked one scene where a girl was washing her hair, I knew nothing of the play and I now thought it was the silliest play by a distinguished dramatist that I had ever read. It hinged on the fact that a young woman, played by Irene Vanbrugh when well into her thirties, equates the lives of her parents with those of characters seen in society plays, and sets out to save her mother (Ellen Terry, then fifty-seven) from an entirely imaginary liaison. This must have been pretty silly even in 1905; in

1945 (the film was to be set in the present day) it was ludicrous and the scenes between the girl and her girl-confidante were embarrassingly coy. There was also a schoolboy brother, said to be thirteen, but created by A.E. Matthews when he was thirty-six! After two full weeks, during which Charlie drove down every Saturday – leaving me just to 'think about things' during the week (on full salary) – I came up with the idea that the film should be set in the period in which it had been written and that the young woman should be just a *child* – say fourteen – who, having been sent home from India where her father was in the Army, had never seen a grown-up play. She and her little brother, sent to a matinée of *Peter Pan*, by mistake got in to see a dashing play called *The Reckless Mrs Rossiter*, which entirely influenced their views of life in London. I scrapped the idiotic confidante and let the little boy take her place and I retained the period atmosphere of 1905.

Charlie liked this idea, begged me to try just a few scenes and, egged on by him every Saturday, I found myself making a complete film script. I had a whale of a time writing scenes for *The Reckless Mrs Rossiter*. Alec typed out the finished job and then we handed it to Charlie, who was enthusiastic. So, surprisingly, were Paramount and all the boys in the front office. The film was to be in colour; I suggested pastel shades to suit the Edwardian period. Wonderful idea! I had drawn plans of the two flats in which the story was set. The scenic department was delighted. Most surprisingly of all, John loved the script, though he warned me it was too good – 'It'll get ruined.' After ten weeks of highly lucrative work, I was free: though Charlie told me he would want me again later, to help with casting and supervise the actual shooting. My dear, kind Charlie – I think he still saw me as becoming that glory of Hollywood, the Producer.

While working on the script I had, in my evenings, coped with forty Christmas letters to friends in England. No doubt this was the reason I reverted to my old habit of sleep walking or rather, sleep talking. After the last letter was airmailed I fell asleep in my chair one evening, then sprang up saying I hadn't written to my Manchester uncles. Alec told me afterwards that I had talked, with my eyes wide open, for a good two minutes before he was able to convince me that my uncles had been dead a great many years. That same night I woke in bed to find myself telling Buzz, very angrily, that *he* hadn't written to *his* uncles. I still remember his hurt and astonished expression at being awakened and told that he was a bad, bad dog.

Writing in my Journal in January I record:

> From my window now I can see a wonderful sunset – a great bank
> of cloudy pinkish orange, the sun having gone. The sea is almost
> cornflower blue and the dark rocks have a surrealistic look. A
> dazzling moon is rising. The little white houses of the Malibu
> movie colony look like a nursery-rhyme town or some neat
> theatrical ground-row. I shall enjoy this house even more when I
> have time to look around a bit. But alas, the rainy weather must
> start soon. I work better in good weather and I wish I could have
> devoted all we have been having to my novel.

I also record that Chris has had a great critical success with his
novel, *Prater Violet*; Time magazine considered it the Book of the
Year. Chris wrote in the copy which he gave us:

> For Dodie and Alec,
>   those great philosophers, who have achieved the Truly
> Organized Life after extraordinary austerities in following the
> little-known path of Dalmatian Yoga,
>   from their friend and worst disciple Christopher, this little
> token of affection and gratitude for the sobering east wind of
> their criticism and the eternal summer of their kindness –
> Santa Monica
November 1945.

John, staggered by Chris's reviews, said – 'Did *you* see all that in
it? Did Chris *mean* all that? Was it in his subconscious? Or is it
merely in the minds of the critics?'

John had had a bad failure on Broadway with his play, *The
Mermaids Singing*. The reviews weren't as rude as mine for *Lovers
and Friends* but, thanks to Katherine Cornell, my business had been
very good; John's wasn't and the play swiftly came off. He behaved
very well about it. No doubt having his two smash hits still running
helped. Chris, though without malice, had said he hoped John
would have a failure because it would be good for his soul, and
failure was so much more interesting than success. Still, I think he
was quite pleased that his own soul lost the benefit that a failure of
Prater Violet might have meant to it.

He had recently had an operation. We never discovered what it
was for, merely that it was something he didn't know he'd got and it
wasn't serious. Later he learned that the operation was unnecessary
as he hadn't really had what he hadn't known he'd got. He was

always much obsessed by medical matters, particularly his 'septic tendencies'. At the moment he was pondering how his life would turn out; it depended on which of his two plans for it eventuated. Plan A was that he would die very soon. Plan B was that he would live to be very old. Alec and I opted for Plan B.

When I got back to revising my novel, I found it difficult. I had elected to tell the story by means of a journal kept by a seventeen-year-old girl. I felt I had made her lively and that all the other characters, seen through her eyes, came to life, as did the castle and its surroundings. But I did not feel the book was well enough written. Of course she must not write pedantically, but she was well-educated, had been brought up in a literary atmosphere – her father was a once-famous author – and there was no reason why she shouldn't write in good English and express her meaning. Combining this with her own idiosyncratic turn of phrase (which made the humour of the book) and making everything she wrote sound natural was one hell of a job. Sentence after sentence had to be rewritten – often several times – before it satisfied my mind, my ear and my conception of the seventeen-year-old journal-writer. And the whole book had to seem as if it had been written easily and, above all, be easy to read. Often as I battled my way on, I remembered Sheridan's saying: 'Easy writing's vile hard reading.' In my case, easy reading was vile hard writing.

And the book was so long. Not having written a novel before, I did not know that would-be light, amusing novels were seldom longer than eighty thousand words. *I Capture The Castle* is nearly a hundred and forty thousand words.

My progress was snail-like, all the more so because we were now indulging in an orgy of sending parcels to England. Friends thanking us for Christmas parcels were telling us that life was now more dreary than during the war, especially as regards shortages (rationing was as strict as ever) of which clothes shortages seemed the most depressing. My job for Charlie had earned so much that we felt we could let ourselves go a bit and in less than three months Alec had packed sixty parcels. I helped with all the shopping. We cheated shamelessly on the customs declarations, marking the price down and saying new clothes were used clothes; I often put face powder on the necks of dresses and coats to indicate this. One of our unused bedrooms became a cross between a grocer's shop and a clothes shop.

By late April I was working with Charlie again, at Paramount, making small improvements to the final script of *Alice Sit By The Fire*, discussing casting, seeing tests. Dear Charlie was on top of the world that spring as the Charles Brackett-Billy Wilder movie, *The Lost Weekend*, had won the Academy Award – indeed, a whole sheaf of awards; best picture, best-written screenplay, best direction, and its star Ray Milland, as the alcoholic, had won the award for the best actor. I had happened to go into Paramount just after the announcement of the awards and had seen that, from each of the many windows facing the courtyard, there dangled a whisky bottle (typifying the film's theme) which had been hung out to celebrate its great success.

Enthusiasm for the script of *Alice* had mounted. Charlie's nice secretary, who always pulled his scripts into shape, told me I had suddenly mastered the technique of film-writing. (News to me). The stars were almost decided on, but the girl whom Charlie had hoped to play the daughter did an unsatisfactory test. I didn't wonder, having seen how badly she was directed. Charlie then asked me to work on her and we at once found she was produceable. Charlie then said I must be on hand for the entire shooting and make sure my lines were said in the way I wished. He would have arranged for a very high fee, but I feared the work would take many weeks; also I was sure it would cause trouble with the director. But could I refuse?

I needn't have worried. A few days later a female voice on the telephone from Paramount informed me I was no longer on the payroll. I said there must be some mistake. Oh, no, there wasn't, and she had already informed my agent. No doubt Mr Brackett would explain.

He came through soon after I rang off. The film had been indefinitely postponed. The boys in the front office had changed their minds about the leading lady; Charlie wouldn't accept the leading man they had wished on him, nor was he happy about the director (neither was I, after seeing him direct tests). We must just wait for a better set-up. The film would be made one day.

(And so it was. Eventually its friends in the front office decided it must be played by Americans and given an American setting. Much of my dialogue survived, but sounded all wrong spoken by Americans, though I must admit that, when I saw the film, the audience seemed to enjoy itself. My scenes from *The Reckless Mrs Rossiter* were saved, but quite wrongly produced. Barrie's title had been changed to *Darling, How Could You?*. I told Charlie my title for it now was *Bastards, How Could You?*)

I had just settled down to my novel again when we heard from one of our greatest friends, Murray Macdonald (co-director with me of my play, *Bonnet Over The Windmill*, in London) that he was in Miami, staying with his friend Ronda Keane, daughter of the famous actress, Doris Keane, now dead. He would have liked to come and see us, but English wartime currency restrictions had made the long journey out to California impossible for him; we persuaded him to let us help.

We met him in the small hours at Los Angeles Airport. It was the first time I had ever been there or ever seen a great plane arrive. I found the atmosphere strange, dramatic. I felt as if I were in the future; I had for so long lived enclosed in my own little world. And the world Murray came from had so long been lost to me. I was almost nervous of meeting him, but as he walked towards us the last seven years were annihilated.

We talked all through the long drive back to Malibu and on through the night, almost exclusively about theatrical London. Murray, seeing the dawn breaking over the Pacific, remembered the last time we had seen dawn together, after a long meeting with Binkie Beaumont to discuss the presentation of my *Bonnet Over The Windmill*. Then we had driven to watch the sun rise over the Thames.

We spent the next day quietly and I began to realise how tired Murray was, but by the following morning he was lively and anxious to be driven to see various old friends who were in Hollywood – Dame May Whitty and Ben Webster (our good friends too), Edna Best, Jessica Tandy. . . But from then on he asked just to stay at home on the beach, except when we drove him into the countryside.

There is a snapshot of us, high in the hills. Murray is looking as boyish as ever though he was now in his middle forties. I am wearing slacks and a tweed jacket made by Motley eight years earlier. I was dressing worse and worse. A Malibu hairdresser, whom I had asked to trust me because I had come out without money, had said smilingly, 'No one who wasn't very rich would dress as badly as you do, Mrs Beesley.' Not that I frequented hairdressers much now; I had given up permanent waves and was growing my hair, which obliged me by growing well below my waist and could be put up in a plaited bun.

Murray was the easiest of guests, appreciative of everything we did for him, charming with the dogs, who adored him . . . and yet I found his visit saddening. For one thing, he did not encourage me to return to England. He did not now think I should ever again like living there; things had changed too much. I felt that, if this proved true, I should indeed be a woman without a country. I would simply be an exile from the past. But he was mainly talking of the theatre world which, he said, had lost all its glamour. I was sure I should never lose my love for the English countryside.

He could only stay a few days. I find in my Journal:

> By the time Murray left we were relieved to let him go and I felt he was anxious to get off. This doesn't mean that our affection for him has dimmed, or his for us. But Alec and I are always happiest to be on our own and Murray has always wanted to get on to the next port of call. He is the friendly dog who goes from house to house. Also days and days of talking can be exhausting. But I felt a real emotional loss when he stepped on the plane, somehow I seemed to be losing England with him. I cried as we drove away. The bright California sunlight seemed pitiless, the Los Angeles streets hideous.

Years later Murray was to tell me that he had felt quite despairing about us. He did not believe I should ever finish my novel, he did not think I should ever write another play. He thought I had been sucked into the world of Hollywood and would just stay on and on. And yet he did not feel he could advise us to go back to a much changed England. But when we did eventually return, it was Murray who organised it.

After he left I struck a bad patch. I say in my Journal:

> I spent the whole of yesterday hammering out one shortish paragraph and ended by feeling that my head might burst at any minute and that my neck was stiff for life. Never have I felt so imprisoned in my body – or rather, imprisoned in my head . . . I have no particular pain, but the 'about to burst' feelings come on as soon as I start to concentrate. How utterly boring! How I loathe being conscious of my physical self. Apart from the damned discomfort, it is against my principles!
>
> . . . An inner voice says to me distinctly. 'You are urging your brain mercilessly all the time because you are revising, not creating.' I know that when the subconscious does work it can be restful, not exhausting. I have known a furious headache to be banished by a flash of inspirational writing. Well, well, maybe I shall one day look back on this period with pity for my pains, but

with wistfulness for the fag-end of my youth, even with its discomforts. I wrote 'youth' but I am really middle-aged; perhaps I shall soon be on the foothills of old age.

I think that some of my discomforts, both mental and physical, may have been connected with the fact that, in that summer of 1946, I was making an effort to find myself some religion. My Christian Science, such as it was, had never been a religion, merely a philosophy, a kind of logic. But after reading Aldous Huxley's *The Perennial Philosophy*, sometime earlier, it seemed to me that there might be . . . well, *something* available. I was now reading book after book by Evelyn Underhill and becoming much interested in mysticism which, it seemed to me, need not be connected with any particular religion.

Writing of one of her books in my Journal I say:

> It helped me at a time when I could hardly work at all – my efforts to do so tired me so much that, in the evening, I could neither read nor listen to music and took to going out and lying on the beach, looking at the stars. I suppose I was trying to get some sort of religious experience or, anyway, help. I can't say I did, really – though once, after I had fallen asleep, I woke, looked at the stars and thought 'Of course, the real proof of God's existence and man's immortality is man's eternal aspiration to that immortality' which seemed to give me some sort of satisfaction.

That summer's Journal contains pages and pages of my religious aspirations, some of which might be interesting if only the seeker had ever come anywhere near finding what she sought, but she never has.

By August I had something less nebulous to think about. My greatest woman friend, Phyllis Morris, after hearing from Murray of his visit to us, sent a cable saying she intended to come, just as soon as she could arrange it.

Of all my English friends she had been the most difficult about my stay in America. She hadn't wanted me to come, she hadn't wanted me to stay and she had been saying so in letters for over seven years, often most angrily. She *missed* me. Well, I missed her and I very much wanted to see her, but when the letter which followed up the cable stated that she was coming for at least three months I became nervous. As young women we had never been able to live together very peaceably; how could we manage it now, in this cramped little house? Still, we at once cabled that we should be delighted to see her and we would of course pay all her expenses. She had said she was quite willing to spend her savings but, though she had inherited a fairly comfortable income and made quite a good living as an actress, we were determined that her savings should remain sacrosanct.

Her letter contained one phrase which struck me as pathetic: 'I will not disguise from you that I would like something nice to eat for a change'.

We next heard that she wished to enter America on the Quota, in case she could get work in pictures, and we should have to sponsor her, the necessary documents for which would have taken us weeks to assemble. We should need letters from *five* banks (we didn't have *five* banks), certified income tax returns, proof of our own legal entry, etc., etc. In the end we sent a notarised statement of our position which she took to the American Consulate in London. Arriving after it was closed, she got hold of someone who turned out to be the Consul himself, who must have been a very kind man or susceptible to bullying (or both), as he arranged for her entry on the Quota.

After some weeks and many letters, we received a cable from her saying: 'I am on standby for call. Plane may leave at any moment. Cannot book railway transport here. Please contact Paramount New York and ask for reservation hotel and overland train journey. Will cable them and you what date I arrive.'

I feared that even Charlie's good nature would not stand for her peremptory assumption that Paramount would help, but when I showed him the cable he roared with laughter and said, 'Isn't she the damndest woman? But she'll sail through all right', and at once started coping. Everything she asked for was arranged. (Paramount plaintively asked who was going to pay: we of course.)

Charlie, with us when we were in the midst of preparations for her arrival, remarked that, having had trouble himself with house guests who stayed on and on, he could foresee a time when I might welcome a job working *at* Paramount; he could always cook something up. But, actually, once I knew she was almost on her way, my main feeling was one of pleasure. And I was feeling better, no longer lying about on the beach waiting for God to *do* something, and even writing fairly well. That, of course, would have to stop when Phyl arrived. Alec had moved out of his room for her, which meant that he and his office would have to exist together in the welter of food and clothes for his English parcels, but he too was looking forward to seeing Phyl. Still, one night when we were quietly reading in our ugly sitting room – always at its best when lit only by reading lights as so much of it disappeared – he suddenly said: 'Oh, the dogs and ourselves and books and peace – it's so *good*!' And I knew just what he meant.

Charlie, having heard from Paramount in New York that Phyllis had arrived, rang us to say, 'The Ice Woman Cometh'. John, at the Chateau Marmont for the winter, rang to say he and Chris had decided she would be an Ibsen Rat Wife character and would cause me to poison all the dogs and commit suicide. Alec would then become a film star. There was no doubt that our three men friends were looking forward to seeing the fun when I had to share my daily life with another woman.

Phyl telephoned from New York. I wrote in my Journal:

The voice seemed curiously high, light, indefinite – nothing like as forcible as I remember it . . . I found myself thinking of her as bewildered, vaguely pathetic. She'd been plane-sick the entire Atlantic flight – 'No one else was; it's just that I'm a hopeless traveller. I ought to be sent by rocket'. She was completely bowled over by New York: 'It's so *lovely*. And the shops! There's everything in the world in them – things we haven't had in England for years'. She wished she could stay longer, but her train journey was booked and the hotel couldn't keep her. She'd managed to see four people she once knew and she'd bought stockings and a blouse. 'And I've had turkey – and I had ice cream as soon as I got off the plane. And I've bought chocolates for the train journey. . .'

After she rang off, I sat remembering our early days together at RADA, our touring days, the times when we shared flats and ran concurrent love affairs in adjoining rooms, our many holidays together. . . It's up to *me* to make her visit happy, to make it bridge over from our past friendship to friendship for the rest of our lives. I must discount my resentment at many of her belligerent letters. *I must make things work out.*

IX

The Friend of my Youth

When, a few mornings later, we drove into Los Angeles to meet her train, I found myself wondering if she would be wearing one of her notable hats. So many of her re-entrances into my life were pin-pointed in my memory by the hats she wore. There had been the Dolly Varden surprisingly worn with loud checked tweeds, the black felt trimmed with a life-size yellow-kid chicken, the gold satin chamberpot, the imposing russet structure in which she had been married. . . She often complained that I make her hats sound funny whereas they were really stylish. The truth is that they were usually stylish *and* funny; and her Los Angeles hat was no exception. It resembled a Salvation Army bonnet, sedately black but, upstanding from the highest part of the brim, there was a bright pink feather curled into the shape of a question mark.

She also wore a dark, well-cut suit and carried a wine-coloured velvet coat; I hadn't seen anyone so formally dressed for years. For a moment she looked older than I had expected – and no doubt she felt the same about me; we hadn't met for nearly eight years. Then she became just the person who had been my best woman friend since we were both on the stage in our 'teens.

Of course we said the kind of things one does say at a reunion – how lovely to see her again. I know I said how attractive her clothes were. She didn't return the compliment and almost before we had settled her into the front seat of the Rolls (the three dogs allowed me a tiny portion of the back seat) she asked me what I meant by wearing slacks. 'No one in England wears them now – we take pride in dressing smartly in spite of rationing.'

I said somehow one did wear slacks on the beach.

'Well, I haven't brought any. And I don't suppose I shall spend too much time on the beach. I intend to get work in films.'

Buzz, whom I was nursing as Folly had kicked him off the seat, created a diversion by trying to eat the pink veil on the back of her hat. I was glad to feel the dogs looked better groomed than Alec and I did and that they hadn't recently found a high-smelling dead sealion on the beach to roll on.

She was in high spirits and interested in everything. Nothing, of course, compared with New York and she didn't think much of Hollywood's famous Strip. But she quite liked Beverly Hills. When we reached Santa Monica she said, 'Goodness, you *are* a long way from anywhere.' (And we still had a long way to go.) Then, after looking at the people on the beaches, she said, 'I suppose I *shall* have to get some slacks.'

I told her we'd go shopping that very afternoon and everything she needed for the beach must be a present from us. She protested but Alec helped me to persuade her.

She liked our Malibu house better than I expected and was touchingly grateful for all the flowers in her room, and to Alec for giving his up to her. 'But I shan't be here long, of course. Just as soon as I get work I must find a flat close to everything.' Then we had lunch, which she adored; Miller had rather gone to town over it. She told us that the food for the four days on the train had been wonderful, but the wastage was awful. 'I showed the people I had meals with that they were leaving far more than we in England got for a full meal. They were astounded.'

After lunch she suggested that she and I should take a little walk on the beach while Alec got the car out for our afternoon's shopping in Santa Monica. I was surprised and pleased as I hadn't thought the beach or the Pacific – both looking their best in brilliant sunshine – had attracted her. No more they had. All she wanted was a few minutes alone with me to get something off her chest. Before we had walked more than half-a-dozen yards she said: 'I'd better tell you this at once. I've told all our friends that I'm going to put a bomb under you. Things here are even worse than I expected. Why are you living out here at the end of the world with no friends? Why aren't you writing plays or doing highly paid work for the studios? You're simply vegetating. . .'

It was a very long tirade but at last I managed to get a word in. I explained we hadn't been able to get the right house in Beverly Hills and now we liked it better here, that we'd three good friends which was all we had time for and that we were going to stay here until I finished my novel.'

'*We* don't believe in that novel.'

I was near to losing my temper. Fortunately Alec called to us that the car was waiting. And as we walked back to the house I reminded myself that she had been bottling this up for years (well, not quite doing that, when I remembered some of her letters) and I must be patient. But to attack me so soon! It didn't augur well for her visit.

We dropped the subject and the afternoon turned into a success. She seemed quite drunk with pleasure at seeing so many unrationed clothes, all of them – according to her – so cheap, so amazingly cheap! It was an expensive shop and they weren't in the least cheap, but I was only too happy to spend some money on her. As well as slacks we got a jacket, blouses, dresses, beach shoes. . . Only next day, when she had asked us to take her shopping in Beverly Hills, did I discover that she believed the dollar was the equivalent of the English shilling. She was involved in the purchase of a really expensive suit and hat which she insisted she was going to buy with her own money, and I felt I must warn her that she would be spending a great deal more than she realised. We got over the difficulty by persuading her to let us lend her the money until she was earning. By now I had seen how dead set on a movie career she was and on starting it at once.

At the weekend Charlie, Chris and John rallied round – Charlie laden with flowers – all of them anxious to help her. Charlie would give her various introductions and try to find her a good agent: John would write to Alfred Hitchcock about her – also he thought there might be a part for her in a play he was writing; and he said he would take her to the theatre and to the opera in Los Angeles – she could stay the night, after these occasions, at the Chateau Marmont with him, as his guest. And as she had already telephoned several old friends in Hollywood, including Dame May Whitty, and been asked to lunch with them, it seemed to me that she had cause to feel cheerful. So I was astounded when, only a couple of days later, she had an outburst of rage.

Though usually very fond of dogs she had taken little notice of ours – with the result that they took little notice of her beyond springing up and barking if she came into a room unexpectedly and in an outfit they hadn't seen before. They would then subside, wagging their tails sheepishly. On the day in question she burst in from the garden through a door that we seldom used. They were fast asleep in the sun on the window seat. All three of them barked wildly and Phyl pretty well exploded.

She screamed that they were near vicious, completely unintelligent, as all Dalmatians were, they were ruining our lives, were responsible for our living out here in the wilds. . . (All of this utterly untrue.)

Suddenly Alec erupted. In a voice any Sergeant Major might have envied he shouted, 'Phyllis, LAY OFF THE DOGS.' He went on to say that she could criticise us and our way of life – which she had certainly done, again and again (that bomb she had brought with her perpetually ticked) – but she would *not* criticise our dogs. 'You've made absolutely no attempt to get on with them. I've given you biscuits to offer them and you won't even try. So I'm warning you once and for all. If you want to live in our house, lay off criticising the dogs.' He then went off upstairs.

Never had I seen him so angry and never had I seen Phyl so shattered. She looked really frightened. He came back almost at once and they made friends – much to my surprise they actually kissed – and the whole violent outburst had most satisfactory results. I think Phyl had been feeling she must not show approval of the dogs. Now she made an effort and they fell for her instantly, showing her great affection, which she very much enjoyed. By the next day she was writing poems to them, one poem for each dog, and she had the nerve to tell me, 'I simply didn't understand them because they simply aren't like dogs. They're like some different form of human beings.' Phyl and I still weren't out of the wood – there were, alas, so many woods – but never again were the dogs a source of trouble.

About a month after she arrived I got a free day to write my Journal, as Alec had driven Phyllis to spend the night at the Chateau Marmont and be taken out by John. I noted that during her first twenty-eight days something had been arranged by us to interest her on twenty-two days: she had met friends in Beverly Hills, been taken to appointments with agents, parties at Charlie's, dinners at different restaurants (I find it hard to believe I survived all this) and she had grown quite fond of Malibu beach. Snapshots show her teaching me ballet exercises; we both look idiotic. Christopher's friend, Billy Caskey, came to take excellent photographs of her which might help her in movies. He also took Chris's favourite photograph of me which Chris insisted had a look of E.M. Forster. Much as I admired Forster, I did not particularly hanker to look like him. On the whole I thought Phyl was enjoying herself. But nothing was happening about her career and she confided to John that she felt wretched at being so far out of everything – not that this was a secret from us; she mentioned it every day.

We finally suggested that we should finance her in a small housekeeping apartment in Santa Monica, from which she could reach Beverly Hills by bus every day, if she wished, instead of having to call on Alec to drive her. She loved this idea and so did I as it would give me a chance to work. Stanley Salmen, of Atlantic-Little Brown, the Boston publishers, who had always encouraged me to write a novel, had recently visited us and begged me to hurry up. Also I was getting worried about money. No doubt Charlie would have cooked up some job for me, but he was now away.

And at this moment – well on into December – a job was offered me by, of all studios, Metro. They told my agent that they knew I hadn't been happy with them, but they now wanted to make this up to me. And they would pay me anything, anything if I would just polish the script of a film version of Margery Sharp's novel, *The Nutmeg Tree*. What was more, if it would help, Louis B. Mayer would ask me himself!

Why? Why was I being so honoured? My agent said Metro had rung up Charlie Brackett and, as he was not available, had asked Billy Wilder what he thought of me. Nobly, he had handed on what he thought Charlie would have wished him to say. Now Metro were avid for my services. A polish job would only take a month or so, and salaries were no longer frozen; I could ask a very large one.

I said, 'Will they pay me $5,000 a week?' I had never heard of a writer being paid so much.

My agent, after enquiries, said they would pay that, if I would just please read the script.

It arrived and it was sheer hell. No polishing would help. It would need to be rethought and then rewritten. The job could take many months. Still, I was begged to come and at least, discuss the matter. So Alec got my kolinsky cloak out of fur-storage – I hadn't used it once for nearly seven years – and drove me in the Rolls, plus the three dogs, to my once so-hated Metro.

I was interviewed by Everett Riskin and George Cukor, who were to be producer and director of *The Nutmeg Tree*. I liked them both, particularly George Cukor. (John loathed him.) From the first, everything went well. They agreed with me about the awfulness of the present script. Wouldn't I please do a completely new one, not just a polish job? I said I was in the middle of a novel and could only spare a month at $5,000 a week. It then appeared there was just a little snag about $5,000. All studios had agreed never to raise a writer's salary too spectacularly. But they would pay $25,000 for the job and, if I could do it in a month, that would work out at *more* than $5,000 a week. I said the whole script (plus one re-write, they managed to slip in) would take me four to six months and that was quite out of the question. Not for any salary in the world would I tie myself up for so long.

'The trouble,' said George Cukor, gently stoking my modest kolinsky cloak, 'is that she's too rich.' Presumably he thought it was sable. (Since then I have changed my mind about wearing *any* furs.)

It was a charming interview. They liked all my ideas, they laughed at almost everything I said, we got on splendidly. But they went on wanting a full script, however long it took, and I kept on refusing to be tied for more than a month. A hovering secretary said, 'Shall I go and get Mr Mayer?', but I managed to dissuade her. At last I said I would take on the job for six weeks, provide a new story-line and do as much of the script as I could in the time. And to my great surprise they accepted. My agents were told to work out a contract.

But next day Metro rang to say that they had changed their minds. They wanted me more than ever and they would up the offer to $35,000, but I must undertake to finish the script. God knows how long that would have taken me. I had to refuse – and see all that fairy gold whisked away from me. This made me all the more determined to get on with my novel. I realised that it might never make as much as Metro's offer; might never even be accepted by Atlantic-Little Brown. But it had got to be finished, immediately after Christmas.

This was the first Christmas for five years that Chris had not been with us. He had again taken Caskey to Mexico. Recently, I had not felt Chris was very happy, and that it was a deadly waste of his talent that he should be doing odd bits of movie writing – not very satisfactorily. We missed him greatly.

Early in December, Phyl had moved from Alec's bedroom to one of our backrooms, which she much preferred as it was prettily furnished. But she still hankered for a Santa Monica apartment and in the New Year she discovered one and moved in. For three weeks all was peace. I wrote five days a week; we brought her home for every weekend and she was much more relaxed. Her prospects were looking up. Her agent, Stanley Kramer, got her some radio work in a Sherlock Holmes series and then she was promised a small part in a Hitchcock movie, to be made in the spring. Although we assured her she could count on us financially, she felt she must now become independent and had sent to England for £500.

And then she quarrelled with the Santa Monica apartment-hotel and was back on top of us. She made a real effort not to interfere with my writing hours but, with me, a good day's work needs a quiet evening, and she would not listen to music or read; she wanted to talk. And she so frequently talked herself into a state of indignation, either with me or with life in general. Alec often cleared out and read in his bedroom. Mercifully, after a few weeks of this, John saved the situation. About to leave for New York to make plans for his recently finished play, he offered Phyl his Chateau Marmont apartment, rent free. He would definitely be away for a month and probably much longer.

By now he had heard her read a part in the play and decided she was not suitable. (She told me his method of directing her was very old-fashioned.) But he had promised her the understudy if she needed it. She never did, and she enjoyed living in Hollywood – eating in drug-stores and shopping in supermarkets. Alec always said that it was the Californian supermarkets which cured her of Communism. I had for years known of her interest in Communism, but only when she came to America did I realise how deep it was. I decided it was partly responsible for her bad temper. She once positively snarled at Charlie that Stalin was a saint. When he protested mildly, 'But what about all the executions?' she shrugged her shoulders and said, 'Oh, well there may have been one or two.' Charlie gave up, but did not give up being kind to her.

Now she was enjoying the lavishness and bustle of American life; it must have been a welcome change for her after the quietness of life with us. We were enjoying the renewed quietness; one evening Alec stopped reading and said, 'Listen to the glorious silence.' I particularly remember that we discovered the novels of Henry Green that spring and became convinced that he was the most interesting living novelist. It was one literary enthusiasm we have always been able to share. Alec could admire Ivy Compton Burnett but not enjoy her. And though he had an affection as well as great respect for Henry James, I think he found reading him a bit like work. But he liked Henry Green almost more than I did.

My writing was now going so well that I broke off every weekend without resentment to make a holiday for Phyl. The pattern of our weekends had changed as Chris was now away in England, enduring the bitter winter of 1947. Charlie was as faithful as ever. It never ceased to amaze me that he would drive so many miles every week for a very mediocre lunch – Miller was getting worse and worse, but we were too sorry for him to get rid of him. He had a wife and baby in Los Angeles and a load of hire-purchase debts he couldn't cope with.

One reason that I look back on this period with pleasure is that Phyl was becoming so much more like her old self. True, she had occasional outbreaks of temper, but she had always had those and, as in our girlhood, she could now sometimes laugh at them. Even when John returned after a couple of months and she came back to live with us, life was fairly peaceful and I carried on with my writing. And within a very short time John decided to go back to New York (plans for his play, *The Druid Circle*, were not too promising as yet) and then to England for the production of *The Voice of the Turtle*. He offered Phyl his Chateau Marmont apartment for an indefinite period, but one which would certainly last well into the summer and he suggested she might pay half-price for it, $100 a month.

Unfortunately this led to one of her explosions. She was outraged that he should ask for anything, when he made so much money. Embarrassed, we offered to pay; John said she need not pay; she recovered her temper and insisted on paying, which she could well afford as she had parts at Metro and at Paramount lined up. And her money from England had now arrived; out of this she had insisted on repaying much that we had spent on her. She was never in the least grasping; her fury with John was due to sudden, unreasoned rage.

In May, when I was finishing the revision of the last chapter of *I Capture The Castle*, my dear, dear Charlie came up with an offer I felt I must accept. I have wondered if he did this out of sheer kindness knowing, as a once unsuccessful novelist himself, how little my novel might earn. But he said he needed me desperately. He wished to make a movie out of Henry James's *The Portrait of a Lady*, as a vehicle for Olivia de Havilland. He wanted 'my knowledge of James, my enthusiasm'. And he only wanted a story-line – he would probably write the full script himself. Anyway, wouldn't I at least put in a couple of weeks re-reading the book (on full pay) and then we could discuss it together. No, I needn't come to Paramount, he would drive down to Malibu for all our meetings.

I enjoyed re-reading the book and our early discussions and efforts to simplify the complicated story. But I was always aware that Charlie, though a well-read man, had never much liked James and his enthusiasm was not for the book, but for the project as a whole. And he hoped I could help sell it to the bosses at Paramount.

My idea of a story-line was to describe it, sequence by sequence, which took fifty pages as there was so much to cover: scenes in America, England, Italy. . . What Charlie wanted were bold dramatic effects to impress the front office. After weeks of work, he suggested I should turn the whole thing into an exciting magazine story. This seemed to me utterly impossible and, anyway, I'd never written a magazine story and didn't know how to. Charlie had written plenty, for the Saturday Evening Post, and after reading my effort, he said he'd tackle the job himself; then he read his version aloud to me. The only line I remember from it was 'a river of ice is now flowing between them' and I'm thankful to say that, when he had finished reading to me, he said, 'Sorry. It's far worse than yours.'

Yet something in his version helped me. I was able to catch his crispness of tone which, combined with drastic cutting of my own work, resulted in something which delighted him – and, he assured me, delighted the boys in the front office. But they felt that all those settings would be impossibly expensive, at a time when Hollywood was being badly hit by a change in the English film quota laws. Oh, they would make it later. I prayed they wouldn't and they didn't.

Never had I worked so hard as during those weeks with Charlie, writing and rewriting, while Alec typed and retyped my work. Now I was free – but I was also sad. Christopher, while in England, had sent me as a present two letters he had found at Wyberslegh, one of his ancestral homes in Cheshire. (He said that he didn't know what use they could be, unless it was to heal scripts.) They had been written by Henry James to the H.B. Marriott Watsons; Chris's uncle had been Marriott Watson's literary executor. Re-reading them with affectionate reverence, I was sad to think that my eight week's valueless work might have earned me more than James had earned by his superb novel, successful though it had been. (*See below)

Well, I had done my poor best and I was thankful for my $16,000, also thankful that Charlie and I had come through all our struggles and arguments with our friendship quite unimpaired.

I now finished my novel without difficulty, and by early August was ready to show it to Alec. I had long ago given up showing him, or anyone else, my work until it was finished as the slightest criticism could put me off, so he knew scarcely anything beyond the fact that it was set in a house built onto the ruins of a castle in Suffolk.

* See Appendix for two Henry James letters.

Remembering he had not always liked my plays on a first reading, I was nervous now, all the more so because the novel was slight, so feminine and, I guiltily knew, too long for such an unimportant book.

I needn't have worried. After reading the first chapter he said he found it fascinating and was quite sure he would go on liking it because of the setting and the characters. He finished it in two days with ever-mounting enthusiasm and I was to find he had not missed one detail. I basked in his praise.

He then suggested that there were a few tiny criticisms he'd like to make, one or two improvements he wanted to suggest. Could he perhaps read it aloud to me and mention them? I loved the idea of this. He reads aloud admirably, so naturally that I have often looked up thinking he has stopped reading and is simply talking. And knowing that he liked the book as a whole, I welcomed the idea of a few suggestions. I was to find myself with fifty foolscap pages of his notes ranging from details of punctuation to particulars of alterations which called for whole pages of re-writing. Often I disagreed with him fiercely but, sooner or later, came to see he was right.

He would say such things as 'You don't make me feel the weight of the stones of the castle', 'The bull-terrier, Heloise, has character but no physique – I can't get the feel of her', 'What did Cassandra *see* when she swam the moat by moonlight'? I had taken it for granted that readers would know what moonlit water looked like. Alec wanted Cassandra to notice that each time her hands went forward they made silver ripples just in front of her eyes. And there would be gold on the water where the candle-lit windows of the castle were reflected. He also pointed out that when swimming a moat you would see the flowers on its banks from a most unusual viewpoint, the stalks first and only the undersides of the flowers. He made dozens of atmospheric suggestions such as these, helping me to create the castle, the countryside, the weather. . . He also pounced on any sentence where the meaning wasn't crystal clear. My problem was that the effort for clarity must always be disguised. And in such matters as the weight of the stones of the castle, I always had to guard against just doling out information to the reader. Cassandra was writing for herself only. I must know what *I* wanted to say and then find some reason why Cassandra wanted to say it.

It took us two weeks to read the book through. It took me over two months to cope with what I have always thought of as 'Alec's revisions'. They were harder work than writing the book, or making my own revisions, but even when they were driving me almost demented I knew they were of the utmost importance. I finished them late in October, Alec retyped seventy pages, and then we sent our script for professional typing.

Phyllis, who read the book during two of her weekends with us, was as enthusiastic as Alec except that she said (with considerable force) that there ought to be a full-size happy ending. I should have found this utterly false.

For nearly two years Alec and I had planned that, when the book was finished, we would move back to New York. I wanted to be there when it was published (if it ever was), go to theatres, return to playwriting and feel three thousand miles closer to England. But where were we to live? Apart from the expense, we doubted if any good hotel would take us with three dogs and John, after making enquiries, reported that there were queues waiting for apartments. And we should soon be faced with renewing the lease of our far from satisfactory Malibu house for a considerable period. I began to feel I should never be allowed to get away from California.

Then Murray Macdonald rang up from Doylestown, Pennsylvania where he was again staying with Ronda Keane, asking us if we would like to rent her old farmhouse as she wished to be away for the winter. We could have it for four months, from the end of November.

It sounded ideal, in real country, surrounded by woods and fields, but only seventy miles from New York with a good train service. We decided instantly. The move was on.

We should need a new car. Now we had three dogs the Rolls would be impracticable for a very long trans-continental journey; also it had no heater and we were certain to run into winter weather. New cars were still almost impossible to get. But not if one had friends at Paramount. In no time at all Charlie arranged for us to buy a De Soto station wagon, a huge car flashing with chromium and pretty vulgar, but the colour was a pleasant green. We took the middle seats out and filled the back of the car with three mattresses, covered in brown fabric. These would be comfortable for the dogs to travel on and could be rolled up and taken in at night for dog beds. And if hotels or motels refused to take the dogs, we could at a pinch sleep in the car full length with them. There was a touch of Covered Wagon days about our preparations for our three thousand miles winter drive. Charlie presented us with a line of tinned goods, hot chocolate, creamed chicken, etc, which could miraculously heat themselves when the outer tin was pierced. The contents were excellent, but I always feared the tins would explode.

Charlie took off our hands the stray canary which had taken refuge with us and been given a palatial cage and every conceivable toy, but had refused to sing. Charlie said he would hang it in his bathroom and teach it to sing while he shaved. It remained mute, but he said he got good ideas for movies while he talked to it. He also took home the stray Persian cat which we had, unknown to the dogs, fed at the back door for months and which had been allowed to sleep in our laundry.

One other animal came to us for help while we were in that beach house. I was reading in bed, after midnight, when I heard some creature whimpering outside. I got up intending to tell Alec, but I found his light out so went down on my own. Outside the back door was a collie dog with a fish-hook caught in the corner of its mouth. This was something I couldn't tackle alone, so I woke Alec and we went down together.

He had brought a pair of thick gloves, but never needed them as the dog was gentle and it remained absolutely still, though removing the fish-hook was difficult and must have been painful; it took several minutes. Once the hook was out our problem was what to do with the dog, our laundry being occupied by the Persian cat. Alec thought it might have come from a farm high up on the hill across the Roosevelt Highway. So we took it to the road and Alec hung on to it until there was no traffic. Released, it streaked across the Highway and up the hill. There was enough moonlight for us to see it reach the farm. Why did it come to *our* house with its fish-hook, instead of going home? When I told John about this, he said 'You are the most extraordinary couple. I have rarely known you to show affection for human beings, but I'm quite sure that if three goats and two bees knocked on your door in the small hours, you'd at once get up and let them in.'

Alec said, 'Well, of course.'

I said, 'What had happened to the third goat's bee?'

John came back to California a week or so before we were due to leave. He had been unlucky. The morning after *The Voice of The Turtle* opened in London we received a cable from him saying, 'Dreadful notices'. And since his return to America, *The Druid Circle* had opened in New York and was now expected to close after only a few weeks' run. I was very sorry for him. I admired *The Druid Circle* – far more than I had ever admired *The Voice of The Turtle* – but it was a grim play about life at a Welsh university, quite unsuitable for New York.

He was only back in Hollywood now for a week; he said his main reason was to see us before we left. He was kind and affectionate, coming down to see us three times and telephoning several times a day. But he managed to infuriate me about my book. After he'd read the first few chapters he rang up to say that he was having a marvellous time, couldn't put it down, etc. *But* how could I, who admired authors such as James and Proust, write anything so *trivial*? How *important* did I think it was? I said I'd never even considered the matter. I'd written it because I wanted to write it and written it as well as I could. He said it was beautifully written, some of the descriptions were perfect. He was often touched, always eager to go on reading. But he resented this, felt it was like eating a box of chocolates without stopping. I suggested he should slow down a bit but he wouldn't hear of it. 'I've got to go on and on; there's so much suspense.'

In the evening he rang up to say he had finished, 'I timed myself. I read it in seven hours'. (This seemed a bit of a rush for a novel 140,000 words long.) He said he'd made himself three lots of tea and hot-buttered toast, 'It's a lovely book to read over hot-buttered toast'. But he still didn't think it was worth writing – 'It's just not *important*'. And he didn't think it would succeed in America. Perhaps it might in England, but there was a shortage of paper for books over there.

Months later he surprised me by saying he had read the book three times and had found far more in it than on the first reading. 'How can you expect me to notice detail when you put in so much suspense?' But he continued to think of it as a hot-buttered toast book, not worth writing. Alec and Phyllis believed that his attitude was due to his own recent failures, but I doubt that. It stemmed far more from long accumulated resentment that I enjoyed authors he couldn't stand. Our friendship remained intact, but my ever present nervousness about the book was increased. Perhaps I had wasted years on a novel that would never even achieve publication.

My only other verdict had been from Charlie. It had been kind, but I suspected this might be just to encourage me. Still, some of his praise had sounded convincing, especially for the humour. Chris was now travelling in South America so I couldn't ask his opinion.

We had many letters from him.

A few days before we were due to leave, we paid a goodbye visit to Beverly Hills.

This was our first outing in the De Soto. Dandy and Buzz roved around happily on their mattresses at the back, looking out of all the windows and often resting their heads on our shoulders to look out through the windscreen. Folly chose one of the back corners and rarely stirred from it, now or in the future. I don't know that she actually liked the De Soto – as she had liked the Bantam station wagon, now sold – but she didn't *mind* it, as she had minded the Rolls, which was now on its way in a freight car to the New York Rolls agency where it would be safe until we needed it again. This had been arranged by the Beverly Hills firm that had serviced it so well for eight years. Eight years! I found it hard to believe we had been in California so long.

We drove past the house in Cove Way where we had lived for a year after I came to work for Metro in 1939. I had some happy memories of it, of Alec and Pongo, but I mainly remembered myself as someone wounded by loss, whose mental sufferings amounted to physical pain. Now I found myself almost envying the poignancy of those feelings, of which I was no longer capable. It was as if I had grown a skin over the worst of my homesickness, but it was still basically there.

By the time we were high in the hills it was dark and we could take our last look at the jewels in the black basin that was Beverly Hills. I remember feeling guilty because I had never learned to love California. Alec had, but even he was ready to leave it now.

Phyl had been staying with us while John occupied his Chateau Marmont apartment. This was now free for her again but she had stayed on at Malibu to see us off. On our final morning I took a last look at my bedroom, now minus my desk and bookcases – half a van-load of our possessions had left the previous day – and went down to the denuded sitting room for a last talk with her.

She was already making a career for herself in movies and beginning to save money. But she would certainly miss me and I should miss her. By now we had retrieved much of the happy companionship of our early days.

She had undertaken to spend the day in the house supervising its thorough cleaning by Miller. Poor Miller, he had wanted to come with us and had even suggested sending his wife, now expecting a second child, to live with her mother. But we had had all we could stand of Miller. He had continued to get worse, was perpetually having to be rescued from financial troubles, had wrecked our smallest Bantam car and once almost set the house on fire by sheer carelessness; but we forgave him all his debts to us and made him a farewell present of money. The trouble with Miller was that he needed driving and I had lost my capacity for driving people.

Phyl hadn't lost hers. When I apologised for leaving her to cope with him she said, 'Not at all. I'm looking forward to it', and there was a grimness in her tone which boded a hard day for Miller. The friend of my youth still retained much of her belligerence.

We sat making plans for her to come and stay with us in Pennsylvania early in the spring. Then Alec returned from giving the dogs their last run beside the Pacific and we loaded them onto their mattressed two-thirds of the De Soto. Then Phyllis and Miller waved us all off into the brilliant morning.

X

Malibu Notebook, 1947

I have always accused myself of failing to appreciate the beauty of California. In 1946 I began a notebook intended to contain descriptions which might be of use to me in some future novel. Here are some extracts. I think they prove I was more appreciative of my surroundings than I realised at the time.

June 14th, 1946
For some reason I don't understand there is a brilliant patch of moonlight on the waves close to the shore, then a vast area of water quite dark except for diamond bright pinpoints of light here and there which twinkle as if stars had fallen into the sea, then beyond, far away on the horizon, a serene stretch of pale gold. This far-away stretch has an unreal, long-ago look as if it were light on a legendary sea.

On the shore, moonlight reflected on the smooth wet rocks is so dazzling that it might be the flash of a strong electric torch.

October 8th, 1946
The season of fine sunsets has come around again. As we bring the dogs back from their walk along the sandy beach every evening there comes a moment when every westward-facing pane of glass becomes a sheet of flame.

October 9th, 1946
I think this is the loveliest day since we came to live at Malibu, though the wind from the hills is just a little too hot for comfort – though not for Alec's; he said at lunch that he could eat this weather or sleep with it.

Brilliance is the keynote of the beauty. When I first looked out, about 7.30 a.m., the sea was a uniform blue, both dark and dazzling. Later, patches of purple, silver, gold and sky-blue appeared. The waves were tiny and regular, reminding me of the line in Tennyson's fragment, *The Eagle*, 'The wrinkled sea beneath him crawls'. When sudden gusts of wind blew, paths of gold appeared momentarily where the blown-back waves reflected the sun. Alec reported that on his early walk with the dogs the blown crests of the breaking waves made many small rainbows.

The hot breeze carries elusive scents so faint that they are like ghosts of those sweet scents that come from flowers and grasses which grow on English cliff tops. They bring back memories of my childhood. But as so often, I am brought up against the fact that beauty here is only visual for me. I still do not *feel* it.

On hot days the dogs sleep on the little terrace below the picture window of the living-room, close to the tall white geraniums. (Yesterday, at twilight, I saw a mother mouse followed by a baby mouse crawl up the thick stem of a geranium to nibble the flowers.) Today a geranium petal fell on Dandy, provoking him to a glance of extreme suspicion. And as he turned to see if he could blame his father, a threepenny-bit-sized butterfly perched on his nose and made him sneeze.

Folly usually takes her ease in the little glass room at the end of the terrace, partly because she likes the extra heat, but also because she has a tendency to segregate herself.

Buzz, having learned that if he is too hot out-of-doors, he can find shade under garden furniture, recently crawled under a small table indoors and, after giving the carpet a merciless going over as if there might be snakes, settled for what he believed would be a cool nap.

October 17th, 1946
Early this morning I heard a curious bubbling noise outside, which I could not place. It sounded rather like a very young child crooning to itself. Looking out, I saw that the sealions were back – from wherever they go to. They were travelling in great clumsy processions, sometimes in single file, sometimes clumped together, or sometimes spread out making an archipelago of sealions. I tried to count them but failed, though I was sure there must have been a hundred. Soon I heard their usual barks as well as the bubbling croon. Do the young ones bubble and the older ones bark, or are the two different sounds indicative of different emotions?

The first rain, for many months – quite heavy – fell two nights ago. When I leaned out of my window next morning I seemed to smell a scent of green things growing – which must have been sheer imagination because one doesn't get that smell here even when they *are* growing. I suppose that lack is due to the dryness of California. But it does puzzle me why there are so few sea smells. The sea is wet enough!

Now, in mid-morning, the sealions have broken up into five large groups. I can see them further south, moving slowly on to Santa Monica. It is odd at what different levels they swim, some low in the water, some with their heads half out. They have great charm for me.

January 23rd, 1947

Waking early this morning I took pleasure in the still life on my bedside table, which is of pale yellowish wood. One dark red rose in a glass vase exactly matched the jacket of Aldous Huxley's *The Perennial Philosophy*, the yellow of the lettering on this repeated the yellow of the shade of my bedside-lamp and the yellow of my glass of apple juice, which I leave unfinished at night so that I can drink it when I wake.

It always pleases me when colours come together on their own like this. I can imagine this note coming in useful some day. I seldom remember such details; I fancy that the born novelist does. Between the rose and the lamp stood my clock, saying 6.45 a.m. Why is 'Between the rose and the lamp' such a pleasing phrase to me?

February 4th, 1947

As we walked along the sands this evening, Alec said it was the last time until the autumn when we should see the setting sun sink into the sea; already the headland at Point Dume was cutting off a small section of the great glowing globe. When we turned to walk home, we saw the huge pale full moon rising over the mist-veiled hills. The afterglow was staggering – apricot, flame, bronze veiled with mauve. Sea and sands were dyed scarlet except where the sea was a shrill cornflower blue. Instead of fading gradually, the magic was obliterated in a few moments by dark clouds.

February 24th, 1947

Notes on Gulls

A lone gull flying towards Santa Monica, its wings turned bronze by the setting sun.

The shadow of a gull on the sand, like a flat painting of a sky-blue bird.

One day as we drove along the coast road, I saw a flight of gulls in the far distance with the morning sun shining on their wings. They looked like a thrown-up handful of giant silver coins.

A few days ago the neighbouring dog, which has twice stolen Phyl's shoes when she left them in the garden, went past my window with a gull in his mouth. He is a smallish dog and the gull was large; he had to hold his head high to avoid dragging the gull along the sand. After him, flying low, came many shrieking gulls.

I went down. The dog had dropped the gull; it was dead. He came towards me wagging his tail – strange that one could feel so sorry for the gull without feeling a flicker of anger towards the dog. Then I saw that the shrieking gulls were now whirling in a wide circle above the dead one. I had feared, when I first saw them, that they might attack the dog, but they showed no interest in him, just wheeled round and round above the dead gull, some of them swooping almost low enough to touch it. Very strange. Were they mourning it?

A Note on Pelicans

So angular and clumsy as they waddle awkwardly along the beach or squat in rows on piles, wings folded, looking like badly packed parcels – but so assured in flight, so confidently breasting the wind. Then, wings folded again, the swift dive to split the waves with a splash and pop up, beaks dripping and pouches holding the catch.

October 28th, 1947

Sunset, high on the Hills

Gold scarlet, flecked by small, almost black clouds. Stretches of turquoise, a great drift of purple clouds towards the land. The hills are string-coloured and olive drab. The moon, rising opposite the sunset, over the hills, in the midst of blue and misty purple. The hills below the moon pink from the sunset, in strange, sinister light reminiscent of Samuel Palmer's work. Alec's face gold, even the dogs pink with reflected light. The beautifully composed sweep of hills beneath the moon. One bright orange star in the middle of the sunset.

I realise more and more that descriptions of sunsets and moonrises can never really convey their appearance. But perhaps the skilful use of words could create their *atmosphere*, surround characters and incidents in it and end by steeping the reader in it too.

November 27th. 1947　Early morning

Last day at Malibu. I woke at 6 a.m., got up and looked out at the sky and sea. The sun was not up, but a glowing band stretched from the east almost to the west. The lights of fishing boats, and some on the Santa Monica shore, shone clear and pale. The shore looked cleaner and smoother than I ever remember seeing it. A mammoth root of a tree that we saw washed up months ago was now bleached white, fantastically twisted.

Only at this time of day and at twilight is the sky so vividly blue. By seven the sun was well up and the sky unspectacular, the sea pale though with a path of gold.

Making that note on our last morning in Malibu surely I must have felt some pang of regret at leaving California and the Pacific? I don't remember it, though I do remember feeling sad when I took a last look around the bedroom where I had worked so hard on my novel for over two years. What I remember best was the great surge of emotion I experienced when we were at last on our way. It was one of sheer, exhilarated liberation.

XI

From California to

Pennsylvania

Alec, though fonder of California than I was, liked the idea of a change, but he did not in 1947 start off in such high spirits as I did. He was worried about the three thousand miles journey, much of which might be in wintry conditions, a new almost untried car and the difficulties of getting accommodation for three dogs every night. Still, he always much enjoyed driving and he had got all the advice he could as to the best route to take. We were told we might never run into any snow at all.

We ran into it on our second day while driving through Arizona, at twilight. We had stopped to give the dogs a last run, in a deserted road beside a vast afforestation of small evergreen trees, all about four feet tall. The falling snow swiftly dotted them with white. I remember noticing the deep silence. During all our years by the Pacific the waves had never been silent. It was nine years since we had seen snow, in England. Our dogs, of course, had never seen it and before we moved on there was enough on the ground for them to play in and show how much they liked it – as most dogs do.

The snow got heavier and heavier so that we were late in arriving at Flagstaff. We were thankful to have our accommodation already booked. We had arranged to meet my London agent, Dorothea Fassett, there. She and her husband, John Watts-Phillips, and their teenage daughter had decided to emigrate to Hollywood where Dorothea meant to set up as an agent. We had warned her that we thought this most unwise. We did not believe she could compete with Hollywood agents. And I had told her for many months that I should be leaving California. As she had originally introduced me to my Hollywood agents, they had worked for me for only five per cent commission, saving five per cent for her. But now I did not intend to earn any more money in pictures and she seemed to have no properties to sell. But she was determined to get out of England for good; though the London Play Company would still remain open.

Dorothea was still the same forceful woman, a brave fighter if a bit short on tact. She had several times involved me in rows. But I liked her and was sorry now to feel I couldn't let her handle the sale of my novel. She knew nothing about the publishing world even in England, let alone America, and if we sold it to Atlantic-Little, Brown we could cope ourselves, plus an attorney to vet the contract. I don't think she bore me any ill-will, though she did later try to muscle in on the book. We sat up half the night talking, then next day she went on her way west and we went on ours east, almost a case of cars that pass in the night.

There was still some snow but not enough to trouble us and our main difficulties were with auto-courts. There were more of them now than on our last coast to coast drive eight years earlier, but few of them were adequate, most of their proprietors were disagreeable and we had great trouble in getting the dogs accepted. Our technique was to say casually, 'You don't mind dogs, do you?' adding instantly, 'They bring their own beds.' If this worked, we carried the mattresses in most ostentatiously and then it was my job to hurry in and draw all the curtains before the dogs rushed in and jumped onto our beds.

By next day, Thursday, the snow was mostly gone but on the Friday, just before we reached Albuquerque, New Mexico, for the night, there was a really heavy fall and we woke to face the worst day I ever spent in America. The pass from Albuquerque was closed, but we were told of a safe detour. It proved less and less safe; the roads were icy. Alec, having had the forethought to buy snow-chains in sunny California, now cautiously had them fitted – much to the amusement of other motorists at the garage who said the snow wouldn't last. We could get no information about the weather ahead of us, cars just started off in a happy-go-lucky mood.

It was in the afternoon that the real fun started. There was a steep hill. Halfway up, one of the drivers who had pooh-poohed our chains was stuck and behind him was a stream of cars, some stuck hub-deep in snow, some held up by the jam. Immediately in front of us was a sportsman's covered truck laden with six dead deer. Every few minutes the two sportsmen, elderly businessmen, rather stout with absurd cowboy boots with high heels, got out to show off their deer to other drivers. My pity for the dead deer was slightly minimised by the thought that they were out of the bad weather and looked far more peaceful than I felt.

I was none too sure we shouldn't end up as dead as the deer. Ahead of us, a truck overturned on the ice and cars started to slide backwards. I had visions of some ghastly accident; indeed, for the rest of that trip my fears continued. I imagined us dead and the dogs running wild in a deserted countryside. I had never been nervous in our cars; I had too much confidence in Alec as a driver. But that day outside Albuquerque unnerved me.

We must have been nearly two hours on that hill – I watched one of the deer, slung outside the truck, become completely whitened by snow – before word came back that a wire fence had been torn down to make a track round the overturned truck. At last we could move on.

For the rest of the day we kept on seeing car after car overturned and deserted. One sad case was that of a small car with a caravan attached which had been fitted up as a home by its elderly owners. They had been on their way to retirement in California. They stood there surrounded by broken possessions. We stopped to ask if we could send help, but they said it was on its way. I started to pick up their shining new saucepans, but they said it was useless. Their little caravan-home, split open, was completely wrecked. They were utterly dazed by their sudden misfortune.

We slept that night at Fort Sumner, New Mexico, in one of the worst auto-courts of our trip, but we were thankful to get into it.

Saturday was as grim as ever, rather less snow but the roads were sheer ice. Alec drove magnificently helped by the chains, again and again avoiding skids. He remained cheerful and patient but I could see he was feeling the strain; indeed, he lost seven pounds during the whole trip. Then, on Sunday, we finished with the snow. The weather was almost pleasant. We relaxed – and in Oklahoma ran into one of the worst incidents of the trip. At a petrol station when I was getting out to fill the dogs' Thermos with water, Buzz saw a dog, scrambled to the front of the car, pushed past me and – most unprecedently – attacked it. Dandy followed. Buzz seized the dog – quite a small one – by the throat and we couldn't make him let go. I gripped his throat, Alec tried to force his jaws open. Dandy milled around, barking. Folly, who rarely got out of the car unless lifted, leapt out and nearly got run over. Eventually Alec got Buzz's jaws apart and we got our three devils back into the De Soto as a Doberman Pinscher running full tilt, arrived just too late to join in the fight.

Not one spot of blood could be found on the small dog; dogs' throats have a lot of loose protective skin. Buzz was also quite unharmed. The only blood shed was mine, a small graze, but the men at the petrol station deluged me with orange mercurichrome, saying there was a rabies scare in the district. They had shown not the slightest annoyance with our dogs. Their only regret was that the Doberman Pinscher had arrived too late. One of them said, 'If he'd got here in time we'd have had a scrap worth watching.'

It is only fair to record that, for the most part, the dogs behaved admirably, frequently softening the hearts of unwelcoming auto-court owners and enjoying themselves far more than we did.

We had lost much time over the icy weather but by Tuesday we were up to schedule and were pretty sure we could arrive at Ronda's house, Netherby Farm in Pennsylvania, on Thursday, November 27th, as planned. Before leaving California we had notified Ronda of this date and she had assured us everything would be in readiness for us. Her Swedish maid, Hannah, would be there to hand the house over, was going to lay in a stock of food and hoped to have found a maid for us – Hannah herself did not want to stay. Ronda was sorry that she could not be there to welcome us and meet us at last.

Poor Ronda, her plans for the winter had changed. She had, some time earlier, had slight tuberculosis which she believed to be checked. It had now broken out again so she had already gone to a sanatorium at Saranac Lake where she intended to stay until she was completely cured (as she eventually was). In these changed circumstances, we could have the house longer than the four months she had agreed to when she expected to get back in the spring. This was a relief to us, but we were deeply sorry for her.

She had assured us that there would be no need to inform Hannah about our arrival, but on the Tuesday it seemed wiser to telephone ahead. A grim voice with a strong Swedish accent answered my call. No, the house would *not* be ready by Thursday, she still had to do much cleaning and pack Miss Keane's clothes and personal possessions. We must stay away till Monday. I told her this was out of the question, but we should quite understand if the cleaning and packing weren't finished and she could carry on after we arrived; we would take things as we found them and look after ourselves, but we must have a roof over our heads by Thursday. Finally, after she had gone on and on about the enormity of her task, I said we would give her an extra day and not arrive until Friday afternoon. She grudgingly agreed to this.

Next day it was a relief to feel we need no longer rush and we reached Pennsylvania and at once liked it. But auto-courts were getting scarcer and scarcer and we were in a mining district where there seemed to be none at all. In the early evening we decided to drive late and get to the Pennsylvania Turnpike as there would be several auto-courts off it. It was dark when we reached the Turnpike and snow was falling again, quite heavily, but even then we loved that road. No pedestrians, no oncoming traffic to dodge and a feeling of security and also excitement. The tunnels were like something in a thriller film. We had fed the dogs and they slept peacefully. I think Alec would have been willing to drive right through the night. But at Somerset we drove off the Highway and found an auto-court. Alec, getting his key, said casually, 'You don't mind a dog, do you?' then drove to our cabin very fast. Nobody noticed that 'a dog' was an understatement.

We were back on the Turnpike next day and that was the happiest day of the trip. We had time on our hands. It was bliss for Alec to drive on that perfect surface. And the great road did not spoil the surrounding country, it merely gave one a chance to see it spread out on either side. There were no houses except a few well-designed restaurants. I recall no advertisements. And no doubt my mood helped. We were now, after over three thousand miles, nearly home – not that it was really *our* home. I remember we spoke sadly of poor Ronda who had so hoped to be back in the spring, to see all the bulbs she had planted.

I thought of her as a romantic figure. She was the daughter of the celebrated actress, Doris Keane, whom I had admired in *Romance* when I was in my 'teens. Ronda, herself, was talented, both as an actress and as a playwright, but she had never quite managed to get going. And she had had two unhappy marriages. But she was still young, had a great many friends and, I was thankful to remember, was very well off. All I could do for her now would be to take care of her house, send her good news of it (and no bad news, I was determined) and get to know her when she was well again.

On Friday we had a picnic lunch with the dogs while the car was washed, then drove slowly to Doylestown arriving in the early afternoon. It was a pleasant town, but with rather suburban surroundings so we were relieved to find that Netherby Farm, though less than two miles away, was in real country. Not another house was visible from it. We pulled up at a narrow farm road leading to a huge red and white barn. On the right of the road was an old orchard; on the left was a lawn as large as a small field, with some fine trees. Facing the lawn was a white house with sashed windows and slatted blue shutters. I guessed it to have been built in the mid-eighteenth century.

On the left of the house, further back, was a gleam of water and a weeping willow, bare now but graceful. 'Oh, a pond!' said Alec gladly. I suggested he should take the dogs into the orchard while I made contact with Hannah. I had a feeling that the owner of that disagreeable Swedish voice might not much appreciate three dogs milling around.

I rang the front door bell, got no answer, rang again and knocked; still no answer. I tried the door; it was locked. Then I heard voices and found workmen near the pond making a rock-garden. One of them told me that Hannah was in the barn and said he would take me to her; on the way I saw a wood of young trees.

Close to, the barn seemed even larger. It had two storeys; it was quite unlike an English barn, the lower part was half-sunk into the ground. Here the animals had spent their long winters protected from the bitter cold. The stalls were still filled with straw which the workman said Miss Keane intended to keep as she thought it romantic. The barn was so built that the upper storey could be reached by means of a ramp up which the harvest wagons had been driven, but the great doors at the top of the ramp were closed today and I mounted an indoor staircase to the upper barn, ill-lit and enormously high. Here the whole floor was still covered with straw and in the middle of it, surrounded by a welter of crates, trunks, theatrical baskets, clothes, books, press-cutting albums was a small, grey-haired elderly woman.

She rose, set her shoulders back, took a deep breath and with the eyes of a defiant woman about to resist rape said: 'The house is not ready. You must go away.'

She followed this with a torrent of words. There had been far more to do than she had expected. She was now having to pack all Miss Keane's mother's possessions. The workmen had not finished the new kitchen. There was no heat in the house, no hot water. Much cleaning had still to be done. We could go to the Doylestown Hotel. They wouldn't take dogs, but there was a vet where Miss Keane's dog had often gone. We must instantly go away and not come back until Monday.

She was so formidable that for a craven moment I feared I might have to give in. Then something stirred within me. There had been a time when I could have made mincemeat of this rude, raging little woman. I remembered my battles when I worked at Heal's, my near free-fights in the London theatre. Had I just become an old pushover? I remembered how tired Alec was after our long gruelling drive.

I said, 'We are not going to any hotel and our dogs are not going to any vet's. We are all coming in here, *now*. You may stay on until Monday and finish your packing. We shan't ask you to do anything for us. Now that's that, Hannah. Give me the keys to the house.'

It was easier than I had expected. For a moment she stared at me in outraged silence. Then she said sulkily, 'I'll let you in.'

When she opened the front door of the house it felt icy. I remembered she had said there was no heating. Imagining the workmen must have turned it off, I said I would now speak to them about it. She said, 'No need. I can do it'.

I said, '*And* the hot water.'

She said she would do that, too. I took it that the lack of heat in the house had simply been a method of discouraging me.

Alec and the dogs came towards me across the lawn. I gave him a brief outline of the battle with Hannah and then we put the dogs back into the car and went in to explore the house. The sitting-room, not large, had windows on three sides, five in all. They were pleasant, with their deep window seats, but they left little wall space. Still, Ronda had managed to get in two antique desks surmounted by high bookcases, two large sofas and three armchairs and a flock of occasional tables; I counted twelve. There was barely room to move. The walls and paint were white and there were spotted muslin curtains and white blinds at every window, as there were throughout the house. Over the mantel was a very beautiful painting which I later discovered was an original Monet, quite unlike any Monet I had ever seen. It was of an avenue stretching into the distance, the trees dimly green, the sky grey. I came to love it dearly.

The dining-room, furnished with valuable antiques, was dark because the porch outside had an overhanging roof. It led into the kitchen which was in the process of being completely modernised and was nowhere near finished. Still, it could be used. And Hannah, suddenly civil (perhaps Alec impressed her) showed us the food which she had got in for us. She said she really had hoped to be ready for us, but the workmen had got her down. (They later told us she had made their job impossible.) She now surprised me by offering to get us a meal, but we begged her to concentrate on her cleaning and packing.

Upstairs there was one room large enough for me to use as a bedroom and a study. It, like the sitting-room below, had five windows with deep window seats. It was charmingly furnished except that it had five unnecessary drawing-room armchairs. There was a good bedroom for Alec, a tiny, inadequate guest-room and a pleasant old-fashioned bathroom. We were thankful to find attics where unwanted furniture could be stored, and one which Alec would make into his study. On the whole we were pleased with the house, so old, so very different from our California houses, and we were enchanted with its surroundings. We took the dogs to explore in the last of the daylight; the wood was quite large, all of it Ronda's property. Then we fed them and drove out for our own meal. We did very little unpacking that night.

By the next day we were on quite good terms with Hannah. She was a terrific worker – every bit of china was washed, every drawer papered – and absolutely devoted to Ronda, whose house she felt must be protected from its tenants. A great many things had been packed away which should have been left out for us, silver, linen, china, but we had more of our own on its way from California. In the afternoon Hannah asked us to come to the barn where she pointed out various possessions that had been Doris Keane's. All the clothes, and theatrical souvenirs had been packed away in padlocked trunks, but such things as fine marble mantelpieces and garden statuary, brought from Europe, were unprotected. 'Please not to use,' said Hannah, unnecessarily.

She also begged us not to turn out the straw which completely covered the floor. 'Miss Keane values everything connected with Netherby when it was a farm, even the hen-boxes.' It hadn't been a working farm since 1931 and Ronda had bought it only within the last year so, presumably, her predecessors must have cherished the straw. We came to value it too as, in very bad weather, our dogs could get exercise in that vast barn searching for non-existent rats in that antique straw; all they ever found were some yellowed press-cuttings of Doris Keane's triumphs in *Romance*.

On Sunday morning, Hannah departed for New York where she would spend the winter in Ronda's apartment, taking care of Ronda's dog. She made no bones about accepting our handsome tip and promised to keep in touch with us. We heaved a sigh of relief and started moving the furniture. We ousted seven occasional tables, one sofa and two armchairs from the sitting-room; also the five armchairs from my bedroom and some heavy mahogany from Alec's. We had come to realise that Netherby Farm was housing all Ronda's furniture and her dead mother's, too.

On the Monday morning the work-foreman arrived to say that he'd no idea when the kitchen would be finished as the contractor had now taken on another job. Alec said forcibly that we would now have to employ another contractor, deduct the cost from our rent and Miss Keane's solicitor would then sue the original contractor. The foreman, who surprised us by looking pleased, did some telephoning and then told us all the men would be back that afternoon. He said they had been driven crazy by Ronda's vagueness. She had taken them off the kitchen to work on making a bar in a henhouse, then sent instructions that they must work on the rock garden. Now they would really get going. He also mentioned that an excellent maid suggested for us had been sent away by Hannah because she didn't want to leave a coloured maid in Miss Keane's house. I said that for the present it was our house and we should be delighted to see a coloured maid in it. He said he would arrange matters.

That was a long, hard day because the removal van from California with all our possessions arrived. Furniture, books, records, household goods . . . how could we get them all into that already overcrowded house? And the van men, though pleasant and helpful, insisted we should unpack everything then and there, otherwise we could not claim for breakages. They did not leave until midnight. All we had been able to do was to stack everything in the hall and dining-room. Alec then took the dogs out for a moonlight walk so I was alone when the coloured maid arrived to be interviewed.

She was a handsome girl still in her late twenties, well dressed and well groomed, with a quietly assured manner and a beautiful speaking voice. I was instantly impressed but, though perfectly polite, she did not seem equally impressed with me; she raised several objections to taking the job. Then Alec returned and walked in on us with the three dogs at their most boisterous. The handsome girl's poise deserted her. She gave a squeal and said, 'Dogs! Why didn't you tell me? Of course I'll come,' and then and there flung herself down in the middle of them, trying to embrace them all. Even that choosey girl, Folly, took an instant fancy to her and competed for attention. I like to think that it was our dogs who won

Dandy, Buzz and Folly

Malibu Beach, California

Christopher Isherwood, Santa Monica, California

The Author, Malibu Beach, California

Harvey, Caskey, Isherwood
(after 'The Boyhood of Raleigh' by Millais)

Dodie Smith, Phyllis Morris, Christopher Isherwood
Malibu Beach

Charles Brackett

Murray Macdonald

Up in the
California Hills

Malibu Beach

Phyllis Morris

and

'ridiculous ballet exercises'

Malibu Beach

Us

Buzz   Malibu Beach

for us the greatest maid of my lifetime. She was also a most lovable woman.

Her name was Esther. She moved in next day; there was a bedroom and bathroom off the kitchen, very badly furnished; as so often, I was shocked by the accommodation provided for American servants. We took a pleasure in making things pleasant for Esther, letting her choose new curtains, bedspread and rugs to cover the cold linoleum. From the first she took over the running of the whole household, chose the meals, shopped for them – she got Alec to drive her down to Doylestown to stock up for a week at a time. She cooked superbly, said she loved doing laundry. She was the only maid I ever had who longed for us to have visitors.

The only criticism ever voiced against her came from John van Druten. He disapproved of her shaking him warmly by the hand and saying, 'Do come and see us again soon.' He thought it officious. It was quite all right with us.

It now seems to me that everything went right at Netherby from the moment Esther arrived. The workmen finished the kitchen and also made us a large dog pen attached to the house; we could never let them run wild on their own as the property was entirely unfenced. And somehow, somehow all our possessions got housed; our bookcases lined the passages, Alec's enormous desk was hauled up to his attic study, my desk – newly painted white by the workmen – stood at one of my five windows facing a great tree that was as beautiful in winter as in summer.

Fairly early in December I was able to cope with my Christmas letters to England, mainly on Christmas cards, quite forty of them. All our presents and food parcels had been arranged before we left California. Then I began a mammoth Journal entry, bringing it up-to-date. Here are a few extracts:

Christmas Day, 1947

A most beautiful day, still, sunny, clear-skyed; there is just enough snow to decorate the countryside. We walked the dogs in Ronda's sixteen-acre wood. Little patches of snow looked like sunlight and, today, there were patches of real sunlight, too. We went down to the stream where the dogs crossed the plank bridge very cautiously before racing off into the distance. Then, suddenly fearing they had lost us, they hurtled back full speed and leapt the stream.

In the more open parts, the ground is covered with a tangle of honeysuckle leaves and there are clumps of tall dried flowers that look like dead meadowsweet. The colouring would have pleased Paul Nash – all the beiges, the various deep greens, the bleached dead wood.

How beautiful it will be here in the spring and how sad that Ronda won't be here to see it. I think of her constantly, also of her mother. There are so many reminders of Doris, especially the books with her bookplate in, many of them about mysticism and the occult. What a wonderful story Henry James could have made out of Netherby, haunted by the dead, famous mother and the delicate living daughter. Indeed, Ronda, with her wealth, ill-health and disastrous lovelife is a very Jamesian character.

December 27th, 1947

In the New Year I must pull myself together and send *I Capture The Castle* to Atlantic-Little, Brown. I am dreading it, in case they don't like it – and even if they do, it will mean worries about the contract, etc. I'd almost like to shut the book up in a drawer, rest – and think about another book. Alec looked at me in horror when I said this and I felt guilty myself – it's like wanting to farm one's baby out and forget it. And I do *like* the book and want it to have a fair chance in life – *and* give pleasure.

Snow has come down with a vengeance. There were eleven inches in our garden by yesterday evening (we measured it); and twenty-six inches in New York which was an all-time record for one day's snowfall. There is chaos there, but we haven't been inconvenienced as we don't want to go anywhere and all deliveries are managing to come as usual. The house is wonderfully warm and looks delightful, decorated for Christmas by Esther with extreme good taste. Her kitchen is as pretty as a toyshop. She cooked just about the best Christmas dinner I ever ate.

Dear Esther! The dogs adore her more and more. She has a pleasing method of giving them occasional titbits. She calls them together and says, 'A piece for Folly . . . a piece for Buzz . . . a piece for Dandy,' and they wait their turn with shining eyes and lashing tails.

. . . Have now come back from a twilight walk with Alec and the dogs. The lower branches of the firs are so weighed down with snow that they look like the paws of giant polar bears. A theatrical moon is rising.

A bath now when Alec has finished his shower – we amicably share the old-fashioned bathroom here. I have a new idea for a play to think about. Could it be that I am happy?

XII

At Netherby Farm

After Christmas I at last sent *I Capture The Castle* to Stanley Salmen and expected to wait some little while for a verdict. But he received the typescript on Friday morning; he and his charming Bostonian wife, Marie, and their seventeen-year-old son read it over the weekend – breaking up the script so that they could all read at the same time – and on Tuesday Stanley rang up full of enthusiasm. I was thankful, on his account as well as my own. He had now been encouraging me to write a novel for nine years, ever since he had seen the provincial opening of my *Dear Octopus* in Boston.

The whole Board of Atlantic-Little, Brown would have to read the script before he could offer a definite contract, but acceptance was absolutely certain. I pressed for criticisms. He said that, from a commercial point of view, the book was a bit long but I was not to worry about that. I was not to worry about anything.

But I did worry, at that mention of length. I was not prepared to sacrifice one line. Still, Stanley's verdict had given me enough of a lift to let me enjoy the beauties of the winter which at the moment were spectacular. I had run out of Journal paper so I turned to my Notebook to describe what was going on.

January 4th, 1948

On New Year's Day the thaw began; rain fell. At first the drops hanging from the branches of the great chestnut outside our sitting-room window were opaque almost like white berries. Then they became clear, then ran together forming a thin line of ice under every branch and twig, from which tiny icicles hung, like pendants from a necklace.

I didn't then know that this was one of the early stages of something unusual, known in England I think, as a silver thaw, but here described as an ice-storm. It was to prove the worst for fifteen years and the centre of it was here in the country around Doylestown. More rain came and then froze again. By Thursday night every tree was encased as if in glass. The weight of the ice was tremendous, branches cracked, split and fell. By Friday morning the garden was strewn with wreckage. I think the weeping willows suffered worst. A car drew up and a man hurried out announcing he was 'Miss Keane's tree-surgeon,' – like a doctor visiting his patients. He has been several times since and reports that the victims, though very badly gashed, should all pull through.

Luckily the roads had been cleared when we drove the twenty-five miles to Trenton, New Jersey, to meet John van Druten's train. Never have I seen such beauty, dazzling frozen forests, crystal arcades meeting over our heads, fields of stubble as bright as mirrors, but the damage everywhere was heartbreaking.

Next morning we took John for a walk in the brilliant sunshine. Of all writers I think Proust would best have done justice to what we saw. I can only jot down a few reminders:

Every twig ice-coated. The smooth twigs were the most brilliant but the perfect outlining of waiting buds was exquisite. The small fir trees were bowed low, their tops looking like jesters' caps. The willow branches were yellow under their ice, the whole trees suggesting frozen fountains.

We crossed the road and walked up the lane to a field where the dead, bleached grass is about two feet high. Every stalk was ice-coated and bending over in a graceful curve. The beige of the grass shone through the ice and, in the morning sunshine, the whole field suggested a pale gold sea, frozen into stillness.

The wood that skirts the field was full of sound which at first we thought must be water running. Then a little wind increased the sound and we realised it was the rustling of icy twig against icy twig. Alec described it as a talkative glitter.

The heads of giant thistles in globes of ice might have been triumphs of a glass-blower's art. Red berries looked like jewellery. And amidst all this, one snow-berry bush was mysteriously free of ice, its little leaves as soft as in summer.

John kept stripping twigs – the ice came off intact – and throwing the little tubes down to Buzz, who crunched them avidly.

I saw one squirrel but no birds, though one can hear faint cheepings in the woods. We have put out suet, coconuts and special racks filled with bird food, but no birds come.

The whole Atlantic-Little,Brown board was as enthusiastic as Stanley, though it did just murmur that it would be nice if I could take, say, thirty pages out of the book. This, I was told, was simply because it would decrease the cost of production; no one suggested that it would improve my novel. Poor Stanley was in a difficult position. He had again and again told me, over the years, that I could make it as long as I liked, *he* didn't think it needed cutting, it was his much cherished baby; and he wanted to keep me happy. But he had obviously been given the job of getting it shortened. I became ruffled during some telephone conversations and then received a telegram to say that Stanley and Marie would be coming from Boston 'with facts, figures and enthusiasm'.

When they came Stanley gave in about the cuts, merely asking me to think about them while I corrected the proofs; and he and Alec got down to discussing the contract. Alec was torn between wanting to be fairly tough on my behalf and hating to bargain with anyone we liked as much as Stanley. But there never was any trouble really; it was an excellent contract, generous in many ways and, all told, Alec saved us a great deal of money by never employing an agent. The only hold-up was when we employed John's attorney to vet the contract. The man who dealt with us split so many hairs that Stanley, rephrasing the contract again and again while pressing on with production, once said, 'This book will be in the bookshops before the contract's signed.'

At that Doylestown meeting I said I thought the book jacket should show the castle and Stanley asked me to send him some rough sketches which could be worked up by a professional artist. There was no hurry so I set to work with finely pointed pencils, india-rubber – much used – and heavy breathing, and turned out a number of drawings which I thought might be a basis for end-papers as well as for the jacket. I did the castle by moonlight, the high-raftered kitchen by firelight, and the girls' bedroom by candlelight, having in mind early Victorian pencil sketches. Stanley liked these so much that he said, though he would employ an artist for the jacket, he would use my drawings just as they were as illustrations inside. It was then found that my pencil drawings could not be reproduced on the paper on which the book was to be printed. So – as I couldn't draw in ink – they were copied line for line; even the lines that weren't correctly drawn were copied, so the amateur, primitive quality was maintained. I was to find that my odd little illustrations did quite a lot to help the book.

While I was still working on the drawings, Stanley telephoned to say the Literary Guild was willing to accept the book. He had always hoped that the Book-of-the-Month Club might choose it, but that book club would not judge a book until it was in proof form and also there were a number of judges to satisfy. The Literary Guild had only one judge, its head, John Beecroft; he would read a typescript and give an almost instant verdict. Now, he would make my novel his Choice for November and he would pay $84,000 (half for me, half for the publishers) for the right to print 550,000 copies in hardback, if only I would cut the book a little.

To get a Book Club acceptance of my first novel! It was something I had hardly dared hope for and the Literary Guild had by far the most members. But my delight had evaporated while Stanley talked. I couldn't, I wouldn't cut ten thousand words.

Alec had picked up the gist of the telephone conversation. He was now standing beside me nodding his head like a Chinese ornament. Stanley went on to ask if he might send me just a few suggestions for cuts, I said yes.

By the time these suggestions arrived Alec, working through the book sentence by sentence, had proved to me that 8,000 words could go. I telephoned Stanley to say we would go on working, but he told me not to trouble. Beecroft would settle for 8,000 words; it was mainly the gesture he wanted. Not a very large gesture seeing how long the novel was, but I still regret some of those 8,000 words. Eventually Christopher Isherwood was to write to me that what made the book was its detail, and you can't have detail without details.

Dear Stanley himself was no slouch about detail. He was soon to arrive all the way from Boston to discuss punctuation. And he had insisted, against the Atlantic-Little, Brown house rules, that English usage and spelling should be used throughout.

I was, of course, more than happy getting the Literary Guild Choice and even more so when, later, A.S. Frere of Heinemann, whom I had known well in London, came to stay with us and secure the English rights, for which he eventually got the English Book Society Choice. But I continued to worry in case something went wrong. Nothing seemed tidily signed and sealed. But at least I allowed myself to enjoy the coming of spring. I wrote in my Notebook:

March 27th, 1948

There was snow on and off until the middle of March and then, after a few mild days, the weather turned miraculously warm just in time for the official opening of spring. The daytime temperature in Philadelphia was 85 degrees.

It was strange to feel such warmth with not a bud swelling on the trees. The snow-harassed grass was a colourless tangle, no shoot from a bulb was showing anywhere in the garden. But now we have had a week of good weather and the difference in the countryside is astonishing. Our vast front lawn is already a brilliant green dotted with daffodil shoots. On the banks of the little stream there are snowdrops, scyllas and tiny crocuses (much smaller than in England). Each day spring's green makes headway against winter's beige.

My bedroom has windows facing east, north and west and through each of them I see different signs of the changing year. The east windows cover the lawn with the great chestnut whose buds are already swelling. Through the north windows I see the large maple which already has tiny leaves – or are they just green buds? It has been dripping sap for weeks; only a fortnight ago I saw the sap frozen into foot-long icicles. The west window looks towards the pond where three wild ducks – a drake and two lady-friends – have settled. The weeping willows there are the most advanced of all our trees. The budding trails, swaying in every breeze, make one think of golden hair.

Strange purple-striped, yellow-green plants are growing in the wood, looking capable of producing exotic flowers. Alec says they are skunk cabbages (or is this a joke? He knows so much more about country matters than I do and sometimes plays tricks on me, as when he once pointed to a solitary stooping figure on a Welsh marsh and told me it was the Government Frogwatcher. I believed him implicitly) . . .

I broke off and drove into Doylestown with Alec to post some letters. The little town has been very gay all this pre-Easter week with masses of flowers in the shops and rows of potted hyacinths outside them scenting the air. As we returned, a sudden storm blew up and the sky over Doylestown was filled with thunder clouds of slate-blue. In the stormlight, colours everywhere seemed intensified. A strong wind made waves across our pond and the wild ducks huddled against the bank. A huge flock of starlings flew from the wood and settled on the topmost branches of the chestnut, so close together that they weighed some of the smaller branches down. Every evening they visit the chestnut, then whirl on to other roosting places.

The storm clouds blew over our heads and still travelled on. As they passed, the intensified colour everywhere paled. A little rain has fallen and we can still hear the thunder, but the storm is far beyond us now.

I am enjoying watching the change from winter to spring here. There *was* a spring in California; the blond hills were suddenly bright green after the rains, but the contrast between seasons wasn't sharp enough for any emotional impact. And alas, even here, the chief emotional impact of the spring is that it makes me miss England more and more. I imagine the country around our Essex cottage, see the garden, the hedges, the woods, remember the elm flowers, the lime flowers, the wonderful variety of an English spring. As always, I come back to the fact that beauty for me, here, is more a matter of seeing than feeling. Still, a garden, a pond, woods with a stream, bulbs coming up everywhere – and an *old* house – are rather better than anything I had at Malibu, beautiful as sea, sunrise and sunset often were there.

When it rained, early this morning, Buzz wore his raincoat – we brought coats for all three dogs in case California-raised dogs couldn't stand the rigours of winter here, but Folly and Dandy won't wear theirs. Buzz waded into the pond after the wild ducks and came out with a large amount of pond water in the underneath of his coat. This remained, suggesting an alderman's paunch, until Alec emptied it out. The dogs love it here, they loved the snow, they love the spring. Folly particularly loves the swamp where there are wild geese. Dandy, as puzzled as a puppy about many things, is pleasurably frightened by all wild life, even rabbits, but boxes very bravely against tall dead weeds. Yes, we like it too – but you dogs should see an English spring.

There was one time when happiness completely conquered my homesickness. It must have been in early April. Stanley had telephoned that the Literary Guild deal was now finally settled. I went out alone and walked along the stream, now bordered with hundreds of daffodils and I remember telling myself: This really *is* happiness; notice it, will you? It's as good as when you had *Autumn Crocus* accepted – better in some ways because *Autumn Crocus* could have failed. Now *I Capture The Castle* is, at least financially, assured of success. What wonderful luck I had had with my first play, and now with my first novel.

That evening I really *felt* the spring – and then I asked myself if that meant that joy in nature comes from within, from one's own welcoming sensibilities. Of course that is true, to some extent, of all enjoyment. But joy in nature is deeply linked with childhood's memories, memories of falling in love, perhaps even with ancestral memory. At least that evening's joy enhanced the spring for me.

April 19th, 1948

What I took to be leaf buds on the maple were really flower buds and they proved to be as exquisite as any elm or lime flowers. Now, as they shrivel and fall, the leaves are opening. They remind me of chickens coming out of their shells, perhaps because of the many tiny creases in the leaves and there is something claw-like about the unfolding shape. I never liked any tree better than that maple. . .

Quite a number of trees are still bare. The oak, in front of the window where my desk is, still has many of last year's dead leaves and not one green bud. A few flowers from the maple fluttered over onto oak twigs, offering them a little fictitious foretaste of spring. Most of our bird-feeding gadgets are hung on the oak so that I can watch the birds while I work. The grey and black nuthatches eat the most, except for the large red bird I have christened Baron Charlus (Alec tells me that he is a scarlet tanager).

Down in the wood the skunk cabbages (Alec wasn't joking) have unfolded their exotic leaves and now look most ordinary. I gather their name indicates that they smell unpleasant, but I haven't noticed it. I haven't noticed any spring smells, pleasant or unpleasant, except for the hyacinths.

Alas, our own personal spring was about to suffer a sudden eclipse as regards flowers. One morning Hannah telephoned that she was in Doylestown and would like to gather some flowers to send to Miss Keane. Of course we agreed though we had already sent Ronda several boxes of flowers, trying to share a little of the spring with her. By now she had come to seem like a friend, through the exchange of many letters. Hers were delightful and full of humour. All was going well with her. But she told us we could keep Netherby until the autumn and probably until next spring as, once her cure was complete, she planned a long visit to Europe. I still saw her as a Henry James heroine and she now had an idea she could make *The Portrait of a Lady* into a play.

We greeted Hannah when she arrived and then went out shopping; we were anxious not to inhibit her in her flower gathering. When we came back there were no flowers to be seen anywhere. There was nothing in the large flower bed on the front lawn but bare earth. Hannah must have set herself the task of taking every bloom, every bud, every leaf. Fortunately she hadn't remembered the daffodils in the wood – or perhaps she was exhausted.

Esther told us she was now by the pond, having a picnic lunch she had brought with her. Well, I took it that she had stripped our garden out of devotion to Ronda so I went along to be pleasant to her. I asked her if she would like to come indoors for a wash. 'No, thank you,' she said coldly. 'I washed in the pond.'

It was fortunate that Esther liked people to visit us. My old friend, Madge Compton, playing on Broadway in *The Winslow Boy*, came for three weekends. John came again and again bringing his young actor friend, Walter Starke, who was becoming a help to him in many ways. As our guest-room was barely big enough for one, let alone two, we put them up at the Doylestown Hotel which John loved. He said it was like an old-fashioned English hotel. He presented me with a novel by Rosa Nouchette Carey (found in its sitting-room) saying it looked my kind of book. While in England the previous year he had purloined (it somehow seems the right word) *The Journals of Miss Weeton* because he knew I liked books about governesses. I begged him to return Rosa Nouchette Carey but continued to cherish Miss Weeton, inscribed by him, 'Criminally, with love'.

And at the end of April, Phyllis came to stay with us. She now had a room in Dorothea Fassett's house in Santa Monica and had been doing well in pictures, but had no work in view at present and would, with us, be on the end of a telephone. It did not ring for two months and, even then, she went back to California without being recalled. But she was now an easy, pleasant guest (America had tamed her) even though I could spend little time with her. At first I had to work on an article for the Literary Guild's brochure, *Wings*. I was asked to make my underlying theme: 'Why I think Literary Guild members will like my book.' The theme didn't remain 'underlying', it was quite plainly said, but anyway, the Guild was pleased. After that both Alec and I were segregated with the galley proofs of the book, so we barely met Phyl except at meals. But she didn't mind.

She walked, she gardened – with a young gardener Alec had

found – and she converted Ronda's hen-bar into a studio which she filled with expensive new garden furniture she unearthed in the barn. She resented anything being kept away from us and I rather expected her to lay hands on those European marble mantelpieces. Once the hen-bar was finished, she sat there happily reading while Alec corrected proofs in the garden and I corrected proofs in my bedroom, listening to a large collection of recently recorded Handel's Concerti Grossi.

I was bad at correcting proofs. I kept losing myself in the story and missing all the mistakes. Alec worked meticulously, and read through the galleys three times. The work took all the longer because we had a charming perfectionist editor in Boston. She was happy to spend a week of letters and long-distance telephone talks as to whether madeira to drink should, or should not, have a capital M.

The galley proofs went off on June 19th and on June 21st I began a Journal entry, the first for six months. In a week I tossed off twenty-five thousand words; no doubt they were a relief to my subconscious mind. They are mainly a chronicle of work and worries; the work necessary, the worries justified, but I find it sad that I should have been so tired and troubled during many months of good fortune – which I rarely had time to enjoy. Only towards the end of those twenty-five thousand words do I allow myself a little gambol about the beauties of Netherby, particularly the fireflies. They fascinated me so much that I would sometimes get up in the night and sit by an open window watching them. It was as if many tiny shooting stars were dashing about the lawn.

Eventually Phyllis went back to Santa Monica and, two days after she left, Charlie Brackett came to stay, having come from California for the saddest of reasons. His wife had died and he and their daughters had brought her to be buried at her family home in Saratoga Springs, as she had wished. Her death had come as no shock as, it seemed, she had been ill for years – though even John, a closer friend of the Bracketts than we were, had never fully realised this. Charlie had been quietly devoted to her, but I had always felt that his greatest devotion was to his movie work, which would stand him in good stead now.

After Charlie left, I was back on the treadmill, this time coping with an enormously long questionnaire from the Literary Guild to be used in publicity. I was asked to answer very fully, describe my whole life, my methods of working, my opinions, give details, include anecdotes. The result was twenty-five pages of close typing, but at least the Guild was appreciative and managed to get quite a lot of publicity out of it. The Atlantic-Little, Brown questionnaire was only slightly less formidable. Some of that was used on the book's jacket. I came to the conclusion that helping to launch a successful novel was far harder work than helping to launch a successful play. I think all my plays had been written and seen through rehearsals in less than a year. *I Capture The Castle* had been begun back in 1940, then laid aside. Since I had gone back to it, in 1945, I had now been working on it, with only a few months off to write for Charlie, for over three years; and I was still working on it.

And I was getting very tired. The heat of the Pennsylvania summer was too much for me and the humidity was something I had never known. Netherby, under its white plastered exterior, was a stone-built house and the walls dripped with moisture. I developed a rheumatic right shoulder – or it may have been arthritis or neuritis or any old itis; I didn't go to a doctor to find out. Esther had the same thing in an elbow and hers was dignified by the name of bursitis. Mine made it hard to write or type, but I went on doing both. I could only sleep with my arm stretched straight out across the bed.

In September Ronda Keane came to spend a night with us. Her cure was now almost complete, but she intended to spend the winter at Saranac, in an apartment she had rented. We found her as charming as her letters, a particularly graceful young woman with beautiful manners and a sense of humour often ruefully operating against herself. She told us we could keep Netherby till the spring when she would return and complete all the improvements she had planned for it.

I remember taking great pleasure in the printed copies of my book when they arrived complete with my little illustrations. I played with them every day, like a child with a toy.

I then had the job of signing dedications to thirty-five friends and Alec had the job of packing the books; many of them went to England. I have always had a dislike for signing my books; it makes me so nervous that I often spoil copies. So I was particularly thankful that Stanley Salmen had let me off making a vast tour to sign books. He said that, though it would help the sales, the expense of the tour would almost offset profits and if I didn't want to go, I needn't. But I felt I must face the Literary Guild's luncheon the week after publication and the Atlantic-Little, Brown cocktail party on the same day, both parties in New York. I'd nothing fit to wear for either of them.

'I'd had no new clothes since we had left Beverly Hills four years earlier and now skirts had descended almost to the ankle. Phyl had been swanning around in a Dior 'New Look' outfit, very long, full and hip-enlarging. I could find nothing possible in Doylestown or even in Philadelphia, but a Doylestown tailor managed to lengthen my one good black cloth-and-taffeta suit, and a Doylestown milliner copied a once-cherished hat I'd had for ten years. I didn't know myself in a hat.

Possibly it was to get my mind off my clothes' woes that I turned to my Notebook:

October 13th, 1948

There was no time for summer notemaking, but here are a few reminders: the riot of vegetation, the long-blooming Queen Anne's Lace, like filigree jewellery, like silver birdcages as it dies. The golden-rod and Michaelmas daisies, both wild here, still blooming. The inkweed with its magenta stalks and black berries. Horse mint, mauve and mahogany coloured, wild asparagus fern with its red berries. Larkspur, peonies, phlox, still blooming in the beds.

A memory of late spring: the slaughter of the wild, orange day-lilies, as tall as garden lilies. Just as they were in full bloom along the verges, the roadmen cut them down and also cut the honeysuckle, though a little of it survives even now. In June the woods were carpeted with it. And did the wild strawberries come in June? There were masses of them. My spring notes never mentioned the exquisite dogwood trees, their white, pink and coral flowers fallen like stars upon the waiting woods.

Now we are in full autumn, but there are next year's buds on the great chestnut next to yellow, dying leaves. Yesterday Alec found autumn violets, exactly like English springtime violets. There were some still blooming when we arrived last November. Forget-me-nots are blooming right in the pond.

Livestock: Charming black turtles – Alec sets much store by them. They sun themselves in a long string on a log in the pond, reminiscent of ebony elephants on Anglo-Indian mantelpieces. Our frogs are wildly vocal; some of them make noises like birds and our woodcocks make noises like frogs. Our rabbits are silent but frisky. They play on our lawn during our dinner each night.

The ducks spend much time on the lawn, too; one of them woke me at four last night by quacking loudly.

Such beautiful birds. Cardinals, flashing blue jays who sometimes drop me a blue feather to use as a bookmark. Robins, rooks, nuthatches; and the bird, never yet spotted, with the six-note call which a composer could build into a passacaglia. And the one who sings 'Figaro, Figaro' rather oftener than I could wish.

The patient rat who sits under the bird-feeders on the oak tree waiting for crumbs to fall from the rich birds' table.

Our orchard is a sorry sight now; few apples and most of them diseased. Earlier in the year the trees became infested with tent caterpillars, very furry, like minute tabby kittens' legs. They lived in white tents of web, tiny houses made of mist. From these they went forth for a full day's work on leaf-eating. Men came to spray them and I felt sorry for them. And the spraying had little effect. We were told that, to eradicate the caterpillars, it would need to be done so often that every apple would cost a dollar.

On the lawn this morning a sudden colony of midget toadstools appeared much the shape of sea urchins, suggesting an elfin village of domed huts.

Blundering grasshoppers are everywhere and, along the meadows, huge black and yellow spiders with the most closely spun webs I have ever seen sit waiting for the grasshoppers. I saw one hop right into a web. The spider wrapped him up so tightly and so quickly that, even had I felt it right to interfere with Nature, I could not have extricated him. (Why 'him'? One can't judge a grasshopper's sex.) But it was very harrowing. I tried to think of the grasshopper's next incarnation, hoped he would progress towards perfection because of his suffering – those frantic, hopeless legs which broke through his webby shroud, only to be instantly tied up again by the spider. I tried to think of the spider's hunger. But to see a hungry spider biting a still struggling grasshopper makes one think of Nature with horror, and hardly wins respect for a First Cause which *allows* Nature. A God who is of purer eyes than to behold evil seems a bit of an escapist. Anyway I prayed – if one can call it that – for both grasshopper and spider. Alec, too, was distressed at seeing a praying mantis devoured by one of those voracious spiders.

Spring, summer and autumn here have been far more riotous than in England, but far less scented. Rarely now can I catch the authentic scent of autumn. I don't think it is only my lingering homesickness that makes me feel the glorious beauty here does not quite enter into the heart as the quieter beauty of English countryside does. The relation with the soil is quite different here. I believe many English people are capable of an almost mystical relation with Nature. English *town* dwellers, conscious of lack, try to assuage it with sooty window-boxes and even aspidistras.

That was the last entry I was ever to make in the Notebook. A week later, on October 20th, *I Capture The Castle* was published.

XIII

I Capture The Castle

On Tuesday, the day before publication, Stanley rang up from Boston to warn me that owing to some mistake over the review copies, there wouldn't be any notice in the *New York Sunday Times Book Review*, as had been expected. There would, however, be a 'quite sweet' small one in the *Sunday Herald Tribune*. No, we couldn't expect any reviews in this week's daily papers; they would be taken up with a new book about Roosevelt. Anyway, Stanley and his wife would like to drive to Doylestown on publication day and stay at the hotel. Would we join them for a celebratory dinner?

Of course we insisted they should dine with us and made plans for an extra good dinner. Alec drove to Doylestown for champagne and returned with the news that the local bookshop had a window full of *I Capture The Castle*, which sounded cheerful. But I didn't find the celebratory dinner particularly cheerful. The Salmens were charming, kind, almost sympathetic in manner, but they were no longer prognosticating enormous success. Indeed, they told us about its being a difficult year in the publishing world and how disappointing the sales of many established authors had been. Both Alec and I got the impression that something had gone badly wrong.

But the next morning there was a long and really glowing review in the daily *Herald Tribune*, by an influential critic, Lewis Gannet. My spirits rose. And Stanley, who had left Doylestown before the morning papers arrived, telephoned delightedly from Boston. He said he could now get on with the advertisements. 'Be sure to thank Lewis Gannet, won't you?'

'Does one thank critics?'

'You do over here,' said Stanley firmly.

No more reviews came our way and there were no advertisements in next Sunday's papers. So I felt distinctly flat when we got ready to go to the Literary Guild luncheon on the following Monday.

The day really began on the night before, when my hot-water-bottle burst. We had to turn the heavy mattress over and put on fresh sheets. My shoulder decided to ache. I got very little sleep. And next morning I hated saying goodbye to our three wistful dogs, safe though I knew they would be with Esther.

Alec had driven very little in New York so we had hired a driver for the De Soto (we rarely used the Rolls now), a very pleasant man who had often driven Ronda's car. About ten miles out of Doylestown Alec happened to mention that our spare wheel was kept in the luggage rack on the car's roof. He added, 'Not that we've ever needed it. I don't remember one puncture since we've lived in America.' At that very instant one of the tyres went flat.

We all of us laughed, but it proved to be no laughing matter as a nearby garage took thirty minutes to change the wheel and mend the puncture. Alec had allowed over an hour more than we needed for the journey, but our driver then lost his way getting into New York so that by the time we reached the Algonquin, where Stanley had booked a suite for us, we were already late for the lunch. Representatives of the Literary Guild, who were waiting for us, rushed us over to the Plaza Hotel.

Mercifully, it wasn't a promotion luncheon, just a meeting with people who worked for the Guild; in fact, just a compliment to me, which made me feel all the worse about being late. We all sat at one large table. I sat next to John Beecroft, the head of the Guild, a good-looking intelligent man, but I found him a little pompous and touchy, which made me nervous. However, he was very complimentary about my book and delighted with its wide acceptance by Guild members, which he thought was due to my description of it in the Guild magazine. The previous Choice, a florid historical novel, hadn't done so well and he couldn't think why. I said I hadn't thought the author's description of the book in the Guild magazine would appeal to women; it had stressed 'the bloody impalement of Basil the Eunuch.' Mr Beecroft gave me a startled glance, then roared with laughter and after that we got on perfectly. Ever since then Alec and I have called a certain type of historical novel 'Bloody Impalements.'

In the afternoon A.S. Frere of Heinemann, over from London, joined us at the Algonquin so that we could hand over the corrected proofs for the English edition. He was resentful because the American edition was coming out first – though he had always known this would happen – and highly critical of the way Atlantic-Little,Brown were handling matters. Why had there been no advertisements? A Book Club Choice should be properly heralded. If we got the English Book Society Choice – as he now expected – things would be very different.

When we met Stanley, later in the afternoon, he told me the Sunday advertisements had been 'crowded out', which I found hard to believe. I still thought his manner strange, kind but evasive.

The cocktail party for journalists was at five o'clock. Most of them arrived late, having been at a party for the publication of a new book by Osbert Sitwell, and they seemed a trifle exhausted. I was asked why Edith Sitwell had been wearing three coats. (Why, indeed, considering how powerful American central heating was.) Three journalists said – one in print – how much they preferred my party to the Sitwell's, but it was the Sitwells that pulled in most of the publicity. I didn't grudge them this as I admired their work greatly. I also admired their talent for publicity as it benefited their sales. As 'Shopgirl Writes Play' when my *Autumn Crocus* was produced, I'd had more publicity than I cared for at the time, but now knew that if one hopes to attract a large public almost any publicity is valuable. Certainly my American image as a novelist could have done with some.

Stanley urged us to stay on in the suite and enjoy ourselves in New York at Atlantic-Little,Brown's expense, but we were dead set on getting home – oh, the bliss of seeing Esther and our three dogs all racing towards us across the garden.

There were no excitements during the rest of the week, no important notices reached me and there were still no advertisements in the Sunday papers. I telephoned Stanley about this and he said he hadn't been able to get the space. I then said I had the impression that the book had fallen completely flat. After a moment's silence, he admitted Atlantic-Little,Brown had felt exactly the same because there had been so little New York interest in it before publication. I could see why: to New York critics it was simply a first novel. It was now five years since my *Lovers and Friends* had succeeded on Broadway and anyway, Literary Guild choices were apt to be slightly despised. I guessed that Atlantic-Little, Brown had not felt like heavily advertising a possible failure. Stanley would never quite admit this, but he did admit that the publicity had been handled disastrously. But it would be all right now. The book was selling well, would be on the bestseller lists, the provincial press looked like being outstanding. . .

I felt aggrieved. With $42,000 in hand as their half-share of the

Literary Guild's payment, Atlantic-Little, Brown could have done better by me – I had been shown proofs of large, handsome advertisements which should have come out long ago. These, I was to find, had been scrapped and what did appear the following Sunday were headed 'This is the novel that begins in the kitchen sink' and included a crude drawing of a girl sitting in a sink. True, almost all critics mentioned the opening line: 'I write this sitting in the kitchen sink', but they mentioned it with amused approval. The advertisements were excessively vulgar.

I let myself get quite ill with anger and disappointment but I gradually recovered. Good reviews were now flowing in from New York and from all over America; in all there were more than sixty good ones. We were steadily mounting the bestseller lists – only the real blockbusting bestsellers remained above us (we were to stay there for over six months) and there was now no doubt about solid success. But after that one outbreak of too late and too crude advertising, the book was mainly left to fight its own way.

However, I had a great many enthusiastic letters and the most comforting of all came from Christopher. I had pretty well taken it for granted that he would not enjoy a long book composed of the journal of a seventeen-year-old girl, so I was staggered by his praise. I wrote back saying I wouldn't accuse him of pulling his punches as it would seem as if the Israelites, presented with manna, said, 'Well, thanks, God, but is it quite fresh?' He wrote assuring me he had meant every word he said. Reading the letter now, (it will be found in the Appendix), I find myself thinking it is both a tribute to the book and a tribute to friendship, and on both counts equally valuable to me.

I would have been glad now to think of some new piece of work, but I was to find that writers of bestsellers get very little peace. Mercifully, the Literary Guild answered all letters which came to them, but many came direct to me; and I was asked to contribute to symposiums, write winning little pieces for Christmas numbers, review books by other authors. I firmly declined the last, being of the opinion that dog should not eat dog and, especially, that new dogs should not eat long-established dogs. And of course we had all our English Christmas cards and presents to get off.

John and his friend, Starke, arrived on Christmas Eve. John's play, *Make Way for Lucia*, adapted from books by E.F. Benson, had now opened in New York to poor notices (it was to last only a short time) but John was reasonably cheerful as he had expected the notices to be far worse, judging by the pre-New York tour. We had seen the play in Philadelphia and thought it very weak, long-winded and dull, most unlike John's usual work. He had gratefully accepted all our suggestions for improvements and generously reported they had all worked well, but nothing could have saved that play. He was now ready to forget it, all the more so because he had finished *Bell, Book and Candle*, which we liked though it needed much rewriting (which it eventually got). He started talking about it when he got off the train at Trenton and only stopped when he got back on the train, three days later.

Soon after John and Starke left us, Ronda Keane arrived to stay for a few days. She was now completely cured, at the outset of a new romance (this time destined for a happy ending) and looking forward to taking Netherby over from us at the end of March – which brought us up against the fact that we had to decide where we were going to live.

I had thought of Doylestown as a sort of halfway house to England but we were, if anything, still more bitterly opposed to the 6 months quarantine for the 3 dogs. Also I did not want to return until I could take a new play with me. I would write one, then force myself to go back on my own, spy out the land generally, including the quarantine conditions, and then. . . Well, perhaps we could at last face taking the dogs; we might even take them to France, where there was no quarantine. For the moment, we must just find another house.

There were plenty to be rented locally, but none that we could bear the thought of living in and none with good surroundings for the dogs. Netherby, with its garden, orchard, woodlands had been ideal. And after several weeks I began to wonder if I could stand much more of the Pennsylvania climate. The hot, humid summer had resulted in the continuance of my rheumatic shoulder and the winter was being uncomfortable without being spectacularly beautiful. I suspected that Alec, though he never mentioned it, hankered for California sunshine. Very tentatively I suggested we might return, not to Malibu but to Beverly Hills.

We discussed it while we continued to house-hunt locally. I soon guessed that Alec would prefer California, though his main wish was that we should live wherever I would be happiest. Well, I *had* missed our friends. . .

We wrote to them, asking what our prospects of getting a house were, and were touched to receive welcoming telegrams from them all. Christopher, Charlie and Phyl would at once start house-hunting. John, though now living at his desert ranch, would make enquiries. None of them had any luck, but Alec thought of writing to the John Balderstons, whose house in Cove Way we had rented back in 1939; happily, that same house was available.

We had paid $350 a month for it before. Now the rent would be $600, but we were not too worried about money, especially as Alec had arranged for the earnings of *I Capture The Castle* to be paid over a period of years, to save Income Tax. The move was on – and at very great expense. The Rolls had to travel by freight car again; all our books, records, household goods had to go back by van. Esther was willing to come with us, plus a coloured girl friend who wanted to work in California and would pay her own fare; we said they could both use the little guest house over the garage at Cove Way. Fearing they might meet with race discrimination on the train, we treated them to a bedroom for two.

We drove off in the De Soto on the morning of April 1st. Ronda had come to take over Netherby. It was a mild, moist day; already the daffodils were out. We were glad to think this would be Ronda's spring, though we felt slightly dismayed to learn that she planned to be quite alone, except for her dog; she did not even intend to engage a maid at first (she had long ago got rid of the horrible Hannah). She just wanted to think, to make plans for all the improvements she hadn't been able to complete. I have always remembered our last glimpse of her, standing at the gate of her domain, an even larger domain now as her millionaire father had given her twenty-five more acres as a Christmas present. I still saw her as a Jamesian heroine, but I doubt if James would have permitted her the happy future that now awaited her.

Much as we had loved Netherby Farm, I didn't greatly regret leaving it – perhaps because I was so relieved that we were at last on our way. All the work on packing had greatly increased the pain in my right shoulder, to which had now been added a pain in my right knee. That word 'my' alarmed me. Was I now landed with 'my' shoulder and 'my' knee for life? Was I turning into an elderly crock? To the best of my belief now, the trouble with both shoulder and knee barely outlasted the journey.

It took us fourteen leisurely days to drive across the continent and though we were taking a new route, I remember little of the journey. I wrote in my Journal later:

I find I have got used to the ugliness of American small towns and rather like the slick gaiety of the well-stocked shops. And the residential districts, with their many trees, are more pleasant than many English suburbs. The big towns are no uglier than many big English towns. I am more inclined to appreciate the likeable things and take the dislikeable ones for granted.

Of the fourteen places mentioned in my Journal only one evokes a vivid memory. On the thirteenth day, at Blythe, California, I was on my way to get an early evening meal (Alec and I usually went separately, so that our dogs need not be left alone in the car) when I saw an old English sheepdog puppy, obviously lost. It was dashing in and out of the traffic; twice I saw it narrowly avoid being run over. I managed to catch it and found it was still small enough for me to carry, so I took it to a nearby petrol station and got it some water (unwillingly given) and was told it had been about all day. All I got for my suggestion that the police should be notified was a surly headshake.

So I carried it to a restaurant intending to buy it some food. There was a pleasant young police officer eating at the counter who told the cashier to telephone the police station. Before I had even got as far as ordering the pup's meal, I heard the strident sound of a police siren and along came a police car, bristling with policemen. They sprang out with guns drawn and hurled themselves into the restaurant, obviously expecting at least to quell a riot – they had only been told they were urgently needed. On being faced with one puppy, now being fed sweet biscuits, they exploded with laughter and set about soothing an obviously eccentric English woman. Sure, they would take the dog to the police station. Yes, indeed, they'd give it a good meal. No, of course, they wouldn't just turn it over to the dog pound; if they couldn't find its owner they would probably adopt it. One elderly Irish cop said he'd personally give it a home – anyone would be glad to have a cute pup like that. It was finally borne away, with the lights of the police car flashing, the siren blaring. I hoped the noise didn't frighten it as much as it always frightened me.

That last night was spent at John's ranch, in the desert at Thermal. It was a genuine working ranch, no horses but tomatoes, vegetables, dates, very successfully managed by John's partner, Carter Lodge. Our last visit had been before John's great success with *The Voice of The Turtle*, since when Carter's talent for interior decoration had been given full scope. John proudly showed me his bedroom which indeed, as he had once told me, resembled the cocktail lounge of a hotel. It was lit only from behind a glass-panelled ceiling, so it seemed to me that one could only read in bed if one stood up. Pride was also taken in the electric light switches, in all the rooms, which worked if one held one's hand an inch or so away from then and willed them to work. If one pressed them, nothing happened – except that the switch, presumably insulted, went out of action for several minutes. The sitting-rooms were charming and John had a study which, as usual, he kept as if stirred with a stick. Revisions to *Bell, Book and Candle* were in progress.

We had to leave very early next morning in order to meet the train bringing Esther and her friend, Margaret, to Los Angeles. They'd had a marvellous trip, holding court in their little compartment to numerous coloured visitors, and were now in high spirits. They were also hungry so we took them to a restaurant for breakfast, telling them to follow us later to Cove Way in a taxi.

We had been warned by Phyllis that the house was now in very poor condition, but it was far worse than I had expected. It had been occupied by James Mason and his wife Pamela and their eleven cats and, though they had left weeks earlier, they had hung onto the keys until the end of their tenancy, leaving Marion Balderston little time to get things in order. During the ten years since we had lived there, much general delapidation had taken place, but what was even more noticeable was the damage done by the Masons' cats. A carpet was appallingly stained, curtains torn, net curtains in ribbons. Loose covers had been clawed or simply removed, and the stuffing was coming out of upholstery. . .

The full horror was only slightly minimised by masses of flowers sent by friends and beautifully arranged by Phyllis, and by Dorothea Fassett who was there to welcome us. (Phyllis was filming.) Nothing could have disguised the state of the kitchen: cracked tiles, broken equipment, an antique refrigerator and much ingrained dirt. Esther made no complaints, simply started preparation for a meal; Dorothea had bought us provisions. Margaret sloped off to the little guest house, only returning when the meal was ready. This was symptomatic of her behaviour for the weeks she remained with us.

In the afternoon Marion Balderston arrived. We had known her and her husband fairly well ten years earlier – it was at their house that we met Charlie Brackett and first got to like John van Druten. Now she was nervous and edgy, insisting the Masons were to blame for everything – she said they had even taken away furniture. But she admitted we couldn't live in the house as it now was. She would come back next day to discuss it all.

In the end she handed the whole matter over to her business manager, a pleasant man who expressed even more horror at the house than we felt. He told us it needed thousands of dollars spending on it. He also told us the Balderstons were in no position to spend them. John Balderston was barely recovering from a serious heart attack; it was unlikely he would ever again work in movies. All they had was their three houses. They occupied one and lived on the rents paid for the other two. Still, they must keep their houses in good condition and he would tell them so.

I felt wretched and Alec did, too. We had liked John Balderston, respected him as a writer. Marion must obviously be desperately anxious about him. We could not harass her now. Alec rang the business manager and said we would buy a new carpet, curtains, loose covers . . . indeed, everything needed if the Balderstons would look after the structural repairs and provide a better refrigerator. This offer, gratefully accepted, led to a lasting friendship with the Balderstons and John Balderston was later to do me a kindness for which I have never ceased to be grateful. For years I had been collecting books by and about Henry James and had managed to get over thirty. John lent me thirty more and said I could keep them as long as I liked. From then on, I chain-read them, usually in bed, and finished the last of them only a few days before we finally left the Balderston house.

It was a particular joy to choose furnishings we really liked after, for so many years, accepting what the owners of our various houses had chosen. And spending money has always had a therapeutic effect on me – especially as, at the moment, we felt we could afford to be extravagant. In England, *I Capture The Castle* was having a spectacular success.

It had been published in early April, but we got little news of it until well into May. Someone at Heinemann had sent notices, advertisements, etc. by ordinary surface mail and had foolishly addressed the package simply to 'Cove Way, California' – it was a miracle it ever reached us. I was touched by the warmth of the reviews and the many kind references to me and to my plays.

Frere had kept his word about advertisements, both before and after publication. Soon he was announcing – 'Top Best Seller; 57,000 copies in print' – a surprising number when there was still a paper shortage in England. When I wrote to thank him he replied that praise from an author was as scarce as snow in the Sahara.

We were still eradicating traces of cats when an emissary from the Masons arrived asking us to pay $250 for a wire-netted outdoor catpen which they had left behind. This was not of the slightest use to us and it was also an eyesore. I had liked James Mason personally when he had been in my play, *Bonnet Over The Windmill*, in London, but I was indignant at the damage the Masons had left behind, so I firmly refused to pay for their catpen and demanded that it should be pulled down. During the subsequent argument the Masons' emissary stepped on Folly, who instantly gave him a shrewd nip on his calf. She had never bitten anyone before, but she had never been stepped on before. Anyway, she victoriously ended the argument and the catpen was pulled down and carted away at the Masons' expense.

By mid-May the house was itself again and long before that our life had settled into a pleasant pattern. We dined with Charlie Brackett every Friday, either at our house or his. We were proudly shown the flourishing condition of our ex-cat and ex-canary to which he had given a home. After dinner he always ran a movie for us at Paramount, managing to get hold of many English pictures to please us. I have a particularly happy memory of those many evenings, of the quiet night-time Paramount lot, where we were able to park the car with our dogs in it and of the special pleasure of seeing pictures for which we were the only audience. Work on Charlie's *Sunset Boulevard* was now in progress.

Phyllis spent every Saturday with us. She was getting plenty of work – she had recently played one of the aunts in *The Forsyte Saga* – and had now taken an apartment and furnished it charmingly.

Chris came every Sunday. He was now beginning work on *The School of Tragedy*, which turned into *The World in The Evening*. Much as we enjoyed discussions about it and having early versions read to us, we were never altogether happy about that book.

John was in Europe, taking Starke on what sounded like the Grand Tour, so our circle of friends was not quite complete, but we had all the company we could cope with. I was longing to start work – if only I could clear off letters, letters, letters – more than ever now that *Castle* was a success in England as well as in America. As always, my lack of time weighed on me. But I was really very happy, constantly comparing my present state of mind with my wretchedness when I had lived in this pleasant house ten years earlier, when war had been raging and my homesickness was at is height.

Was I still homesick? In late May I wrote in my Journal that if quarantine should ever be removed and we could at once take the dogs back to England, I should feel ninety per cent joy and ten per cent dismay. 'So I am ten per cent nearer to feeling this exile is not an exile. And I have come to think that when I cease to mind being here, I shall at last be allowed to go home.'

XIV

Towards Esmeralda and The Cloth

Having cleared my decks a bit, I at last turned my thoughts to writing and delved up an idea for a play I had had some years earlier. It was about the vicar of an English village and a famous London dressmaker. He thought her luxury dressmaking, with its fantastic prices, was almost immoral. She thought his religion was mumbo jumbo. Yet they fell in love. How would things work out for them?

I invented a story-line and a set of characters. From the beginning my dressmaker and her business were fully alive for me. Not so my clergyman. I had drawn clergymen before: an amusing one in *Autumn Crocus*, a much-liked vicar in *I Capture the Castle*. But I hadn't the knowledge to draw a full-size leading character who was a normal Church of England vicar. I knew very little about the Church of England. I got together a number of modern books on religion, by C.S. Lewis, Dorothy Sayers and far more conventional authors. I went back to Evelyn Underhill whom I had admired years earlier. I told myself to take my time, really feel my way into my subject.

Meanwhile, I very much enjoyed the summer. Alec encouraged me to do more therapeutic money-spending, on clothes now – of which I had been starved since we had last lived in Beverly Hills. There were beautiful shops: Saks–Fifth Avenue, Magnins, the couturier Adrian, and less expensive shops where one could buy charming summer muslins and sunbathing dresses. All these gave much pleasure to Alec who took a great interest in my clothes; as did Charlie and John. I can't remember that Chris ever showed a flicker of interest in what I wore except once, years earlier, when I went to his Vedanta Temple in a conservative outfit which included long suede gloves. Chris thought this elegant and assured me Swami had noticed. I had only visited the Temple on such special occasions as hearing Chris read aloud, or John lecture. And as Chris had told me that Swami said anyone connected with the Temple in any way would be liberated after death, I always had to be assured that merely entering the place would not constitute a contract, and I should not find myself unwillingly hauled into Nirvana, or wherever.

Life was extremely pleasant. Esther gave us lunch by the pool and dinner on our little terrace. By the pool we were plagued by meat-eating wasps, a breed which bit rather than stung and would very neatly cut small segments out of cold meats. One of them got away with a tiny segment of my finger. However, we found that if provided with a thin slice of meat, they would carry little pieces of that away to their nests.

Bees troubled me more because they fell into the water and could not get out. Catching them in one's hand was a risky business and one could not always reach them, so I bought a long-handled fishing net. Landed and placed in the sun they recovered, but if there was no sun they died. If one took them indoors it was dangerous for the dogs. I said, 'What I need is a bee-cage' and an admirer Esther had acquired made me one, out of wood and wire window-netting, like a miniature meat-safe. In this, comatose bees could be warmed back to life in the kitchen, to be let out only when they were in full buzz. It gave me enormous pleasure to fling the cage open at the window and see the resuscitated bees soar away. This had to be done before sunset; I found they never lived through the night indoors. Chris considered the bee-cage one of my top eccentricities; I had once asked him and John if they considered my attitude to animals and insects a little eccentric and they had replied, as one man, 'Eccentric? You're *mad*.'

Not only bees were in need of rescue. Late one evening a piteous miaowing drew our attention to a cat up our tall mimosa tree by the pool. The tree was fairly easy to climb, Alec went up fast, but the cat went up faster; it got nearly to the top – the tree was well over fifty feet tall – where it resisted all coaxing. Alec came down and did some thinking, then got a sack which he tied to himself. He reckoned he could grab the cat and drop it into the sack. Unfortunately, this operation required three hands: one to hold on to the tree, one to grab the cat and one to hold the mouth of the sack open. How he managed I never quite knew because I was suddenly dazed with terror for fear he might fall, in which case he would have crashed down onto the stone flags surrounding the swimming pool. But he got down somehow and released the cat from the sack. It dashed out under the garden gate and we never saw it again. We later learned that it was customary to send for the fire-brigade whenever cats got stuck up trees in Beverly Hills.

Another cat was to become known to us as the 'karma cat'. For some weeks Esther fed, at the back door, a black, much dishevelled but obviously Persian cat, gentle but nervous. I watched it sometimes, from a distance, but never got as close to it as Esther did when she put its food down. One day she reported to me that she thought it had broken its jaw; its mouth was crooked and though again and again the poor creature would rub its face in the food Esther offered, it could not open its mouth enough to eat – or to drink. It would eventually leave, unfed. This went on for several days.

I was deeply harrowed. There was no way of catching the cat nor of getting a vet's advice as, when approached, it dashed up the wild hill at the back of the house. It occurred to me that Christopher would say, comfortingly, that the suffering was the cat's karma and would be of benefit in its next life.

I was thinking of this next morning on my way down to the pool to rescue my bees when it flashed through my head that I wished I could take over a bit of the cat's karma, somehow help it that way. The next moment I slipped on the sloping concrete path and sat down very heavily on the hard concrete. It was the worst pain I ever remember feeling. It jarred my spine and my whole body. I think I must have, for the first time in my life, come near to fainting. A black curtain seemed to rise up from the ground and block out all light. Then the curtain slowly receded and left me sitting on the concrete, fully conscious but in very great pain.

At the back of my mind I held the thought that I must rescue bees – a job I did every morning. Somehow, I crawled the rest of the way on all fours, picked up my bee-rescuing net and rescued six, thankful that the sun was out so I need not take them indoors. I then lay down and closed my eyes. By good luck Alec saw me from a window, ran down and helped me into the house. He then remembered he had some champagne and hurried to get it.

Champagne – the only drink I really like – and at eleven in the morning! Feeling both dissolute and pampered I swiftly recovered. And then Esther came in to tell us that the cat had just turned up with its jaw quite normal and that it was eating ravenously. I instantly thought, 'I must have taken on that cat's karma.'

Of course, neither Alec nor I really believed this but when, later, I told Christopher about it, he did. He told me one *could* take on another creature's karma, but it was a very wrong thing to do and I must never, never do it again. Apparently, I had done the cat out of suffering which would have been useful to it after death. All I knew was that it was now a well cat again – and it went on being a well cat until it ceased to visit us, some weeks later. And I had – I think – had the experience of fainting and certainly come by champagne in the morning.

We had an easier time with an opossum which we found down a deep hole with an injured leg. It was in a part of the garden to which the dogs had no access, so we were able to feed and water it until its leg got better. Even then, it still couldn't climb out of the hole so Alec made it a small ladder and it then managed perfectly.

In June, Charlie invited us to the filming of one of the last scenes in his *Sunset Boulevard*, to take place in the garden of an old house (old by Hollywood standards) on Wilshire Boulevard. Gloria Swanson had to shoot Bill Holden when he was standing on the edge of the swimming pool. He then had to fall into the pool face downwards. The scene took place at night, with lights blazing on the pool. Large, beautiful moths fluttered on the surface and were carefully rescued by someone with a man-sized version of my bee-net. Out of consideration for the feelings of the invited spectators, rescued moths were allowed to fly away. When word came that the director, Billy Wilder, was ready to shoot the scene, lagging moths were swiftly exterminated.

Bill Holden stood there in his well-cut suit. The fatal shot was fired. Bill fell in, smack on his face – and had to stay with his face underwater for what seemed to me a considerable time and, when he came out gasping, he was told by Billy Wilder he must do the fall again. He went off uncomplainingly to change into a replica dry suit.

After two more falls which didn't satisfy Billy Wilder, Bill Holden said he'd only been supplied with one more suit. Billy settled for the fourth fall.

I talked for a considerable time to Gloria Swanson – or rather she talked to me. I am so short that my face is seldom on a level with anyone talking to me. Gloria's was, and she had the habit of getting very close to anyone she was talking to. Automatically, I backed a step; she took a step forward. This went on and on until I found myself backed against the wall of Bill Holden's travelling dressing-room. I almost felt I should be bitten, or expected to rub noses, but having now got me into the talking position she liked, all was well.

Much as I admired her fantastic performance I was, when Charlie took us to a sneak pre-view of the whole picture, a little disappointed. It seemed to me that Billy Wilder's direction was self-consciously heartless and turned a story which should have been ironically moving into sheer melodrama.

By August I felt ready to start my play. My religious reading had, of course, been mainly to help me understand my clergyman's beliefs, but I had half-hoped that some of them might rub off on me. They didn't, but at least I acquired a fairly sympathetic knowledge of the Anglican Church. I felt I could bring my clergyman to life. He must have charm, humour, never be priggish.

I started in my usual way, just counting on the inspiration of the moment and expecting the characters to come to life at the pencil's point. Most of them did, especially my great dressmaker, Esmeralda, but not so my clergyman, Colin. I found I could not be interested in a man who could accept conventional Christianity. Should I scrap the play?

Around this time both my English and American publishers wrote urging me to write another novel. Stanley Salmen said that if my second book was even half as good as the first, it would sell twice as many copies on the strength of the first one. Frere of Heinemann told me that *I Capture The Castle* had had the largest acceptance of any novel offered by The Book Society. It was silly not to follow this up, but I had no idea for a book and I desperately wanted to take a play back to England. And I liked all my characters except my clergyman.

I struggled on until mid-autumn when it was time to cope with Christmas presents for England. Rationing still persisted there and people seemed to need food and clothing even more than during the war. And I was floundering in a sea of unanswered letters. I would give the play a rest until the New Year.

Phyl was now doing very well in movies and had bought herself a beautiful Chevrolet which she drove about Hollywood with great pride. I remember she came with us to help decorate Charlie's large Christmas tree. He had amassed around a hundred silver witch-balls and dozens of yards of tinsel and he insisted that all his decorations should be put on. He wanted his young grandson, known as Tigger, to remember this tree all his life. Tigger was now Charlie's greatest joy. My main reason for recalling him is that when Hollywood was conducting its famous witch-hunt for Communists and a dozen suspects were lined up in some newspaper photograph, the little boy asked, 'Which one is Jesus Christ?'

Phyl and Chris spent Christmas Day with us. Chris rang up a few days before to find out if Phyl was going to give him a present. I said she had made a tiny pottery figure for him – she had recently taken up pottery. My Journal notes:

Chris: (horror stricken) Oh, God, I shall have to get her something.
Me: Nonsense. It's only a little thing she made in her kiln.
Chris: (bitterly) *I* haven't got a kiln.
Me: Well, don't spend more than fifty cents. Buy her some little decorative book.
Chris: (astounded) A book? (His tone implied that books are now seldom seen and dangerous to track down). It would take me days to choose one.
Me: Look, you give her the Penguin *Gordon Craig Designs*, which you gave me. It only cost seventy-five cents. I'll get Alec to gift-wrap it for you.
Chris: Wonderful. (Sternly) I shall replace it, of course.
Me: Well, we'll see. The point is that you oughtn't to spend time hunting for a present when you ought to be *writing*.

Unfortunately Chris and Phyl arrived together on Christmas Day and I had difficulty in getting him alone in order to give him the package. And when I did, he seemed incapable of writing on the attached gift card. He was still arguing about the spelling of 'Phyllis' when she was coming into the room. 'I always have the same trouble with spelling "syphilis",' he said plaintively.

Esther had a happy Christmas. We deluged her with presents and she had many more. She now had four men friends. The only cloud in her sky was that an unsatisfactory boyfriend, named Al, whom she had left behind in Doylestown, was giving her trouble. He had got a lift to California in the summer and implored her to marry him. She didn't want to, but obviously feared she might eventually give in to him – and so did we.

After Christmas, I let myself go in my Journal, writing much about my religious reading and inventing a myth which came near to satisfying me. It was to the effect that God and the Devil are equal partners in one firm, that good can only be proved by means of contrast with evil. In fact God and the Devil are one. Nothing else would be fair. (This vaguely linked with one of my greatest strikes against Christianity, in which Christ's need of a betrayer victimised Judas.) This was hardly a good basis for a play about a conventional English clergyman, and it dawned on me that my leading man must not be a *conventional* clergyman.

I found that the only thing connected with religion I could believe in myself was that mystical experience was possible, and need not have anything to do with religion. My Colin should be a completely irreligious man who, after a particularly hellish war and a nervous breakdown which leaves him on the edge of suicide, has such an experience. Though utterly beyond his comprehension, it illuminates his life and he longs to recapture it. Eventually he is persuaded that his best hope of doing so is to adopt conventional Christianity, trusting that faith in it will follow, which it does. He becomes a clergyman and, through family influence, vicar of a country parish. It is here that Esmeralda, who turns the decaying village guildhall into a weekend home, erupts into his life.

I had to change my story-line, invent new characters; I was much delayed by a working notebook which ended by being longer than the play. Still I did get going. In the first act Esmeralda discovers the guildhall, adjacent to the vicarage; I brought in characters from the surrounding village. There was a good deal of comedy, a happy atmosphere. I was hopeful.

Act II takes place at Esmeralda's London dressmaking establishment, a few days before her Spring dress show. She is putting the final touches to her Collection, dresses are being finished, models instructed when, into this highly feminine atmosphere, Colin unexpectedly arrives. Her maid, a village girl, is shortly to have an illegitimate child and he brings the news that its father, an American soldier, has returned to the village and is anxious to marry her.

From then onwards, Colin and Esmeralda are involved in the maid's story – she gives birth to a premature child. While waiting for news in the small hours they at last get to know each other. He sees that her business is *her* religion, her many superstitions are her ritual. She realises she is in love with him, but has no idea what he feels about her.

I was well on into this complicated three-scened act when I had to break off and work for Charlie. Apart from the fact that I never liked to refuse him, I felt that a few weeks at a high salary would come in useful, all the more so as we had not yet, in spite of much interest, sold the film rights of *I Capture The Castle*. And it was pleasant work, on *The Mating Season*, which was already being shot. I just had to be around making suggestions for last minute improvements. I had many friends at Paramount and enjoyed seeing them again.

I was looking forward to getting back to my play and then, in unhappy circumstances, Esther left us. She suddenly said she must have a month's holiday. Up to now she had refused to take holidays, preferring to be paid double instead. Now she said she must return to Pennsylvania and see her mother and Al. No, she wasn't going to marry Al, she was coming back to us – and as she left most of her clothes behind we believed her, cheerfully paid her fare and set about making do with a friend she had found to replace her, who proved to be utterly hopeless. We were counting the days till Esther's return when she telephoned asking for more time, just a week. . . But at the end of the week she asked for another and finally admitted she wasn't coming back at all. She was going to marry Al.

We were too fond of her to be angry. We could only wish her well and set about packing her clothes and sending them to her – and finding another maid. The first one we engaged was white, elderly and plain, but had striking red hair. Christopher became convinced she was a Communist spy and spent happy, fruitless hours searching our house and cellar for hidden microphones.

I now found the long brilliant summer too hot for work – though not too hot for me to enjoy the garden, with which Alec had done wonders. There were flowers everywhere – I remember them in a jumble of seasons, possibly because California does jumble its seasons, thanks to much sunlight and continual watering by sprinklers; though presumably Nature alone is responsible for the fact that orange and lemon trees have blossom and fruit on together at the same time twice a year. We had a charming little orange tree near the pool. I remember bougainvillaea, hibiscus and so many flowering trees. I think my favourite was the blue-flowered jacaranda. Ours had branches stretching across one of my bedroom windows. This tree was responsible for one of the rare disagreements Alec and I ever had. He did not believe trees, however beautiful, should be allowed to keep out too much daylight so, without warning me, he lopped off a branch – though not, I'll admit, when it was in full bloom. I said with extreme dignity, 'I'm not going to make a fuss about this; I am simply telling you that you have behaved like a beast.' He took umbrage and said that in no circumstances should I call my husband a beast – thus somehow putting *me* in the wrong. We must have remained on bad terms for fully five minutes. Some of our friends would have paid good money to witness this scene.

Actually, the only thing that offending branch had cut off was the view of part of the Selznick swimming pool which could just be seen, raised up on ugly concrete columns, across the road, which reminds me that, late in the summer, we were to make the acquaintance of the swimming pool's owner, Mrs Irene Selznick. When John had almost given up hope of placing his *Bell, Book and Candle*, she had said that she would produce it if he would make numerous changes. He was summoned to Beverly Hills to discuss them.

Mrs Selznick was Hollywood royalty, doubly so as she was the daughter of Louis B. Mayer and the ex-wife of David Selznick. Her house, protected by a large garden, was not visible from ours. I was much impressed by the fact that she kept a day staff and a night staff, so that there was always a chauffeur available and, say, a steak could be cooked and served in the small hours. John worked with her day after day, usually staggering across the road to us for strong drink and sympathy in the late afternoon. It seemed that she was unpicking his play line by line.

Charlie said that if there was one woman qualified to work on a play about witchcraft it was Irene Mayer Selznick. But she certainly showed no love for witches. One of her first demands was that John should remove anything to do with real witchcraft – she was horrified to know that witches worshipped the Devil. His heroine must just be a girl who had a sort of knack for magic. She just spoke a few strange names or had a word with her cat and, well, things happened. And seeing that the play was a comedy and love story, I think she was right. More important for success, she set herself to build up the part of the leading man which had been refused by various actors because the leading lady's part was so much better. And here, via John, she taught me something I have never forgotten.

She said no leading man should ever be expected to say simply 'Yes' or 'No'. He must always substitute something, or add something which was interesting. Every line he spoke must have some importance and, in a comedy, he must have frequent laughs. She would say to John, 'You must put in a laugh there' – and it was surprising how often he could. And though nothing would have persuaded me to go through what he was going through, it seemed to me she was doing a pretty good job for the play.

Towards the end of their work together John informed me that he would have to bring her to see us – 'And it's no use reminding me you don't like meeting people because she *insists*. She's *got* to come.'

So come she did. He brought her with him after a hard day's work and they sat in the late afternoon sunlight on our little terrace. My Journal describes this:

> She is in her forties, probably; small, dark, quite attractive. She uses more gestures than a French actress playing a French actress. Her excitability is nerve-shattering. She had asked to come to see us so that she could tell us about staying with Binkie Beaumont at our Essex cottage, but she tossed this off in a few minutes, telling us scarcely anything except that she hadn't minded having to unpack for herself. What she really wanted was to talk about John's play and various changes she was still rooting for. In the end she insisted on being left alone with me and then told me she was determined that he should learn how to create virile men, vital love scenes. She gave me glimpses of real life love scenes she had figured in herself, how an insulting remark from a man may be the highest form of compliment to a woman, indicating that he has 'had another erection'. I said mildly, 'Well, you can't show that on the stage, can you?' But in view of Tennessee Williams' latest play, in which someone drops a French letter on the floor, perhaps you can.
>
> Still, I quite liked Mrs Selznick even if I wouldn't work with her for a fortune. When she left she clasped my hand warmly and said, 'And I may come again?' I said, dubiously, 'Well, just,' which made her laugh.

She told John I had a pungent mind. Odd word, pungent: I didn't believe I'd ever in my life used it. No doubt she meant it as a compliment, but somehow I didn't feel it was quite me. She certainly improved *Bell, Book and Candle* and managed to secure Rex Harrison and his wife, Lilli Palmer, for the leads. John was off to New York with a successful production ahead of him before I'd begun my third act.

It was to be set in the old guildhall, now Esmeralda's charming weekend home, at Christmas time, with snow on the ground. There was plenty of comedy and village atmosphere, but resolving the love story was extremely difficult. Esmeralda, knowing that Colin will never ask her to give up her business and knowing, too, that she cannot be a full-time wife to him if she hangs on to it, finally relinquishes it and does so before she is sure that he loves her, thus making an act of faith similar to the one he made when adopting Christianity before he believed in it.

I was in the midst of this when, in October, Murray Macdonald, after directing Edith Evans in *Daphne Laureola* in New York, came to stay with us. Since our last meeting in Malibu he had had a nervous breakdown, but was now well and cheerful and anxious to get me back to London to do a play with him; he wished to go into management. I told him a little about the one in hand and he seemed so eager that I promised I would do it with him instead of with Binkie. He undertook to come back in the spring to read the finished script and discuss casting and, encouraged by Alec, I said I would go to England for rehearsals and presentation. Murray got on well with Charlie and Christopher and his whole visit was a stimulating success. It greatly helped me to finish the play.

I was able to show it to Alec and Phyllis early in the New Year. Both of them liked it. Chris thought it the best thing I had ever written. Charlie felt sure it would succeed in New York as well as in London. John, on arrival back from successfully directing *The King and I* in New York, kindly awarded me ten for effort and thought I had ninety per cent succeeded in drawing a good man who wasn't dull. He added that he had once thought of writing a similar play himself, but he didn't want to talk about that now. (Neither did I.) He then borrowed a copy (Alec had retyped the whole script with carbons) to take back to his ranch to study before making suggestions, but as it was several weeks before he sent them (they were minimal) the final version had been professionally mimeographed without them in time for Murray's visit in March.

Alas, Murray was not at his best during that March visit. After he reached America he got the news that Ivor Novello, a great friend whose most recent musical Murray had directed, had died. This saddened him greatly; and I had recently heard from friends that his nerves were bad again. He seemed unsure if he was ready to go into management. But he cheered up after he had read the play (now entitled *Esmeralda and The Cloth*) and felt sure he knew the right woman to play in it, an actress new to London, named Eileen Herlie, whom he had helped to recent success. He now suggested he should present the play with Binkie, directing it himself and keeping control of it.

Both Alec and I were greatly relieved as Binkie was still the most powerful theatrical manager in London. All that worried us now was that he might refuse to share. But he cabled enthusiastically only two days after Murray got back to London with the scripts, would love to present the play and was 'thrilled' that I was coming home for it. Long letters followed, mainly about finding a star leading man. I should be needed in early summer. All I could do was to answer letters promptly, buy clothes suitable for England and feel thankful I no longer had to work every day.

In early May, Phyllis went back to England for good. She had had a disappointing year, like almost all members of the English colony in Hollywood. Owing to film quota complications, fewer and fewer English stories were being made into films and far longer-established and better known English players were having to go home. What she most disliked was giving up her car, but she was comforted by the thought that I, too, would be going to London shortly. And she was pulling out with a fair amount of money saved. We weren't worried about her.

But we were worried about Christopher. He seemed far from well, his private life was full of difficulties, he was getting poorer and poorer and saw no immediate probability of earning anything worth mentioning. He continued to write and rewrite *The World in the Evening* and had recently begun it again on new lines. There seemed nothing we could do except be ready to help him out in any sudden financial emergency.

We were talking about him one day in May as we drove down past Palm Springs to spend the weekend with John at his desert ranch. Alec said, 'If only John would make a play out of the Sally Bowles story in Chris's *Goodbye to Berlin!*' We had discussed such a play before and I had never believed it could be satisfactory. I still didn't but Alec persisted, pointing out the interest of the setting in pre-war Berlin, the character of Sally . . . anyway, couldn't I just suggest it to John? Anything to help. . .

I said, 'If I suggest it, John will turn it down flat. But if *you* suggest it and I say it's impossible . . . John's very fond of contradicting me. But how will you lead into it?'

'Oh, I'll find some way,' said Alec blithely. It was a deliberate ploy between us to help Christopher.

We arrived in the late afternoon when it was still very hot and soon went down to the ranch's reservoir which did duty as a swimming pool. Alec swam, John and I were on the bank (so was a horrible electric fly-trap which made frizzling noises every time a poor fly electrocuted itself). Alec, after swimming underwater, popped his head up and said, 'John, why don't you turn *Sally Bowles* into a play?' I can't say it was a subtle approach; Alec then retreated underwater.

I said, 'It couldn't be done.'

John said it could be, but the idea didn't attract him. I continued to say it was impossible, unless . . . I threw out a few suggestions. John improved on them. Alec joined us and greeted John's suggestions with enthusiasm. We went on talking all through dinner until Carter Lodge said, 'John, are you serious about this? If not, it mustn't be mentioned to Chris.'

'Of course I'm not serious,' said John, 'I'm just playing with the idea,' and went on playing all evening.

Fairly late he pulled me up by saying, 'Don't *help*, Pongo.' This was an old joke between us. My first Dalmatian, whenever he saw packing afoot, would climb into suitcases, tread on dresses, massacre tissue paper, causing me to tell him not to *help*. John loved this story and always used my phrase when he didn't want me to interfere. 'Don't help', now meant *Sally Bowles* belonged to him.

Ten days later he brought his finished play to Beverly Hills and Christopher, Alec and I detested it. Alec and I thought it dull and dirty. Christopher thought it cold and dirty – a combination he particularly disliked. We criticised it but tried to be tactful. John cleaned it up a bit and added a character of his own invention. He then sent scripts to New York to his agent, Monica McCall, and to Alfred de Liagre, a great friend who had presented *The Voice of The Turtle* and other plays by John. In both cases the verdict was worse than ours.

Meanwhile, the contract between John and Chris had to be arranged and we were astounded to learn that John intended to give Chris only twenty-five per cent of the play's royalties, keeping seventy-five per cent for himself. We had taken it for granted that the split would be fifty-fifty as the fame of the story and Chris's prestige as a writer were a good balance for John's great success as a playwright, and all the enquiries we made supported this view. John would have none of it.

He entrenched himself at the Chateau Marmont, refused to talk on the telephone and wrote bitterly aggrieved letters. I made myself answer tactfully. Chris answered humorously, but saying John was a bit kinked about money. (John never answered that letter.) Walter Starke, now at the Chateau Marmont with John, rang me up asking me to be more understanding. Monica McCall, whom I knew only slightly, wrote from New York. Would I please stop making Johnny so unhappy? Surely I knew how he felt about money? One just had to accept his attitude. I found this hard to do, seeing that money was pouring in on Johnny whereas Chris was pretty near broke.

It is only fair to say that John's 'funniness' was not simple meanness. He could be generous. From Monica's letter, from talks I had with Starke and from my own intuition, I came to believe that the earning of money compensated him for the fact that, in spite of all his success, he had no great literary prestige. He was jealous of Christopher's, which he frequently said was inflated. For John, the earning of huge sums was his way of feeding his ego.

After a bitter struggle, John grudgingly agreed to give Chris forty per cent. Chris accepted, with grace and humour. Amicable relations were resumed between us all – but were they ever quite so amicable? Incidentally, John still had a financial trick up his sleeve which he didn't disclose until much later.

Even while the battle raged I had been busy with work of my own. By the end of May I had begun to feel guilty because I wasn't doing any writing. Murray had now been back in England for over two months and no star leading man had been found. I thought Michael Wilding, then in Hollywood, might be a possibility so Charlie kindly invited him when next running a movie for us. Michael Wilding brought with him Marlene Dietrich, elegant in black satin and eye veil. I had always admired her but that evening she was so rude to Charlie and to Michael Wilding, for no apparent reason (us, she merely ignored), that I took agin her for life. And Michael Wilding wasn't free for my play or very suitable. One way and another I didn't think I should be wanted in London for a considerable time and then I remembered that I had once thought of making Henry James's novel, *The Reverberator*, into a play.

I began it early in June, scribbling away in pencil as with my earliest plays; it was bliss to be writing so easily. By early August I had a typed revision ready for Alec to read. He liked it (did anyone who read that script not like it?) and we hastened to get professionally typed copies. Just as these were ready I received, most opportunely, a letter from Terry Helburn of the Theatre Guild reminding me of the success of *Call It A Day* and asking if I couldn't let her have another play.

I sent her two copies of the new play, which I called *Letter From Paris*, telling her that, if she liked it, I very much hoped the Guild could present it in conjunction with Jack Wilson, to whom I owed so much. If she approved, would she send one of the copies to Jack and discuss the matter with him? Terry telegraphed surprisingly soon, saying the play was 'enchanting' and she hoped to get a film star to play in it. Meanwhile, the other members of the Guild were reading it.

By the time we heard from Terry, Alec and I were in a whirl of activity. Murray had written saying that, unless I returned to England *soon*, *Esmeralda and The Cloth* would never get produced by Binkie who, having failed to get a blazing male star, was now making no constructive suggestions.

However, he hadn't yet admitted he was bowing out and, if he did, the excellent management of Rea and Clift were anxious to present the play with Murray. And there were good actors available who were better casting than the stars who had been approached. But I *must* come over.

It was now well into August. It amazes me that Alec was able to make the necessary preparations for my trip, cope with permits, passport, arrange for me in New York, get rail and steamer reservations (still very difficult), supply me with a dossier of information about our London solicitor, accountant, bank, (even so, I went to the wrong bank, but they kindly supplied me with money), help me pack and finally get me onto a train in Los Angeles on September 4th. But so it was.

XV

To New York, 1951

After the train started I realised I was in for a very painful experience. Of course I had known I should miss Alec, but during our wild rush to get me off I hadn't had time to think just how *much* I should miss him. On the train I was suddenly smitten both mentally and physically. I felt *ill* with a sense of loss. I remember thinking, 'I just don't know what to do with myself.' Mercifully Alec had got me a compartment to myself, so I could suffer in seclusion.

During our thirteen years in America we had been separated for less than half-a-dozen nights. There had only been Alec's few visits to pacifist camps and organizations, and the three days he had spent in the famous Death Valley, which he had long wanted to see. I didn't want to myself; I was sure it would be too hot for me and for the three dogs. Also I hadn't been willing to break off my struggles with *Esmeralda*, so I let him go alone. Our three men friends had rung up repeatedly to make sure that I was surviving and Charlie had suggested we should have an aeroplane sky-writing, 'Welcome Home', to greet him on his return.

Now we shouldn't see each other for months. Was he as distressed as I was? Later he told me that, having at last got me on the train, his main sensation was one of relief. He went home exhausted and slept for hours, surrounded by the dogs. Only later did he feel much as I did.

At least I could be sure he would be well looked after as we had now acquired our best maid since Esther. (She had succeeded a stout lady who told me she had a first edition of Dickens, handwritten on vellum; and she was apt to build up our anticipation of meals by saying such things as, 'How would you like some freshly opened, thoroughly chilled, thinly sliced SPAM?'). Our new maid was half Negro, half Red Indian and particularly proud of her Indian blood. Her Christian names were Rosa Lee and we were expected to make them sound like that, not like Rosalie. She was fussy about that.

Christopher would continue his weekly visits. Charlie would dine with Alec every week and run movies for him at the studios. (Charlie had now left Paramount for 20th Century-Fox, an important step-up for him, but I never liked the atmosphere at Fox as much as I had that of Paramount.) John was in New York hoping to arrange for the production of his Sally Bowles play.

Alec who, on boyhood visits to America had travelled across the continent by train, had told me how much I should enjoy the journey. He was wrong. I was too miserable to enjoy anything. Looking out of the window didn't interest me. I took no pleasure in reading. I slept badly. In Europe I had always liked sleeping on trains. I didn't enjoy meals and I especially disliked getting to the dining-car, being flung about by the madly swaying train. On my first evening someone at my table had a bad cold. Soon that was my bad cold, too. I couldn't remember having any colds in America and had forgotten what a really bad one was like.

All that I did enjoy was receiving two encouraging telegrams from Alec which were handed in to the train during the four days journey. They were a comfort. But what I really looked forward to was reaching New York and telephoning him.

I was to stay at John's hotel. He had very kindly offered to be my host in New York, taking me to a theatre every night. Alec had asked him to choose me 'a suite that would cheer me up'. I didn't need a suite, but Alec was determined I should have one. It was something of a shock when I was shown into a dark sitting-room where the carpet was badly stained and there were glass rings on every table. In the bedroom the walls of the clothes closet were growing mould, the bath was uncleaned and much of the paint was off the lavatory seat. John later admitted he hadn't had time to inspect the suite, but had 'asked for a nice one'.

His own penthouse suite was considerably better if not exactly glamorous. You could call it comfortable or frowsty depending on if you were John or me. He said he liked the hotel because it was 'cosy'. He had decided that Starke should present the Sally Bowles play (eventually called *I Am A Camera*) in conjunction with Gertrude Macy, who was Katharine Cornell's business manager. This meant that financial backing would have to be arranged, which would depend much on the casting. Discussions were in full swing and I felt unwilling to take up John's time; indeed, I would have been more than willing to go to bed and nurse my cold. But he insisted on taking me out to dinner and then to *The King and I*, which he had directed.

He had reserved two stalls, but said he couldn't sit through the show again; he would meet me in the first interval. When he did so I said, 'John, I think this may be the best musical I've ever seen and, quite certainly, it's the best directed'. He said, 'In that case, I can bear to see the rest of it with you.' His pleasure at my praise was so extreme that I found myself wishing that I had, more often, praised his work whole-heartedly; though I had, sometimes pulling my punches, praised it more than he had praised mine. He was to tell me that he quite liked my *Letter From Paris*, but he interrupted himself to say perhaps *he* ought to adapt something by Henry James. Could I suggest any particular book? To the best of my belief, he had never even got through any book by James or even any of the short stories.

I had arranged to have Sunday supper with Terry Helburn. She told me her fellow Theatre Guild directors all found my play 'enchanting', but didn't like it quite as much as she did, 'they don't know Henry James as well as we do'. I formed the opinion that all she knew about James was that *The Heiress*, adapted from James's *Washington Square*, had been a big success. That, she pointed out, had a strong story-line. Perhaps the story-line of *Letter From Paris* needed to be made more dramatic – 'the way Jed Harris fixed *The Heiress*.' I pointed out that my play was a comedy – 'Oh, yes, of course the comedy's enchanting but. . .' She got vaguer and vaguer, didn't seem quite to remember what the play was about.

I asked her if she had sent it to Jack Wilson. Oh, yes and he felt much as the Guild did. Well, we must all go on thinking. Perhaps if we could find just the right star. . .

By the end of supper I didn't believe the Guild now had any intention of doing my play. Still, I went to see John's agent, Monica McCall, and asked her to keep an eye on things should Terry's interest prove to be serious. I also saw John's attorney, John Wharton, and asked him to get me the right to do the play in England, where *The Reverberator* was still in copyright. In America it was already in the public domain. Mr Wharton put the matter in the hands of the young man who had coped with my contract for *I Capture The Castle* and taken a hell of a long time over it, but I was in no particular hurry as I had no intention of offering the play in England.

John was extremely kind throughout my stay. He took me to five theatres, the only one of which gave me pleasure was *The King and I*; John disliked most of the others even more than I did. His *Bell, Book and Candle* was now off as the Rex Harrisons had determinedly left the cast. We dined together every night and I insisted I should pay my share of those very expensive meals (John's 'funniness' about money did not extend to the cost of meals), but he would not let me pay for my theatre seats. He said he could take them off his Income Tax. I said so could I, but he said his Income Tax needed them more than mine did.

What I most looked forward to each day was getting back to my awful rooms at night and telephoning Alec. I never told him what that 'suite to cheer me up' had turned out to be, as I knew he would have wanted me to do something about it and I didn't want to bother. I only used it for sleeping in and telephoning him from.

I rang Jack Wilson's office the day before I was due to sail and his nice secretary told me he was desperately busy rehearsing the tours of two musicals, so I just sent him my love and hardly expected to hear from him. But she rang back arranging for me to lunch with him next day.

I thought he looked very tired with new lines on his still youthful face. But he was as charming as ever, interested in my coming visit to England. It was some little time before he mentioned *Letter From Paris* and then his verdict was on the same lines as Terry Helburn's. His main criticism was that it would be hard to get modern American audiences to feel strongly about the distress of a dignified American family long resident in Paris when their most private affairs are pried into and exposed by a crude American journalist. People wouldn't take it seriously.

I said, 'But the play's a comedy – and a love story; not a strong drama that's somehow missed fire. There are only occasional touches of drama.'

He stared at me, then covered his eyes with his hands for a moment. Then he said, 'Darling, you don't have to say any more. You've sold it to me.'

He went on to explain that the Guild had only lent him the script for a few hours; tired after rehearsing all day, he had rushed through it, influenced by the Guild's verdict. Now his whole attitude had changed and, in spite of his very rushed reading, he knew far more about the play than Terry did and could go through it commenting on the comedy angles. He interrupted my fuller explanation by saying, 'You don't have to say any more. I've *got* it.'

He would really prefer to produce it on his own, but if the Guild knew he wanted to, nothing would get it away from them so he'd leave them alone for the moment. If they did decide to do it he would co-produce and direct. As for their desire to 'fix it', 'Forget it, darling. They're always fixing at least five plays and never know which is which.'

That lunch gave me a real lift of spirit, all the more so because I could hand on the good news to Alec. Then, on my way to the Queen Mary and in that slightly heightened emotional mood always induced in me by leaving one country for another, I wondered if Jack's sudden change of attitude could have simply been due to kindness; perhaps he didn't really mean to do the play. But, on board, I found a bottle of Bristol Cream from him; I had asked to have it at lunch and he had told the waiter to show him the bottle. There was a note with it saying 'Darling Dodie, Bon Voyage. It was a lovely lunch and good luck to us both, Jack.' 'Good luck to us both' had been on the telegram he sent on the opening night of our *Lovers and Friends* and I knew it meant that we should be working together again with my *Letter From Paris*.

I still find myself touched that a tired man, who had to dash off to a rehearsal, should have found time to write me that note. And though his secretary no doubt ordered the sherry, she didn't *think* the sherry.

During the voyage I spent much time on my Journal, catching up on over four months' gap. Part of the entry written the day I landed has an immediacy which retrospect cannot achieve.

Wednesday, September 19th, 1951 11 a.m.
No time to finish last night – I packed till after midnight. I have Alec's huge Hartmann trunk, my old Asprey wardrobe suitcase, a shoe-box, two suitcases of clothes, two suitcases of stationery and scripts, an attaché case, a typewriter, two boxes of food for presents – and Jack's unopened Bristol Cream which I shall have to carry like a baby.

I originally planned to have far less luggage. But Alec could not bear me to leave things behind which might conceivably be of use, especially warm clothes, cashmere rugs and the like. Conversely, he wanted me to bring my California muslin dresses in case I had even one chance to wear them (he particularly likes me in those); but I drew the line at them with the English autumn ahead.

Oh, my dear Alec! I think it is due to you that I feel so much less than I expected to about this return to England. The heart cannot take in too many emotions at once and I have been so shattered by parting from you that I seem capable of feeling little else.

It was painful enough saying goodbye to the dogs. They stayed behind with Rosa Lee and my last glimpse of them was when, high up on the terrace, they turned their heads watching the car pass the garden wall. But it was infinitely worse seeing the last of Alec from the train. . . It has been a terrible, terrible wrench. Alec says it is like the loss of a limb. To me, it is more like the loss of some important part of my brain. As well as caring for each other very deeply we have, over the years, achieved a companionship so closely interlocked that, separated, we simply are not complete.

But separation seemed necessary if I am to continue as a playwright. Alec has felt for a long time that I ought to come. If he hadn't and hadn't coerced me, I couldn't have done it.

My array of luggage reminds me that he cleaned every bit of it for me. He brushed my suede shoes and handbags – jobs I rarely bother to do. He spent hours and hours preparing me to be on my own. I no longer remembered how to make out a cheque, what stamps letters need. Every document I need had to be explained and labelled. Perhaps it's a bad thing to let myself become as dependent as I have.

I am gradually becoming a little less sad – or perhaps I am just getting used to sadness. And in some ways it's a relief not to talk to Alec every night as I did in New York. I shall hope to telephone from England sometimes, but we both feel we must break the habit of telephoning every day. Those calls were a bit too painful.

I looked forward to them all day, but there was something terribly distressing about them – the nearness as well as the farness and, always, the misery of ringing off. Alec was usually in bed with the dogs around him – Buzz's nose within a few inches of the telephone. Alec has moved into my room and has my big bed. All the dogs sleep with him and he covers Buzz up in the early morning, just as I always did.

I haven't missed the dogs as much as I expected to, mainly because I know they are happy with Alec. Buzz hunted for me at first but is quite all right now. I have been up to the ship's kennels and made friends with a gentle Alsatian on his way to quarantine in England. The thought of our dogs going into quarantine can move me to tears at any time, but that is for their sakes, not mine, I find. I can bear to be without them as long as I know they are happy.

Well, I must look forward to my return to California, and work hard so that I can take back good news. On this trip depends what we do with our future. We might go to France, to keep the dogs out of quarantine.

It's so damnable that I don't like travelling and Alec adores it. If only *he* could have had this trip! And he would so love to be back in the London theatre, watching over the details of one of my productions, fighting my battles. I don't think I'm quite the fighter I once was.

I had hoped to have some feelings about England this morning. But they are not there and I'm not going to fake them. I shall close my last suitcase, then go up and watch our approach to the coast. Perhaps the feelings will come – or perhaps all greatly looked-forward-to-happenings are always anti-climactic. I'm not really unhappy; even missing Alec is now only a dulled sense of loss. I'm not really *anything*. But perhaps my subconscious mind is busier than I know.

XVI

A Traveller Returns

I can't recall that I ever did work up any acute feelings. With all my luggage, getting through the Customs was complicated and, though Murray Macdonald was close at hand, he wasn't allowed to join me and help. Only when I was on the train did I have time to think about being back in England.

Gazing out of the window I was most conscious of a lack of strangeness. The fields and the houses did *not* look unexpectedly small. The grass was no greener than I had remembered, the countryside just as I had treasured it in memory. So much of my mind had always remained in England that I was less like a traveller returning after a long absence than a sleeper waking from a brief dream. The dream seems long in itself, but life is so much more vivid that it ousts the dream instantly.

On our way from Waterloo we drove along The Mall. It had been such a wet summer that the trees in St James's Park were still in full leaf with scarcely a hint of autumn. The greenness and furriness of English foliage were just as I had remembered them.

What Blitz damage I saw made curiously little impression on me then – because I was so fully prepared for it. I found it impressed me much more by degrees.

Murray's house, where I was to stay, was in Cheltenham Terrace, a little street of old, cream-painted houses off the King's Road, Chelsea; they faced the grass at the front of the Duke of York's Barracks. The basement was let to an actor who was away on tour. Murray's elderly Yorkshire housekeeper, Frances, had the downstairs front room, with her kitchen at the back. Murray had the first floor rooms (very well furnished with some good original paintings) and on the top floor I had a front sitting-room, a small back bedroom and a tiny bathroom which was adequate except that the lavatory was disinclined to carry down the formidable, tough 'Bronco' paper, then in use all over England. I got over this by using facial tissues.

Murray had asked Phyllis to dinner so she was waiting to welcome me and my rooms were crowded with flowers; there had been so many that Murray had filled his own living-room with them, too, where I should have most of my meals. It had never occurred to me that people would send welcoming flowers. Murray must have been a powerful bellringer to let so many friends know I should be arriving.

During the evening he warned me that Binkie was annoyed at my coming to England, which he interpreted as an effort to force his hand. But he had sent the most beautiful flowers and there was no sign of annoyance when I dined with him alone, on the evening after my arrival, in his enchanting house in Lord North Street, Westminster; really two houses now joined together. They were perfectly preserved 17th Century houses, the rooms small but admirably proportioned. Sitting with Binkie late in the evening, the silence was such that I remembered a line from Henry James's *The Sense of The Past*, 'He longed for the ticks of the old stopped clocks.' In Binkie's house I almost heard them.

He had all his old smiling charm, with occasional touches of playfulness in his manner – *not* indicative of a playful nature. He talked a great deal, rather more than in the old days and with greater confidence, but he also listened well and the evening passed most pleasantly. But it was mainly an evening of gossip and again and again he slid away from discussing my play. Not until shortly before midnight did he, quite suddenly, make a suggestion for casting. He then plunged into action, telephoned Murray asking him to join us and the three of us went on talking about the play until after 2 am. Eventually Binkie telephoned for a radio cab to take us home. This drawing of a cab out of the night from this tiny old panelled sitting room fascinated me.

My Journal, made up some little while later from my expenses notebook, gives the day by day record of my first week: meetings with friends, meals in restaurants, visits to theatres and films. I enjoyed everything, so presumably what John van Druten had called my 'hermititis' only operated in America. Of course I still missed Alec, but not quite so painfully and airmail letters from him, almost every day, helped. Often I longed for his opinion and advice and wrote asking for it, but by the time he wrote back the circumstances had usually changed.

Binkie now seemed willing to do the play without a star leading man so it was only a question of *right* casting. And he had hinted that I just might not think Eileen Herlie was ideal.

She was fully occupied with the final rehearsals for the televising of *The Little Foxes*, which took place the Sunday after I arrived. I was not impressed, but told myself not to count television against her. When she dined with us next day I realised she had quite a strong personality. She was dark, vivacious – I could believe she was talented; but she had none of the sunny charm my great dressmaker needed. Also, I found her annoying. She thought I ought to cut most of the religion out of the play and let my clergyman play a good game of cricket. Obviously she had no understanding of the play as a whole. Still, I hadn't the heart to tell Murray what I felt. She had been waiting months to play the part.

The next day Murray took me to the first night of the Jean Louis Barrault French Players at the St James's Theatre – a very grand occasion; I regret to say I fell asleep. Murray nudged me awake and then fell asleep himself. Afterwards we went to the Oliviers' even more grand party at Claridges. Vivien Leigh, receiving the guests, looked unbelievably beautiful in grey chiffon and antique jewellery. My Journal records that I talked to Diana Wynyard, Peggy Ashcroft, Emlyn and Molly Williams, Edith Evans, Sybil Thorndyke, Noel Coward, the Bronson Alberys . . . the list goes on and on. I mention that 'everyone was charming to me – in fact, rather nicer than they would have been in the old days'.

I also talked to John Gielgud with whom I had had an earlier meeting two days after I arrived. Walking along the Haymarket, I had stopped to look at His Majesty's Theatre. I was wondering about the room in the dome, which I had never been in, and thinking about a play I had once wanted to write about a young girl in the London theatre world. (It got written as a novel some fifteen years later and was called *The Town in Bloom*.) An unforgettable voice behind me said, 'It's all right, Dodie. His Majesty's is still there'. I turned and saw John Gielgud.

Since the old days when he had played in my *Dear Octopus*, he had aged scarcely at all – unlike many of the people I had met at the Oliviers' party. I am bad at remembering faces and again and again it had taken me some seconds to recognise people I had known quite well. I was reminded of the last book of Proust's *Remembrance of Things Past* where, at a party, the narrator thinks the guests are in fancy dress and make-up, and then finds they have merely grown old. I was even more conscious of this when Phyllis invited me to the Three Arts Club (now like a hostel – and such an elderly hostel) where there were still members who had been young when I was young.

By the end of my first full week we were considering two leading men, one better known than the other. Eileen, when she came to dinner, had asked for him. She now said she wouldn't consider playing with the other. I found her grand leading-lady manner over this annoying; and during the week I had become more and more sure she wasn't right for the play. Murray finally got this out of me and, to my surprise, agreed. He said she had changed, become affected. But he still felt he could get a good performance out of her. He went to his Brighton flat for the weekend and on the Sunday I went to Manchester with Binkie who had invited me to the dress rehearsal and opening of a new play. He thought it would give me the chance to see my Manchester cousins and it was typical of him that he should remember I had some.

He was particularly kind throughout the trip. I recall that when, on the train journey to Manchester, I said I was going to get a wash, he told me lavatories on British Railways were no longer fit to use – 'Anyway, if you must go, we must find you one that's reasonably clean.' He then marched me along the corridors opening doors until at last he said, 'This one'll do – just.'

The play was *Figure of Fun*, by André Roussin, adapted from the French by Arthur Macrae whom I very much liked. I also liked the company whom I met at meals at the Midland Hotel where we stayed, particularly Brenda Bruce who was giving a most sympathetic performance – but nothing told me how she was one day to affect my fortunes. The whole occasion reminded me of my own out-of-town openings though it was, seemingly, more peaceful than mine had been.

Binkie kindly gave all my family seats. My cousin Esmé, once notorious for eating the arms off her dolls, was now happily married. She had become a dazzling blonde and, when I remarked that I liked her new hair, said, 'Oh, did you notice it?' My cousin Ronnie who, as a small boy, had warned me that I had 'such a frail chance' as an actress, was now a prosperous business man with his perfect wife, Frances, and two beautifully mannered young sons. Alas, none of my uncles and aunts, those playmates of my Manchester childhood, still remained.

I spent a day with Ronnie and Frances and met their local vicar, Peter Hamilton, a clever and likeable man who was shortly to take up an important religious appointment with the B.B.C. We had corresponded while I was writing *Esmeralda* and he now assured me the play was correct in all details connected with the Church of England and that, in spite of Esmeralda's invincible lack of belief (and my own), nothing would give offence. He also told me that pain was said to be God's last gift to man, which I have now come to equate with my own belief that without evil – perhaps the loan of it, rather than the gift – man cannot recognise what is typified by the word 'God'.

During that Manchester weekend I told Binkie that Murray and I now shared his doubts about Eileen and he said frankly how angry he had been because Murray had only offered to do the play with him if she was engaged. We must review the whole situation at the weekend, which I was to spend with him at The Barretts, my much loved Essex cottage, which had now been on loan to him for nearly thirteen years. I was still far from sure we could ask Eileen to bow out. As well as thinking her wrong casting I had found her criticisms annoying – not to mention her request for a new scene in which she could 'bubble', whatever she meant by that – but she had waited so long for the part that I almost felt in honour bound to her.

Another complication was that Binkie had now definitely decided against the actor she wanted, on the score of 'unreliability', but we must on no account disclose this reason to her.

Back in London on Wednesday evening I had to inform Murray of this decision, which put him in a difficult position as Eileen was pressing for news about her leading man. Feeling that for the moment he must try to keep her happy, Murray rang her up, intending to have just a pleasant chat. I gathered it didn't turn out to be pleasant. He rang off and said ruefully, 'She's coming here.'

She arrived on a very high horse. Why was she being kept waiting? Why wasn't the actor she wanted being engaged? She had been in touch with him and knew he was willing. Murray could only say we didn't think him quite suitable. Wouldn't she consider the other actor? He had offered to read the part with her, so that we could all judge his suitability. (I had never seen him act.) Very few leading actors would have made such an offer, but she refused it indignantly. Her manner throughout was so rude that I felt she must suspect we had turned against her. When she left I could see she was really angry.

We rang Binkie. After careful consideration, he said he'd give her time to get home and then telephone her, just feel his way around. Later that night he reported that she wished to give up the part and would like to see us all at the Globe Theatre next day 'to explain'.

The lapse of over thirty years has not dimmed my memory of that meeting. On a chilly October afternoon, and at a time when most women dressed very casually, she arrived in a navy-blue silk dress, coatless, but wearing the longest fox stole I had ever seen. It reached from the ground on one side, went round her neck, and then down to the ground on the other side. At each end it had a fox's brush. She wore a yellow satin hat with a gold-sequined veil, and long black suede gloves, outside one of which was an enormous topaz ring.

She explained with extreme graciousness that she was wrong for the part and had always known it. She had only accepted it because she thought some star leading man would 'pull her through'. One not being forthcoming, she felt she must ask us to release her. I supposed we expressed conventional regrets, but her manner at that interview left us wondering why we had ever considered her. She finally bade us an emotional farewell and left after kissing everyone.

Poor Eileen Herlie! She had wasted as much time as we had over a part that should never have been offered to her. Murray, in his liking for her and desire to help her career, had made a bad error of judgement. It was simply a question of suitability. I was never to see her act, but I am sure she was, and has remained, an excellent actress. She has had a successful career, much of it in America. And if I remember her appearance – and performance – that chilly October afternoon with a tinge of malice, I also remember that, when Binkie admired her impressive two-tailed fox stole, she endearingly told us it was second-hand.

It was then agreed that Murray should take the script to Ann Todd over the weekend. She wasn't perfect casting – Binkie gently pointed out various actresses who would have been better, but were no longer free – but she was extremely talented, a film star and I knew her work well; she had been very good in my play, *Service*, in 1932.

The next evening I went to a party at John Gielgud's and he suggested Valerie Hobson for the part. But she was mainly a film actress with little stage experience and Binkie was much against her. I met her a year or so later – too late alas – and knew she was dead right in type, with all the unaffected warmth the part needed.

John's little Westminster house was very like Binkie's though more sparsely furnished. Binkie was an addicted collector of glass, china, personal souvenirs. John had some good modern paintings, especially some Matthew Smiths. My Bluthner grand piano was in the upstairs double drawing-room and John showed me what good condition it was in – probably better than when it had been with me as he played on it more regularly. It had now been lent to him for over twelve years and was to remain for several more. When it eventually came back to me, I felt like a neglectful mother taking her child away from a devoted foster-parent.

As well as people I had met at the Oliviers' party, there were many who had appeared in my plays, whom John had specially asked to meet me. I also had a long talk with Mary Martin whom I had known well in Beverly Hills. She was shortly to open in *South Pacific* at Drury Lane. It was a pleasant intimate party, in spite of the many guests.

The next morning Binkie drove me down to the cottage in his big black Rolls. He took an ugly, quick way that Alec and I had never taken, so reminders didn't start until we reached Dunmow; after that they were continual. Duck End, where Pongo invariably woke up and did the rest of the journey with his elbow nonchalantly on the grey armrest of our Rolls . . . Great Bardfield, then Finchingfield . . . so little changed; our village, still unspoilt. Then we were on the by-road to the cottage. Soon I could see the two poplars we planted outside our white fence in 1934, now grown unbelievably tall. And still topping them, in the orchard, the old, old poplar still with the dead branch at the top.

When Binkie at last stopped the car and said, 'Well, there it is', my first impression was of increased wildness. Dead leaves covered the whole of the large front lawn, all creepers and hedges were overgrown, the brick path was in very bad repair, the barn music-room in need of thatching. The effect was picturesque, but it was also melancholy and particularly melancholy to me, remembering my much loved home as I had known it.

I fear some of my dismay must have shown, for Binkie assured me he hoped to get together enough old bricks to re-do the path entirely, and re-thatching the barn would be his next job. He had already partly re-thatched the cottage itself. And as we walked round I realised he was doing all he could for the property. Though the war had been over for six years, labour and materials were still hard to come by and there were various difficult government regulations. Still, dismay continued. The paddock, once lush grass and the home of wild violets and cowslips, was now a wilderness of elm suckers. In the orchard the hedges were quite twenty feet high and during the weekend a farmer called to say that if something wasn't done about one that overshadowed his land he would burn it down. Binkie gently reassured him – and me; something would be done.

Indoors, dismay continued – but I trust decently under control. Almost all our furniture had been moved into positions it didn't fit and had been augmented by pieces belonging to Binkie, most of them valuable, but wrong in scale and period and far too ornate for a cottage. Every room was overcrowded, curtains were faded or had been replaced by makeshifts, the kitchen floor sagged under wornout lino. As for the bedrooms and bathroom. . .

I turn away from the lamentable details in my Journal and remind myself – as indeed I did then – that Binkie had had to see the place through thirteen very difficult years and that, for him, it was merely a weekend home, not a cherished possession. There, indeed, lay the trouble; it was not *his*. And it must be hard to spend money on someone else's property. It is true that even a low rent would have amounted to far more than his expenditure over the years. Still. . .

In lending my most valued possession I had felt I was doing a kindness, but I am far from sure Binkie ended up feeling that was the case. And, on the whole, *I* ended up feeling I had reason to be grateful to him.

Lunch had been cooked by his local help, from the nearby hamlet of Howe Street. She was shy and unobtrusive; indeed, beyond noticing she was pretty, pleasant and softly spoken I barely took her in, though I did realise she was a good cook. Nothing told me she would one day work for Alec and me. At this moment of writing, she has been helping us for over 30 years.

After lunch Binkie suggested I should go for a walk while he worked in the garden. He was a fervent gardener, particularly interested in roses and flowering shrubs. He had a rose hedge outside the white fence and dozens of shrubs in the orchard, each one encircled by a neat round bed which to me somehow suggested a jam tart. I prefer shrubs to grow out of grass, and not to be in an orchard. I hope I didn't say so.

As I wandered along our still narrow road, various people came from cottages to waylay me having, it seemed, known I was coming for the weekend. They all asked after Alec, all hoped we should soon be returning. I was touched by such friendliness.

I found the countryside quite unspoilt and much wilder. Not only Binkie's hedges were fantastically high, almost all hedges were overgrown so that I could no longer see the cottage from what Alec and I had called the high crossroads. How often had I stood there marvelling that I owned it. Now I could only see the tops of our poplars . . . and think about it. I had so often longed to be back, but now my longing was confused. I longed for the cottage that had been and was saddened by the cottage as it was now. I found it hard to believe that Alec and I would ever be living there again.

It was a most beautiful afternoon. I wandered far over the fields, remembering walks with Pongo. Now, three other dogs stood between me and permanent return. I thought about them and Alec in California and wondered what he would think about the cottage now. He had loved it as much as I had.

Eventually, I had to hurry back to tea as Binkie, most thoughtfully, had invited my dear onetime housekeeper, Bertha, to bring her husband and two children to meet me. He provided a handsome tea, then vanished. His help returned to give us supper, after which he and I talked till the small hours. During that weekend we must have talked for more hours than all our pre-war conversations could have added up to.

We said very little about my play – there was really nothing to say until we heard from Ann Todd. For the most part we talked of the theatre world in general and Binkie told me many things about his life and unhappy childhood – which made me realise more and more what a remarkable person he was. Nothing short of a combination of devotion and genius could have achieved his enormously powerful position in the London theatre world.

I slept in the room that had been Alec's, now the guest-room. John Perry, Binkie's great friend and business associate, had mine. He was absent that weekend. I went into that room, saw my well-remembered view of the orchard and pond, the great yew overshadowing the front window. Then I hurried out. That room, most painfully, was no longer mine.

On Sunday morning the telephone rang – and from that moment Binkie was a different man. All was not well with the play he had taken me to see in Manchester. Changes would have to be made before the London opening. A new director must take over. More telephoning, a meeting at midnight in Lord North Street was arranged. We must leave that night instead of waiting until Monday morning.

Noting Binkie's eager anticipation, I asked him if he actually enjoyed occasions like this. He gave that a moment's consideration, then said he did not like distressing people, which such occasions usually entailed; but if he felt they had to be coped with then he did enjoy coping with them. I suspected this gave him a sense of power and that the love of power was his deepest motivation. He rarely displayed this and, whenever possible, avoided personal publicity. What gave him pleasure was his inner satisfaction.

We drove off after supper through a fog that grew so dense that Binkie actually stopped talking. I was sorry, because I always liked listening to him, and his silence gave me too much chance for melancholy thoughts.

I see in my Journal that I suspected Binkie of wishing to buy the cottage. He had never before wished to, but now he was combining great affection for it with a noticeable desire to minimise its value. I thought, with amusement, that this might be an attempt to keep the price low. Nothing would have persuaded me to sell unless Alec wished to. But I made it clear to Binkie that there was no question of our asking him to move out in the near future. And when he dropped me at Cheltenham Terrace, I thanked him not only for my weekend at the cottage, but also for all the years during which he had taken care of it for us.

Murray was away in Brighton. Frances was in bed, but she had left a thermos of cocoa in my bedroom. As in my youth, I still found cocoa comforting.

XVII

Changing Horses

The next morning Ann Todd rang up full of enthusiasm. I was reminded of her youthful excitement about my play, *Service*, and of how good she had been in it. She was now ninety per cent certain she would accept the part, but wanted to read the play once again. Next day her agent, Aubrey Blackburn (once my own agent, who had so wrongly advised me to give a third option to Basil Dean) rang to say she had changed her mind – and I strongly suspected him of helping her to. He had done the same thing about an actress offered a leading part in my *Dear Octopus* – for which she later blamed *me*. Well, both actresses worked in films and it pays agents best to make sure they go on doing so.

During the week Binkie sent the script to yet another star leading man and a married couple of stars – all of whom, I am thankful to say, realised their unsuitability. Murray and I discussed possibilities, but he was now rehearsing the tour of Ivor Novello's *King's Rhapsody*, which left me free to meet various friends. I remember pleasant meals at the Ivy; Abel, the proprietor, still eager to offer the footstool by which he expressed his deep respect – and at Caprice, now owned by Mario who, in the old days at the Ivy, had always been so kind to Pongo. I went to the first night of *And So To Bed*, with Murray's great friend, Kenneth Carten. The Vivian Ellis music was charming and I foretold that Keith Michell would become a star. Most important of all to me, I got time to write fully to Alec, not only about the cottage, but also to catch up on some earlier letters.

I had not realised what a brilliant letter writer he had become. It must be seldom that such good love letters have been written by a near middle-aged man to his fully middle-aged wife. I was proud to have inspired them. And he could make the most trivial details of his daily life absorbing: conversations with Chris and Charlie, the garden, even the California weather and, above all, the three dogs.

He was now taking them, and Rosa Lee, on regular visits to the drive-in movies where the dogs much enjoyed barking at any dog that appeared on the giant screen. They not only saw the dogs, they also heard them, as the sound was relayed into every car. Occupants of nearby cars, far from objecting to the noise, urged our dogs on.

I was to be slightly perturbed by a later letter, in which I learned that Christopher Isherwood sometimes brought with him young male friends – no doubt to cheer Alec up. They were apt to get playful and swim about with flowers in their hair – Alec sent colour snapshots – and, on one extra playful occasion, they threw all our garden furniture into the pool, which didn't do it any good. It was Alec's habit to go out for an evening meal at a drive-in, when Rosa Lee had her nights off; the dogs stayed outside in the car. One evening he was at the counter when a pleasant, intelligent boy (even if he had thrown our furniture about a bit) joined him and said, 'You see that guy over there? He's a plain clothes cop. I just may get arrested.' Alec, distinctly scared, had visions of getting arrested, too, and my having to dash back to California to bail him out. Fortunately it was a false alarm, but he gave that drive-in a miss for the future, as he now realised it was a well-known meeting place.

Incidentally, Chris had once said he believed that all men had some seeds of homosexuality in them. But then added, 'Except Alec. I somehow can't imagine it ever appealing to him.'

At the end of the week I received a cable from Monica McCall in New York saying she was now starting negotiations with the Theatre Guild which had decided to buy *Letter From Paris*. This was because Betty Field, a suggestion of mine, was interested. She was now married to Elmer Rice whom I had known well when he was married to an earlier wife. He was a member of the Playwrights' Company and, if Betty accepted the part, the Playwrights would want to share the management. I was surprised and pleased and cabled Monica to go ahead. But what had happened to Jack Wilson?

I suddenly felt I wanted to discuss the matter with Binkie. He knew about *Letter From Paris* and had several times asked to read it but Murray, who greatly admired it, had begged me not to let him. With its scope for scenery and dresses it was, Murray thought, just Binkie's type of play and he might easily want to do it before *Esmeralda*. Now, I felt I wanted Binkie's opinion both on the New York setup and on the play itself. I telephoned him – he was away in Leeds – and he arranged to have the script delivered to him by his Rolls which was being driven up to him that day.

I spent the weekend with my old friends, the actors Laurier Lister and Max Adrian, in Laurier's house in Sanderstead which had a wonderful garden running down a hill. The house still retained its William Morris wallpapers which, nearly twenty years later, found their way into my novel, *A Tale of Two Families*. Max, remembering I had once liked Sole Veronique, cooked it for me. It was a peaceful weekend and I attach to it one particularly happy memory of my journey back to London. It was a cold, foggy morning. My train got stuck at Clapham Junction. The station looked extremely dispiriting. I had quite a few things to worry about. Yet I remember feeling supremely happy, just because I was in England. I told myself, 'Well, if that's enough to make you happy, stuck at Clapham Junction in a fog, you are obviously in the country you ought to be in.'

During the afternoon I was telephoned by Binkie's secretary to say he had read the play and liked it, but wanted to read it again before discussing it. I suspected that what he really wanted was the opinion of his play-reader, Dick Clowes. I had known and liked Dick as a young man and valued his opinion; he was always telling me to 'dig deeper'. I should have been depressed by an adverse criticism from him; but two days later Binkie rang and said – I can remember his exact words – 'It's a wonderful, wonderful property.'

He wanted to see me at once. I had arranged to spend the day with Ambrose Heal at his Buckinghamshire country house and could not now cancel this, but I said I could be back by the late afternoon. Binkie said he would come to Cheltenham Terrace for a drink by six-thirty.

I was glad to have his enthusiasm to think about during what, for me, was a sad day. Sir Ambrose, now getting on for eighty, was a shadow of the vital man I had once worked for and known so well. He was a widower now and obviously greatly missed Lady Heal. I was sure that he also missed his shop, from which he had retired some years earlier. He spoke of it in a distant 'watch the world go by' way. His eldest son, Anthony, was now its managing director. As a boy he had accompanied me to Leipzig Fair as my interpreter. He and his delightful wife, Theo, now lived with Sir Ambrose at Baylin's Farm, Beaconsfield. Speaking of her affectionately he said, 'She's a wonder', so I was irritated to find he didn't like to have her dog, a most gentle spaniel, in the house. She told me it only came in when he was shut in his study, 'And if he sees it, we say it got in by accident.' I didn't feel he should need such humouring and I firmly took the dog into his study, where it spent most of the afternoon on my lap. Sir Ambrose regarded it tolerantly, remarking, 'The creature appears to have taken a fancy to you.' He had often referred to my Pongo as 'the creature' and always considered my attitude to dogs ludicrous.

I think my firmness about the spaniel amused him, probably reminding him of the days at Heal's when I had always stood up to him. Certainly we got on better as the afternoon proceeded. But we had little in common now. He never went to a theatre and, though he liked to read, was difficult to please. I had sent him books for years, scoring a particular success – impossible to duplicate – with the reprinted novels of Ada Leverson. Few modern novels gave him pleasure, though he had quite liked my *I Capture The Castle* – 'especially the weather, very well done. But the sentences are too short.'

I felt the real trouble was that he was not himself without his shop, just as the shop – though admirably run and most go-ahead – was not, for me, itself without him. I had already visited it and talked to many old friends on the staff, reflecting, 'Here but for the grace of God – and a trip to the Austrian Tyrol following toy-buying at Leipzig Fair – go I, growing older and older.'

I had to leave Sir Ambrose after an early tea and got back only as Binkie was arriving for his drink. I hope he got it, one of my failings being that, as I rarely drink myself, I forget other people do. And Murray was not there to play host, being away with the tour of Novello's *King's Rhapsody*.

Binkie stayed well on into the small hours. In mid-evening Frances came in and asked if she could supply a meal, but Binkie said no, he had a supper date. However, Murray returned around midnight and firmly ordered bacon and eggs. No more was said about Binkie's supper date.

What did we talk about before Murray arrived? Binkie expressed great enthusiasm for *Letter From Paris*, but he couldn't have gone on expressing it for all those hours. It was one of his talking marathons, in which he dashed backwards and forwards between London and New York, and he also covered the Paris theatre. I enjoyed every minute of it and certain definite facts about *Letter From Paris* did emerge. He wanted to do it soon, preferably before New York did it. And this play needn't depend on stars though he would certainly try to get them; he fancied Glynis Johns for the heroine. What was essential was superb decor, how about Oliver

Messel? And Peter Brook as director? Murray wasn't the right director for this play. He was sure Murray would understand that. (Murray, when I broke the news to him after Binkie left, understood no such thing and was deeply hurt.) Anyway, Murray must stick to *Esmeralda* – which Binkie showed no sign of jettisoning except for remarking that Murray just might prefer to do it with one of two other managements that were interested, rather than wait for a cast that would satisfy Binkie – after all, *Esmeralda* always had been Murray's play.

I had discovered by degrees how much Binkie had disliked sharing it with Murray – but that wasn't his only strike against it. He insisted that he liked it as a whole, but admitted that he disliked anything to do with religion. I pointed out that my heroine did, too, but that both she and he were intensely superstitious. Oh, he had plenty of sympathy with *her*, but a *clergyman*! Only a star actor could make him bearable.

Anyway, I knew I could never force him to let Murray direct *Letter From Paris* and I must say it was a pleasure to see Binkie when he was really enthusiastic about a project.

I spent most of the next day writing to Alec, who was feeling frustrated, longing to help things on in London. Here was good news! And I regret to say that was the last really cheerful letter I wrote to him during my remaining weeks in London for a steady stream of worries was now in store for me.

The first arrived in a letter from Monica McCall saying she was making good progress with the Theatre Guild, but felt she ought to warn me that our attorney had made no headway with obtaining the English rights of *Letter From Paris*; in fact, Paul Reynolds, who was in charge of the Henry James Estate, had flatly refused them. I rang Binkie who told me that Reynolds was 'a monster', impossible to deal with. Still, he would hardly go on refusing once he knew a first-rate London management was waiting to do the play, and would I please get things in New York cleared up quickly?

I wrote to Monica, asking her to do what she could. I wrote to Alec, asking him to get in touch with our New York attorneys. He had dealt with them over the book contract for *I Capture The Castle* and I grimly remembered just how long that job had taken.

Within the next few days another worry had descended on me. I did not intend to let the London Play Company handle my new plays and had not been to see Laurence Fitch, now in charge of the agency, with which he had been ever since it had placed my first play, *Autumm Crocus*. He now wrote to tell me that he had received

Netherby Farm

Doylestown

Pennsylvania

John van Druten
and Author

Netherby Farm,
Doylestown,
Pennsylvania

Cove Way   Beverly Hills

Rescuing bees   Beverly Hills

Pearl and the
De Soto

The House at Wilton,

Connecticut

Back View

Hugh (Binkie) Beaumont

Peter Barkworth

The Barretts, Winter

The Barn, converted

Foal at foot   Sugar and Spice

The Barretts, Summer

Home at last

With Gratitude

a letter from a Mrs Winchester of New York, who had, some years earlier written a play called *Scandal Sheet* which was an adaptation of Henry James's *The Reverberator*. She had sent this to the Theatre Guild which had lost it. Now she had seen in the New York Times that the Guild was about to produce my play – which must be a plagiarism. By a coincidence she had also sent her *Scandal Sheet* to the London Play Company which, disliking it, had refused to handle it and had returned it. Now, she asked, could she be given some help in establishing her rights? It turned out that she had no idea I had any connection with the London Play Company.

I hurried to see Laurence Fitch and found him much changed from the handsome boy I had known twenty years earlier – not that he wasn't still handsome. He had acquired great authority and I at once realised he was highly efficient. He undertook to set about convincing Mrs Winchester that she had not been plagiarised – and he eventually did so. (But not, as I was to find out later, before she had done irretrievable damage.)

Even at that first interview I knew I should want Laurence Fitch to be my agent in England, but on his own, not as part of Dorothea Fassett's London Play Company. Trouble with Dorothea had been another of my worries during those worried weeks.

Against my better judgement I had allowed her to handle the film rights of *I Capture The Castle*. In spite of much interest she had never managed to sell them. We did not really blame her; it was a bad time for selling books with an English background. But we had come to realise that she had made some bad mistakes. It was now three years since the book had been published and I thought all interest was dead. But while in London I had been rung up by a Hollywood agent named Jules Goldstone, who was convinced he could make a sale to R.K.O.

I was so impressed by Mr Goldstone that I asked him to get in touch with Alec whom I then telephoned myself. (This was one of our very few trans-Atlantic conversations as I found it so difficult to make myself heard.) Alec, too, was impressed with Jules Goldstone, told him to go ahead and notified Dorothea that she must no longer consider herself the agent. She replied that she had contractual rights that could not be terminated. Alec had a carbon of a letter from me telling her that they could be, at any moment. All the same, he felt he must make sure of our legal position and it cost us $250 to get the information that her claim was 'impertinent bluff'.

I am fairly good at forgiving injuries to myself, but incapable of

forgiving them to people I care for. I never forgave my stepfather
for his treatment of my mother, I doubt if I ever quite forgave John
van Druten for his meanness to Christopher Isherwood, and I never
forgave Dorothea Fassett for distressing Alec when he was on his
own and particularly anxious not to worry me. Beyond one meeting,
later, to end our association, I never spoke to Dorothea again. She
had contractual rights to handle anything connected with my first six
plays, but eventually Laurence Fitch took over the London Play
Company and so acquired these; and for later plays, film rights,
novels he became my personal representative, and no writer could
wish for a better one, or a better friend. So I can find it in my heart
to be grateful to Mrs Winchester who caused me to go to his office
that October afternoon in 1951.

My Journal covering my next weeks in London (written during
my return journey to America) lists a welter of theatres and parties:
a large party at Binkie's on the night of the General Election and an
even larger one, in a house where David Garrick had lived, now the
headquarters of the famous amateur theatrical publishers, Samuel
French, whose plays I had first known in my childhood. This party
had been for the head of the firm, Cyril Hogg, who had now been
with French's for 50 years. And there were weekends out of
London, at Murray's attractive but chilly Brighton flat, and with
Alec's beautiful step-sister Laurien, her husband and two children,
in Buckinghamshire. They had a cat and a free-roving hamster and I
lived in fear that the cat would get the hamster. I was thankful we
were still helping this charming and brilliantly intelligent family with
regular parcels of rationed food – they had kept one so that I could
see it opened.

Not that *I* ever suffered from food rationing – possibly because I
had so many of my meals at restaurants. I was astounded to find that
the cost of admirable food at first rate restaurants was sometimes
less than at an American drive-in.

I spent an afternoon with Basil Dean (early producer of my plays)
whom I had met at the Garrick Club when I was dining with my old
friend Madge Compton and her husband, Gerald Lawrence. I had
been particularly nice to Basil and he had asked me to tea. He was
now living in an old house in St John's Wood, a most attractive
house but somehow sad, perhaps because Basil now was curiously
muted. Divorced from his third wife, Victoria Hopper, he lived
alone with a gentle Boxer bitch, which made me long for my own
three dogs. He gave me tea on the *Autumn Crocus* china Heal's had

designed in honour of my play. I never bought any myself – so ungracious of me; but I should have felt self-conscious about using it. He was longing to be back in the theatre and spoke of being short of money, but as he had a full-time housekeeper and a full-time secretary – he was dictating his memoirs – I felt he must be fairly well off.

I did not, for some time, realise I should have to return to America to clear up various problems. I thought it could all be done by letter. So for hours and hours, day after day, I pounded on my typewriter, writing to Alec, to Monica McCall, to our New York attorneys . . . and Alec did the same. And neither of us got anywhere at all; indeed, we reached a state when our attorneys simply ignored my cables. Then, well on into November, Binkie begged me to go back and make sure of the English rights for *Letter From Paris*. He wanted to announce it and begin definite plans for an early spring production. And I found I wanted to go and not only for business reasons. I longed to get back to Alec.

But I had Murray on my conscience. He was now planning to do *Esmeralda* with Paul Clift who had already booked Christmas dates at Brighton and Blackpool. I had told Murray I would see the production through, but I had no confidence in the cast he was, still very vaguely, suggesting and I doubt if he had, himself. Now, as always, he was understanding and he had another play he could do with Paul Clift to fill the Christmas dates. I assured him we would do *Esmeralda* together in the New Year.

I had a rush to get off, many people still to see, many jobs to do, first among which was buying presents for Murray. He would not tell me what he needed but his housekeeper, Frances, helped. She suggested bed linen and told me he had what she described as 'fallen in luv' with my portable radio because it could be taken into the bathroom. I got him an English one, towels as well as linen, a case of champagne . . . but they nowhere near compensated for the cost of my board and lodging, let alone for all his trouble and wasted time.

During my last London days, Alec cheered me on in his letters by pointing out that my life might be worrying, but it was also full and interesting, and all the problems could be solved. He reverted to my distress over our cottage and assured me that he could one day restore it to what it had been. I was no longer worrying about it. My main worry now was whether I should ever get on a boat – not until two days before it sailed did Binkie manage to get me on the

Mauretania. I looked forward to writing my Journal during the voyage, summing up my two months in England. I note with pleasure that, at the end of a lengthy entry, I wrote 'Oh, I do long to get back to California. In spite of the beauty of England what matters most to me is Alec, and the dogs, and our way of life together. And yet I love England just as much as I knew I should'.

XVIII

London Notes, 1951

In that eighty-page Journal entry written on the Mauretania I record having moved around 'in a daze of love for England'. Apparently that daze of love didn't prevent me from making a few criticisms, for I find:

> Everywhere I stayed everyone did everything conceivable to make me comfortable and yet my total impression was that most English people live highly uncomfortable lives. And this isn't a question of lack of money, rationing, post-war conditions; at least, not in most cases. It is that their *standards* of comfort are low. They don't *mind* about hard beds and pillows, inadequate lighting and heating, draughts; in icy weather they not only fling windows open, but leave front doors open – for no reason whatever. And yet they don't strike me as impervious to cold; out-of-doors they wrap up more than I do.
>
> Actually there were only a few days of anything approaching 'icy' weather – when everyone talked about it a great deal and it didn't worry me at all. But I was often cold indoors. Murray would light an enormous coal fire in his sitting-room, then open his windows and door. I think the English like to *see* warmth, but are careful to let it out of the house.
>
> Yet they are perpetually cheering themselves on with cups of tea, coffee, drinks – mid-morning coffee arrived at Murray's before the breakfast tea was taken away. Perhaps this habit of what I called 'little pampers' derives from when food was *really* short. They think it's short now but, except for some rationed food, it isn't really. It is merely rather expensive, by pre-war English standards. The shops are now packed with unrationed tinned goods such as we are still sending from America in all our parcels – and at much cheaper prices here than we pay over there. Most of our friends can afford these, but either won't or haven't noticed the stuff is there. I was amazed at the muddled ways some

of our friends live. Madge Compton (really well off) walks a mile
a day to the shops because 'food must be fresh'. And she has a
refrigerator.

But that seems to have exhausted my criticisms. For the most
part, my 'daze of love' persisted. And I'm happy to note that I
fiercely defended Londoners from Phyl's criticisms – she sadly
misses California. 'She is wrong. People on buses do *not* smell. They
are clean, civil, and quite nicely dressed. And their voices, even the
Cockney voices, have a pleasant ring. And their eyes are bright.
And their faces have noses, not just nose-intentioned blobs, and
good bones and are, to me, twice as interesting as many quite
good-looking American faces'.

On the last page of that Journal entry, written just before
reaching New York, I record a list of 'high spots' which I had meant
to write about and hoped to, later. It was many months before I did,
but I will add them here, to round off this record of my first return to
England after so many years.

DOGS

I was astounded by the number of them and their general
joyfulness. Each dog seemed to say with its eyes, 'I am among
friends. I have complete confidence in life.' Food shortages or
not, they all looked well-fed. And I never saw a lost dog. In
America one is always seeing them and the un-lost ones so often
have a lost look. In America one curses the owners who let them
run wild on the roads and come to agonising deaths. In England
the non-leashed dogs have the air of being able to cross busy
roads alone and unscathed. And often they *are* leashed. It is a fine
sight to see two dogs leashed to the owner of a full perambulator
all happily proceeding through a busy shopping district. One has
to be pretty nippy not to get entangled, but who minds? All dogs
here seem happy, friendly, brimful of intelligence. I don't believe
any country in the world cares for dogs as the English do.

(Hindsight Note.) The daze of love was certainly operating when I
made that note. What about all the dogs the English leave stranded
on motorways?

MIST IN PARKS

I have never before realised how often there is mist in England,
especially in the parks. Sometimes, in the distance, it looks quite
purple. I got little time to walk in parks, usually saw them from
taxis, always softly green, as if painted by Pissarro or Renoir.

When I did find time to walk in my most-beloved Regent's Park I was a little disappointed. Too many people, the atmosphere seemed disrupted. And yet I liked the people for seeming so happy – and so English. I can look at any English face with pleasure, listen to any English voice.

ST. PAUL'S CATHEDRAL

After lunching with Cyril Hogg somewhere in the Strand – Simpson's, I think: it was a very meaty restaurant – I went along to St. Paul's. I don't believe I've been inside since I was confirmed there. I was most disappointed in it now. There seemed to be no religious atmosphere at all. I wondered if this was partly due to the temporary and very plain altar. An altar should draw one's thoughts. The altar at St. Paul's seemed to shut a door in one's face. All I really liked were the listed names of some of the Saxon bishops. I chose Eggwulf, Beowulf and Swithwulf for the dogs and told Alec our Buzz was to have Swithwulf.

Outside the back of St. Paul's was the tower of a bombed church and in this tower was an altar and a few chairs. An old woman sat on the altar steps, keeping guard – she said that if the place was left alone people stole the chairs, the candles and anything else that could be carried away. I felt more religious atmosphere, more sense of the not-impossible God in that ruined tower than in the whole of St. Paul's.

The City was very sad but very beautiful. I believe London's ruins add immensely to its beauty, perhaps because they stir the imagination. Beauty cannot exist without the responsive mind.

RIDING IN TAXIS AND BUSES

Riding in taxis was a particular pleasure, provided I was alone in them. It gave me a chance to sit back, look out, and think about London. Again and again I could have wept with love for it.

Taxi drivers so often drive one past Buckingham Palace that I think they must like it. And I like it, too. I never got tired of thinking about life in the Palace. How do they feel about it, the Royal Family, enacting a sort of fairy-tale to please the public? Do they feel imprisoned, never quite natural, never quite able to be themselves?

Riding on London buses is more hazardous now than when (so long ago) it was my usual means of transport. The speed is now terrific, the pulling-up so jerky. Once I rashly stepped off before the bus quite stopped – at which I used to be adept in my youth.

The result was disastrous. Kind people, picking me up, advised me never to do that again. Still, I liked buses, especially at night. Once when I had been to a theatre alone I came out to find a fairly thick fog and no taxis. I managed to get on a bus, went on top and particularly enjoyed careering through the fog. It took me back to my years on the stage, when I so often played in the outer suburbs; though our speed through the fog on that 1951 night seemed faster than on a clear night in my youth.

ARMISTICE DAY

Written while I was packing to leave England: I was up in my little sitting-room which looked out onto the Duke of York's Barracks. The large building there is, I suppose, a church, for men swept their hats off as they went in and many women carried flowers. I had the wireless on so that I could know when the two minutes silence began. While it lasted, several small children ran around outside the church. They weren't old enough to remember any war. They played, autumn leaves scurried around them, the flag on its flagstaff idly flapped. I thought of all I had experienced in the First World War and of all I had missed in the Second, and of all the years that had passed. And now, youth has vanished – yet there is always something within me which insists that youth is eternal. *My* youth? The youth of all the men who died in two wars? And is this sense of ever-living youth an intimation of life eternal?

If I had a moment of illumination it wasn't lasting. Now all that comes back to me is the idly-flapping flag, the playing children, the restless autumn leaves . . . and my room littered with half-packed luggage.

LAST GLIMPSE OF BINKIE

It was an endearing one. He had asked me to Lord North Street on my last evening in England for a farewell drink. The little drawing-room was softly lit, the long curtains closed. A large fire glowed behind a fan-shaped brass fireguard, clipped to the bars. We talked of my forthcoming return to England for *Letter From Paris* and he promised, when announcing it, also to mention *Esmeralda and The Cloth*. Then he sent for his Italian housekeeper, Elvira, with whom I had made friends over our shared love for animals. I had brought her a book of animal photographs. She came up with her dog and her tame pigeon, which promptly settled on Binkie's head. There he stood, in the glowing little 17th Century room, imploring the pigeon to remember its manners – it mercifully did.

After that, I drove with him to see the new opening scene of *Figure of Fun*, so my real last glimpse of him was when he shut me into his Rolls, in which I was then driven home. But I prefer to think of him with the pigeon on his head. Dear Binkie! He can be so kind and I am so fond of him. Yet I have known since the nineteen thirties that he is a liar and it's never quite safe to count on him, nor indeed to count on the London theatre world. Can I ever get back enough of my old toughness to cope?

XIX

Theatrical Allsorts

I landed in New York late at night on November 19th to find Ronda Keane waiting to meet me, with her husband, Carl Muschenheim, the doctor so largely responsible for her complete cure. She had been alerted by Alec when he found that John and Christopher were in Philadelphia for the provincial opening of *I Am A Camera*. I had sent cables of good wishes to them and to Walter Starke and that morning received a puzzling Marconigram saying, 'Cast changes here all hands needed deep regrets and love'. And signed 'We three'. Only now did I realise the regrets were for not meeting me.

It distressed me that Ronda should be waiting on the dock on a bitterly cold November night. And I had a maddening Irish customs official, who decided I was 'a lady movie writer from Hollywood' and treated me with both admiration and suspicion, examining the contents of piece after piece of luggage. When he started on my largest trunk I said, 'If you would tell me what you're looking for perhaps I could help you.'

He took this at its face value and said eagerly, 'Labels from English shops.'

I said, 'Don't you realise that if there had been any such labels I should have taken my little pair of scissors and unpicked them?'

He gave me a bitterly disillusioned look and no more trouble.

Monica McCall (she too was in Philadelphia) had booked me a suite at the Hotel New Weston, which was a lot more comfortable than John's hotel. (I was told that prices at my favourite hotels, the Pierre and the Sherry Netherlands, were now astronomical.) I could hardly have looked impressive when I reached the New Weston for the desk clerk, before he found out I had a booking, asked if I'd like a nice little room at five dollars a night.

Now I could telephone Alec and at last make myself heard. I had telephoned from the Mauretania but with very poor results. Good though it was to talk to him, what I really wanted was to get on a train and go back to him, but there were things I had to do in New York. And when I lunched with Monica McCall, back from Philadelphia, next day, she said John particularly wanted me to go to Philadelphia and give him some advice.

I had hoped to have good news from Monica about the New York production of *Letter From Paris*, which I had understood to be almost settled. But she said the Theatre Guild had now become maddeningly vague. However, things were going better with the Henry James Estate, over the English rights. Monica herself had got in touch with Paul Reynolds and found him pleasant. He appeared to have nothing against *me*, but couldn't stand my attorneys – or rather, that member of the firm who was handling the job, whom I will call Mr S. Thanks to Monica it was now agreed I *could* have the English rights and only the details of the play contract had to be worked out.

After lunch we went to see Mr S. and I found him specious and arrogant. However, he assured me he had now completed the contract. I didn't really believe him and Alec had asked me to see the head of the firm, John Wharton, before I left New York, so I made an appointment.

That evening Chris came to dinner with me. I gathered that *I Am A Camera*, now in its second week in Philadelphia, wasn't doing well. He was angrier than I had ever seen him, having just discovered that John planned to give him no share of the royalties on the printed version of the play (which John had dedicated 'to DODIE who started the whole thing'). Chris had already put up with something far worse: the fact that John having cut down his normal royalties (in which Chris would share), had greatly increased his royalties as a director (in which Chris would *not* share); John had then also arranged that he would get a ten per cent share of the play's gross profits – entirely for himself. I suppose Chris had no way of fighting this, but it seemed to me almost ludicrous that, after accepting such an outrage, he was now prepared to end his friendship with John simply over the printed play – which, unless its fate was unlike that of most printed plays, would earn very little. And the letter to John which he had drafted would certainly have ended the friendship. After a long discussion, I reminded him of his habit of offering his troubles up to God (or whatever he meant by God) and I said·that if he would offer *this* up – and forget it – he would whoop right into the saint class. This made him laugh so much that he agreed to tone the letter down. (And John eventually gave in and shared the printed play's royalties.)

I saw John Wharton the next afternoon and a very depressing interview it was. He could only instruct Mr S. – pretty brusquely – to hurry up and give way on all the points Mr S. still wanted to hold out on, as we were now in a bad position (thanks to whom?). Mr Wharton then informed me that the New York chances for *Letter From Paris* were no longer rosy. He didn't believe the Playwrights' Company – with which he was closely associated – would ever do it, because they would never all make up their minds at the same moment. As for the Theatre Guild, it now felt itself threatened by Mrs Winchester. She *had* sent her play, *Scandal Sheet*, to the Guild and it *had* somehow got lost. And the Guild now felt that, if it produced my play, Mrs Winchester would certainly sue for plagiarism. No other management would be so vulnerable and I had better take the play from the Guild and start again. I was not then to know that Laurence Fitch would eventually rescue me from the menace of Mrs Winchester. And I doubt if that poor lady was ever a menace.

I had to hurry away to catch a train for Philadelphia in time for the evening performance of *I Am A Camera*, but when I got there John asked me to wait until the next night as he was trying out a new scene. I filled in the evening by going to the try-out of Jack Wilson's show, *Nina*, and talked to him in an interval. He was looking grey with worry, as well he might with that show on his hands. After telling me some of his troubles he asked about my visit to London and I told him *Letter From Paris* was going to be done there. He seemed vague about its New York troubles and said he would still do it on his own if he could find the necessary backing. But there was none of the light-hearted confidence he had shown at our last happy lunch. No doubt life, with Gloria Swanson in *Nina*, had become grim.

I spent the next day with John and Walter Starke, both of whom were nervous and irritable, and saw *I Am A Camera* that night. It was the Thanksgiving holiday and the audience was depressingly small and not appreciative. But the show was far better than I had expected. John had improved the script and directed it most admirably, and Julie Harris was giving a superb performance as Sally Bowles. So I could say, quite sincerely, that I thought there was a good chance of success in New York.

When we got back to the hotel John asked me to come to his suite to see if I could help to improve the new scene. Before we started talking I asked if I could have some tea at which John said, 'Do you mind if you don't? You see, I don't want you to stay long. I want to work.' He then kept me talking for two hours and was aggrieved when, after two o'clock in the morning, I departed, dead beat. I'd have gone on much longer if I'd had the tea. I now not only needed it, I was annoyed because he hadn't let me have it, and even more annoyed when a substantial supper was carried through into Starke's room, as he could never sleep without eating.

Work with John continued over breakfast, after which I firmly left to catch my train. That trip to Philadelphia had delayed my return to Alec by two days and cost me quite a lot of money; my most pleasant memory of it was meeting Rex Harrison and Lilli Palmer after I got off the train in New York. I didn't know either of them, but when I found myself standing on the next step of the escalator I felt impelled to introduce myself. They had been to Philadelphia to see *Nina* about which they were even more gloomy than I was. Their niceness to me went far beyond mere civility, leaving me with an impression of a type of good manners which has almost vanished from the world today. Rex spoke with admiration of *The Sofa and The Window* which he had read five years earlier, Lilli praised *I Capture The Castle*. They drove me back to my hotel and, on the way, asked if they could read *Esmeralda and The Cloth*. When Rex returned it, he said it needed the late Leslie Howard and Gertie Lawrence – within a year, alas, also to become 'the late'. Perfect casting indeed.

Chris dined with me again that evening and took me to the ballet. He said he knew I didn't like ballet much, but it was the only thing he could get free seats for. I'd probably have enjoyed any entertainment with Chris – except circuses, boxing matches and bullfights; and anyway, I did enjoy *La Valse*. It was hardly surprising that he couldn't afford expensive theatre seats as it was costing him a lot to live in New York and he couldn't, as yet, have had any royalties from *I Am A Camera*, nor did he have high hopes of it. He would have been staggered to know that it would succeed as a play, as a film, as a musical (*Cabaret*), and as the film of that musical, thus providing him with an income, perhaps for life. It was indeed a fortunate moment when, as a result of our deliberate ploy in California to help Chris, Alec had put his head out of John's swimming pool and said, 'John, why don't you turn *Sally Bowles* into a play?'

The next day I was at last free to take a train for Los Angeles and this time I enjoyed the journey, mainly because I was on my way back to Alec, but also because I suddenly saw how I could make a play out of *I Capture The Castle*. I had been asked to do this again and again and I had thought of a way of managing with only one set, but I had never been able to see how I could cope with the many shifts of time that were necessary; the curtain would continually have had to come down. And the construction would have to be so odd, with some scenes long and some lasting only a few minutes.

It now occurred to me that the cinema had accustomed audiences to dissolves and that the radio had accustomed listeners to disembodied voices that bridge from scene to scene. Why shouldn't I use dissolves to cover time-lapses and the voice of my young heroine, speaking her journal, to supply any information necessary? The voice would avoid dead-stops between scenes and also keep the journal form of the novel alive. And I might achieve a slightly new form of play and one in which the necessities of the subject originated the form rather than an effort to be original – it being my belief that efforts to be original, just for the sake of being original, were apt to end in stuntiness. Anyway, it was an interesting project to play with during the long train journey.

Dressing on the last morning, I knew I was in for a bit of happiness that nothing was going to do me out of – unless the train crashed. It didn't. And seeing Alec at the Los Angeles station was one of the high moments of my life.

He had arranged that, when we got home, I should stay in the garden and one dog at a time should come down to me. Buzz came first, barking, and even when he reached me, it was a few seconds before he took me in. Then he nearly knocked me into the pool with joy. I was careful not to have my back to it when I received Folly and then Dandy.

I had a wonderful couple of days and then went down with one of my fiercest colds again, no doubt caught on the train. I told myself that Fate seldom allows one to be happy for long – and then told Fate I was *still* happy. Day after day Alec read to me. He is the only person I ever enjoy being read to by. He achieves the happy medium between 'putting in the expression' and leaving it out. He began reading the whole five hundred pages of Henry James's *The Golden Bowl*. I had, of course, read it before, but Binkie had asked me to consider making it into a play. I did map out a synopsis, but I doubted if I could ever have been persuaded to lay hands on such a blazing masterpiece. It is my favourite of all James's books.

I was barely better before we were overwhelmed with nonsense letters from Mr S. in New York about the contract he was trying to work out with the Henry James Estate. It proved to be a colossal document largely copied from the film contract for that other James adaptation, *The Heiress*. I knew Paul Reynolds would never sign it. I shortly received from him a carbon of the letter he had written to Mr S. saying he would have nothing to do with all the 'legal verbiage, hocus pocus and donkey work' and would prefer to get together with Monica McCall and work out something on half a sheet of notepaper. Mr S. responded with an even longer contract which was again spurned. Then, after weeks more of obstructions and weeks more of letter-writing from Alec, Paul Reynolds himself drew up a short letter-contract which was perfectly satisfactory.

What *was* Mr S. up to? It was suggested to me that his delays were in the interest of 'fee-pushing' but I doubt that as he was employed by such a highly reputable legal firm. And in the end John Wharton refused to accept any payment from me – though Alec insisted that we must pay something if the play proved a success. At the moment all we owed to Mr S. was a long and infuriating delay in production, for Binkie now said he could not present the play until well into the spring.

(I eventually met Paul Reynolds, who was said to be one of the three best literary agents in America. I liked him greatly and he was particularly kind to me. But he undoubtedly was formidable – had not Binkie said he was a monster? Mr S. from the outset had got the monster's hackles up.)

In spite of a wild rush to arrange Christmas presents for England, I got started on the play of *I Capture the Castle* in mid-December and finished it in early February. I could hardly believe my own speed. While I was working, Jules Goldstone, the agent who had hoped to sell the film rights, came to life again. His early hopes had fallen through, but he now had other hopes. I hadn't been able to find out anything about him and had begun to have doubts about his status as an agent. Now Jules invited us to lunch at a Hollywood Country Club where famous movie producers, directors and stars greeted him as a valued friend. He was beckoned to Louis B. Mayer's table and stood with his arm round Mr Mayer's shoulder and, a few minutes later, was asked by our waiter to speak on the telephone to another movie mogul. While he was gone, Alec and I played with the idea that he had hired the whole Country Club to impress us and had engaged movie extras to represent waiters and guests. (If so, he'd got a good double for Mr Mayer.) Later, our Jules got Howard Hughes of R.K.O. to telephone me about his interest in the film rights of *Castle*. Charlie Brackett told me this was so unheard of that I wondered if someone was impersonating Mr Hughes. But there was nothing phoney about the offer Jules secured from R.K.O.

This was for $15,000 for an option to buy *Castle* at a price which would depend on the fate of the play-adaptation I was writing. For me, this was ideal, as I wouldn't have cared to sell outright now I had the play in hand, and the $15,000 would be a godsend, as we were now in one of our impoverished periods.

Where *did* our money go? I suppose mainly in rent and living expenses. I spent a fair amount on clothes but not an enormous sum. As for Alec, he had ordered only one suit to be made during our thirteen years in America – and ended by repudiating that because it didn't fit. Of course my recent trip to England had been expensive. Anyway, the really large sum earned by the novel of *I Capture The Castle* was now almost used up.

Alec rarely worried me about money, but I had recently decided I wanted to move across the continent again. (All told, we saw far more of America than most Americans see.) Monica McCall knew of a suitable house in Wilton, Connecticut and I wanted Alec to be three thousand miles nearer to me next time I went to England. The new house would cost less than half the rent of our present house in Beverly Hills, but the move would cost $2,000; so Alec felt he must warn me this wouldn't leave us with very much in hand. But I was still determined to move. And we signed the lease for the Connecticut house before Jules Goldstone landed the R.K.O. option. As so often before, I had to involve myself in expense before the means to meet that expense turned up.

We were now in high spirits. We had money in hand, the house ahead of us looked charming in photographs, and our dear coloured maid, Esther, agreed to join us as her husband had gone to the Korean war. Binkie had now told me he wouldn't need me before May so I should have plenty of time to settle into the new house. We started from Beverly Hills in early March and spent the first night at John's ranch where I had to dash through a book on playwriting he had just written, which took most of the evening.

After that, I remember little about our sixth and last three thousand mile drive across the American continent, except that the De Soto (Alec again shipped the Rolls by freight car) recently serviced, developed the peculiar vice of refusing to start when it was hot and no garage we consulted could cure the trouble. This meant that, if we stopped to give the dogs a run, Alec had to keep the engine running by leaving a brick on the accelerator pedal. I now recall, too, that we drove into full spring in the Middle West and then out of it into full winter in New England, arriving at Wilton in a snowstorm so heavy that it was hard to find our way. Seen through the snow the countryside looked completely unspoilt – as, indeed, it was – and there was no house within sight of ours, which we recognised from its photographs.

Esther, who had been there some days ahead of us, came running out into the snow bringing three biscuits and crying: 'A piece for Folly, a piece for Dandy and a piece for Buzz.' She had used these words countless times to them in Pennsylvania and in California and they recognised them, and her, instantly. When we let them out of the car they nearly knocked her into the snow with delight. It was some minutes before she managed to say, in her musical, gentle voice, 'I think perhaps I should go in or I may take cold,' – she had rushed out without so much as a cardigan over her overall.

Showing us over the house Esther told us we should like it better than Ronda Keane's, which we did. It was an Eighteenth Century weather-boarded house, very well restored, painted pale yellow, with good old furniture and numerous original American primitive paintings. It was built on a hill so there were two storeys at the front and three at the back where the dining-room, kitchen and Esther's bedroom and bathroom looked onto a wild garden with a large pond. Nothing separated the garden from very tangled woods, so we had to do a lot of fencing. Then the dogs could run free.

When the snow melted we found neat lawns at the front, but no indications that there would ever be any flowers. We heard that the long, bitter New England winters and the hot, humid summers discourage gardeners. But, apart from its flowerless state, we found this last of our eleven American rented houses delightful.

And it had particularly nice owners, a married couple who lived not far away in a larger house. They called on us and offered to give a party to introduce us to our neighbours, but when I said, as politely as I could, that I had writing to do and needed peace, the wife said, 'Right. Then we'll protect you. Come to us if you need anything, but otherwise we shan't trouble you – or let anyone else.' When we left, over eighteen months later, she refused to let us pay for any of our breakages, remarking, 'My husband would never allow me to accept one cent from people who have looked after our house the way you have.' I like to think that, in spite of our three large dogs, we did take good care of the houses we rented. Even Eleanor d'Arrast, the formidable owner of our Beverly Hills hill-top house, grudgingly called me 'a good housekeeper' – an odd description of anyone as undomesticated as I have always managed to remain.

We enjoyed settling in and exploring the surrounding country, mainly by car as the weather was bitterly cold. And I worked hard, and fast, turning out suggestions for a film treatment of *I Capture The Castle*, which I had promised to R.K.O., and making some changes in the play, which I then sent to Binkie. He was a long time in expressing his opinion, which was a mixture of enthusiasm and nervousness about my 'new technique'. He had again postponed my trip to England, from May till June. So I went back to work on a play I had begun seven years earlier, set in an Austrian monastery, and dashed off a second act, only stopping work when the weather, in early May, turned spring-like and I could go for walks.

I found the country almost too wild. So many once-cultivated fields had been allowed to become wildernesses. I gathered that New Yorkers had bought out many of the farmers (who must have had hard lives with such stone-strewn fields), converted the farmhouses and left the land to Nature. The result was great beauty, but you could not walk in the fields and woods. As well as being pathless thickets, they were full of poison ivy. However, there were compensations, particularly all the lilac hedges, the fact that I rarely met anyone on the roads and that there were few cars.

We were only fifty miles from New York and had planned to go there often but, in the end, we only went there once, to lunch with Paul Reynolds with whom we had kept up a correspondence. He had offered to extend the period during which I had to get my contract for *Letter From Paris* signed, as Binkie was being so slow about this and had had many arguments about terms with Laurence Fitch, but I think the real reason for delay was the difficulty in finding the right leading lady, who needed to be very young and enchantingly pretty. Glynis Johns was no longer available. Eventually Binkie chose Brenda Bruce, whom I had seen in Manchester in *Figure of Fun*. I hadn't thought her either very young or very pretty, but I had thought her charming, both as an actress and as a person, and as he was enthusiastic I agreed. He then signed the contract, paying me generous advances for both the English and

American rights, and giving me a handsome travel allowance – for which I hadn't asked.

He also went to great trouble trying to find me somewhere reasonable to stay. So did Laurence Fitch. But I suddenly decided I wanted to stay at the Ritz. No one could have called this 'reasonable', but I was dead set on it, feeling that of all London hotels it was the one most likely to be useful to me as a writer. (I did indeed make use of it in novels written over ten years later.) The only snag was that the Ritz said that, at the height of the season, they could not offer me a suite, and they went on saying it. Then Guthrie McClintic wrote to ask me if I could follow up *Lovers and Friends* with another play for his wife, Katharine Cornell, (alas, I was never able to) and I remembered they always stayed at the Ritz. They kindly used their powers of persuasion and the Ritz graciously agreed to let me have a very *small* suite. This cost seven pounds a day which seemed a huge sum to me, but I knew I could get it off our income tax as a legitimate business expense. I am told that a comparable suite would now cost more than ten times as much.

I left for England on June 18th, 1952, having remained in Wilton long enough to see the first exquisite fireflies and experience some days so hot and humid that the dogs showed disinclination to go for walks, though they were – just – willing to amble round the large pond frog-hunting, giving excited yelps whenever a huge frog plopped into the water. I wondered how Alec would get on if most of the summer was so hot and humid.

He came to New York to see me off on the Queen Elizabeth. My Journal entry, begun on the day after I embarked, states:

> The maimed feeling of being separated from Alec is back. I can still see his determinedly smiling face and then his white handkerchief waving until the direction taken by the boat cut off the view of it. I just don't know how to face the months that lie ahead.

That long Journal entry, covering six months since I returned from England, is a mass of details of daily life, work done, business matters, reports on friends. . . Only if I were a female Shakespeare, whose very laundry bill would be a treasure, could it be of much value except as an *aide memoire* to me. But there are two passages I want to quote, partly for their memories of those first months at Wilton and also because they seem to be written by a gentler, more emotional woman than I remember myself being. Surely I had been more formidable during my business career at Heal's and, later, in the London theatre of the nineteen thirties? And surely I was now less well-equipped for a return to that theatre, though I doubt if that occurred to me at the time. Early in the voyage I wrote:

> I reckon it must now be twenty-past-ten at night in Wilton. Soon Alec will take the dogs out for their last run, with the fireflies dashing about like stars on the loose. Then all three dogs will go to Esther's room for two 'Friskies' each – little biscuits they love. Then Folly will settle with Esther for the night – they both decided on this months ago. Alec will get himself a drink then he and Buzz and Dandy will go up to bed. Oh, first Alec will feed his tropical fish. He has a long tank of them on his desk, the first thing he has bought for himself for years. I was so delighted and encouraged him madly. Goodnight, my dear Alec, Buzz, Folly and Dandy. Goodnight attractive tropical fish, and kind Esther, and fireflies and frogs and goldfish in the pond and even the marauding turtles who have got through our fencing and eaten some of the goldfish. Goodnight and sleep well, all in and around the yellow house at Wilton.

Last Entry on the Voyage:
> It must now be early evening at Wilton. Perhaps Alec is still at dinner, with the twilight deepening outside. We have so enjoyed these last months. We've both read a lot and taken to playing the gramophone again. We now have a long-playing record of Schubert's Octet which Alec particularly likes – so do I. I shall always associate it with this spring. Oh, I do hope I can bring back good news this time. But whatever happens I think we already know we possess the things that matter most.

XX

Letter from Paris Ahead

During my last evening on the Queen Elizabeth, Peter Glenville, who was to direct *Letter From Paris*, telephoned to the boat to ask me to dine with him on my first night in England and then go with him to a party at Oliver Messel's. I later discovered from Peter that the telephone call had been organised by Binkie, who wanted Peter to get in touch with me before I 'fell into Murray's clutches' – though what clutching Murray could have done I can't imagine. Anyway, I had already asked him, along with Phyllis and Laurence, to dine with me on the night of my arrival, so I could only accept for the late-night Messel party.

Phyllis met me at Southampton next morning and Laurence met us in London – with a large hired car as he had felt that a taxi wasn't grand enough, and also that I might have a lot of luggage. So I had, but it was instantly whisked away at Waterloo by the waiting Ritz porters, which greatly impressed me. I was, however, less impressed when I arrived at the Ritz. My suite, on the seventh floor (I had asked to be high up) was nowhere near ready. Maids were still cleaning it, none of my welcoming flowers had yet been brought up, and there were workmen outside my windows, where the narrow stone balcony was littered with ladders and building materials. The receptionist assured me all these would soon go (they didn't) and I should soon be offered a suite overlooking the Green Park (I wasn't). But I find my dismay of that morning difficult to recapture for I was to become so fond of the suite that, even after nearly thirty years, I cannot think of it without loving nostalgia.

There was a small, dark entrance hall from which opened the sitting room, bedroom and bathroom. The sitting room – very small – had cream and gold walls and cream and gold furniture, the easy chair and sofa were upholstered in bronze brocade, the carpet and heavy satin curtains were reseda green – it was so long since I had heard the word reseda that I am surprised it came when called.

There was a crystal chandelier and electric candle-brackets. I imagined that the fireplace, black-leaded with bright brass fire-irons, was merely a survival from the days before central heating, but my floor waiter assured me I could have a fire in it any time I wanted – which seemed hardly likely as I had arrived at the beginning of a heat wave.

The colour scheme of the very large bedroom was pink and grey with satin-wood furniture and a vast brass bedstead. The clothes cupboard was as large as an outsize American closet. And once I got the sagging hair mattress changed for a better one, I was very comfortable. Both the sitting room and the bedroom had French windows opening on to the narrow balcony, with a view across Piccadilly and down Berkeley Street to the great trees in Berkeley Square. I became so fond of that view that when, eventually, I could have had a suite overlooking the Green Park I preferred to stay where I was. I suspected that, in moments of loneliness, Piccadilly would be better company than a park.

The bathroom was twice the size of the sitting room and almost as large as the bedroom. The whole of one wall was of clouded glass, facing into a deep well. One wall was painted glossy white, two walls and the floor were of irregular little tiles, pale tangerine and somehow suggesting Alma Tadema Academy paintings. Silvery, pre-chromium pipes were much in evidence. Water came out by the side of a huge porcelain bath in a complication of taps. There was a low white chair, a white dressing-table and a very old-fashioned lavatory with a mahogany seat and no lid. I got so fond of that bathroom that I often sat there.

Laurence and Phyl departed obviously horrified by my suite. Phyllis, always belligerent, wanted me to leave at once or at least 'send for the manager'. I had an inkling that things would look better once the place was tidy, as indeed they did, especially when my flowers came up. Soon after that, Binkie telephoned and asked me to lunch with him and Peter Glenville, so I asked them to lunch with *me*. Living at the Ritz was going to make it easier for me to entertain. If I went to restaurants with men I had either to let them pay, or have an embarrassing struggle over the bill.

Binkie arrived bringing a noble present of two dozen eggs, reminding me that rationing and food shortages still existed in England – seven years after the end of the war! He said that even the Ritz could run out of eggs. Indeed it could; one night it ran out of bread.

I got on with Peter Glenville from that very first meeting. My Journal (written much later) describes him as 'wonderful company, charming, amusing, light-hearted. He is short and slight, with very dark hair and eyes. . . Dresses carelessly and is apt to have food stains on his clothes. It is hard to believe he is in his late thirties; he seems like a boy.'

Binkie left after lunch and Peter asked if he could come up to my suite for a short discussion – which lasted most of the afternoon. He began, diffidently, by saying that he knew I never changed anything in my plays, but he felt he ought to tell me there was just one scene-ending he didn't feel sure about. I said there were nine scene-endings and I didn't feel sure about any of them, as I considered myself weak at getting curtains down effectively. So what did he suggest? In the end he decided he liked the scene-ending just as it was and he stopped being diffident. Either Binkie had been building up a picture of me as a formidable author or my reputation – according to John van Druten – of being 'a martinet in the theatre – and Alec was worse,' was still intact.

My dinner party at Caprice for Murray and Phyllis and Laurence was saddened because Murray was so aggrieved at not directing *Letter From Paris*. I could only urge him to find a cast for *Esmeralda and The Cloth* – I felt quite capable of attending two sets of rehearsals at the same time. But there was no getting away from the fact that Murray, so largely responsible for bringing me back to England the year before, was now out in the cold. And it made matters more difficult when I had to return to the Ritz so that Peter Glenville could call for me and take me to Oliver Messel's party.

Oliver, who was to do the scenery for *Letter From Paris*, had two old terrace houses joined together, in South Kensington, with a large garden. I was enchanted by Oliver, short, dark and very good looking, in his middle forties. He had a gentle, uncertain manner. I was to find that manner was belied by a rock-like hardness and utter pig-headedness. Soon after that first meeting I happened to say to Binkie that 'Oliver was very kind'. Binkie said, 'Oliver is a fiend'. And so Oliver was – but also kind.

The party was in full swing when Peter and I arrived. I had barely got into the drawing-room before a male voice said, 'Dodie!' and I found myself embraced for so long that I had time to think, 'This must be someone you know really well, so you must respond warmly.' I was glad I did because it turned out to be Dick Halliday, to whom I had never ceased to feel grateful for his kindness to Alec and to me in Hollywood during a difficult period of our life. I had a long talk with him and his wife, Mary Martin, eventually interrupted very rudely by Oliver's Danish manager, Vagn (pronounced Vaughan) Reiss Hansen, one of the rudest men I ever met. He was also one of the funniest and intensely likeable.

I talked to a number of people and then a famous troupe of Spanish dancers broke out. This meant the end of all conversation. There are a few noises I like less than Spanish stampings and shouts of Olé! So, around one a.m., I told Peter I would like to go but didn't need seeing home. He and Oliver put me into a taxi, Oliver assuring me that I should soon see the models for my scenery. It had been a pretty busy first day for me, but I enjoyed it all – except for those Spanish dancers. Peter told me later that they went on and on right through the night.

The next day George Bishop, of the Daily Telegraph, lunched with me. He had been the first journalist to ring me up after Basil Dean bought my first play, *Autumn Crocus*, and had always written about me with great kindness. Now he wrote that it looked as if I might soon have three plays on at once. I wasn't banking on this – which was just as well.

In the afternoon, I went to Binkie's office at the Globe Theatre to meet Brenda Bruce. She looked to me completely wrong for my heroine and not young enough, but her personality was charming and, as before, I greatly liked her. I also met Nicholas Hannen whom I had admired as an actor for thirty years. I liked him as much as I liked Brenda and couldn't have been happier to have him – except that, with a highly sympathetic personality, he had been cast for an unsympathetic part.

Later, Peter escorted me to a large press conference at Binkie's house. Many of the journalists were old friends of mine, most of the young ones hadn't heard of me. Everyone asked why I had stayed in America so long and I got the impression that no one believed this was because I didn't want to quarantine the dogs. Still, it was faithfully reported.

Those first days come back to me vividly. After that, memory offers mainly a blur of the three weeks before rehearsals started, a blur of hot, sunny weather, auditions, restaurant meals and theatres. But a few days restore themselves by means of my Journal, written later. One such was my first Sunday:

Except for a brief lunch with Laurence at my old favourite Café

Royal (much changed), I had spent my time writing to Alec, then gone by myself to the film of *The Importance of Being Earnest* at the grandiose cinema that has replaced the old Alhambra. I came out into one of those English summer evenings when the sky seems to grow more luminous after dusk. Down in the streets it was already twilight, but up above it seemed as if there were lights behind the blue bowl of the sky. Even Leicester Square, my least-loved London square, looked to me romantic.

I was wearing an old, expensive, printed-silk dress, white butterflies on emerald, with some of the butterflies cut out and appliquéd onto muslin fluttering round my neck. I was hatless and had flat-heeled white shoes. I found it wonderfully pleasant to be wandering through a London summer evening. I felt rather like a ghost, a happy ghost, back in my youth and, ghostlike, able to move without effort.

I went into the little streets between Leicester Square and the Haymarket, vaguely looking for a theatrical agency I had often been to during my earliest years on the stage. It had been in an old, tumble-down building – even then I had been fascinated by its age – so I wasn't surprised that a new office block had replaced it. But I was soon in streets that were not new, little Eighteenth Century streets of old houses, food shops, pubs. These were not business streets, people *lived* here, lights were on above the shops, there was laughter and occasional singing. The pubs were busy. I had forgotten that so many people manage to live right in the heart of London. I had noticed this when, at nineteen, I had combed these same streets hunting for theatrical agencies.

It was strange to come out of this little world, still belonging to the past, into the blaze of colour and noise that was Piccadilly Circus. It was crammed with people, far more girls than men. Some of the girls wore sunbathing outfits and there was a general milling around as if at some seaside resort. I heard one girl say, 'If only my feet weren't killing me.' The many neon signs intensified the blue of the sky and the whole scene was a brilliant, raucous jumble, both appealing and repulsive. Perhaps the appeal was mainly due to my mood for I saw crudity, many bad make-ups, ugly clothes; but I certainly felt affection for the crowd – and much sympathy for that girl's poor feet.

I was thinking about this, standing in front of the Criterion Theatre, when a young man said: 'Well, fancy seeing you again! Isn't that nice!' I shook hands, while trying to place him. He was the right age for a gallery boy, but the gallery boys of my day would now be mature men. I asked questions. He said, 'Oh, what does it matter where we met? Just come and have a drink.' And then I saw from his expression that this was just a pick-up, ('pick-up' to my mother's generation, 'get-off' in my youth, now 'pick-up' again). I just managed not to laugh and said, quite gently, 'Oh, don't be silly,' and left him gaping.

Perhaps he was short-sighted or perhaps the fluttering butterflies on my dress attracted him, or perhaps as a child he had adored his grandmother; or could I have been surrounded by an aura of remembered youth?

After Piccadilly Circus, Piccadilly itself seemed both quiet and dull. I turned into St James's Street and here there was a different kind of quietness, highly romantic. I walked in the little streets on the right, near St James's Palace. There was a smell of hay from the Park and the sound of running water which I traced to a hose with which boxes of geraniums were being watered. There were some well-kept houses with lights only in their basement kitchens where servants were entertaining their friends. And I saw a great house, deserted and barricaded, with the name 'Stornoway House' on it – a house asking for a book to be written about it. I caught a glimpse of the Green Park through the windows of a blitzed house. Then there were some small shuttered shops, dim passages leading to courtyards, a sleeping cat on a window sill . . . I decided I would like to live in this part of London.

Actually, before deciding to stay at the Ritz, I had asked Laurence to find me rooms in St James's. He had replied that it wasn't now a respectable neighbourhood.

I doubt if he's right but, anyway, I wouldn't give a hoot. Why should I mind a few tarts? Some of the best friends in my youth were only just hanging on to their amateur status.

It was almost dark – and one cannot for ever go on looking and loving and longing. So after a last look at the Palace and the Grace-and-Favour houses (surely their inmates are respectable enough?), I went back to the Ritz and had a blissful supper of bacon and eggs in my sitting-room, expecting Alec to telephone; but his call was so long delayed that I was fast asleep in bed when he got through at two-fifteen a.m. And he then had great difficulty in hearing me.

From then onwards, Alec telephoned every Sunday night and, later, on Wednesday nights, too. I enjoyed falling asleep looking forward to his call; it always took him hours to get through. Sometimes I woke to find it morning and then would get a cable saying he had been unable to get through at all. And our talks were pretty unsatisfactory and not only because of my quiet voice. There were loud cracklings – which would suddenly clear and it would almost feel we were in the next room to each other. It was eventually discovered that there was something wrong with our Wilton telephone which the telephone authorities there could not put right. They gave us a large reduction in our enormous bill, but that didn't atone for those frustrating conversations. The Ritz operator, always sympathetic, insisted the trouble was due to Atomic Bomb experiments.

At the end of my first week Peter Glenville went to Paris to hunt for a young leading man, who needed to have a French accent. He returned with a youth who, I knew at first sight, was hopeless. But he was given a long audition, with Brenda Bruce, at the Apollo Theatre after the curtain fell on the current show. Binkie then took us all to supper at the Ivy, during which the poor young Frenchman, who could barely understand a word of English, let alone speak it, couldn't have had any idea he wasn't getting the job. It was thought kinder just to feed him. Peter broke the news to him after Binkie escorted me back to the Ritz.

In the taxi Binkie told me that Peter Brook had now read *I Capture The Castle* and thought it would make a fortune, but he wouldn't be free to direct it for at least nine months. So we must consider other directors – this was the first time Binkie had plainly intimated that he wanted to do that play. I loyally suggested Murray but had no luck. Binkie then said he'd like to come up to my suite for 'just a few minutes' talk'.

It soon reminded me of the evening when he had decided to do *Letter From Paris*. Then he had arrived at Murray's house at six-thirty and stayed until two a.m. Now he stayed until after four a.m. There wasn't much to say about *Castle* until we got a director and a star, but there was plenty to say about *Letter From Paris*. It was then that Binkie warned me that Oliver was 'a fiend' and that, sooner or later, there would be hell about the scenery and that, owing to a one-time romantic attachment (Binkie's phrase was 'more than friends') Peter would never go against Oliver's wishes. In all the many years I had known him, this was the first time Binkie had ever referred to the existence of such attachments. Peter himself had no such inhibition and neither did the Messel household.

Around three a.m., having refused earlier offers of drinks because he was 'just going', Binkie agreed that I should try to get some tea, which my night-waiter willingly brought. Soon after that the conversation took a new lease of life. It is a night I look back on with great pleasure, in my tiny ornate sitting-room high above Piccadilly, with Binkie at his nicest and my hopes high for both plays. We squeezed cup after cup out of the teapot until we were drinking faintly tinted hot water.

The next night was the London first night of *The Innocents*, William Archibald's adaptation of Henry James's *The Turn of the Screw*. It had been brilliantly directed by Peter Glenville. I invited Murray to come with me, but he had to be out of London and he asked me to take his great friend, Kenneth Carten, a most admirable theatrical agent whom I greatly liked. The play was a great success, partly due to the acting of two quite young children who, Peter assured me, didn't know what the play was about. A number of adults didn't either including, according to Peter Glenville, its leading lady Flora Robson. He told me she believed the mystery was to do with the dead servants having been smuggling gold into the garden.

Kenneth took me to supper at Caprice where Valerie Hobson, one of his clients, joined us. She seemed to me ideal for my Esmeralda and she said she would 'like to have a bash' at the part. I sent a message back to Murray asking him to try to build a production round her. She finally endeared herself to me when back in my Ritz sitting room, she walked up to Alec's photograph and said, 'What a handsome man.' Both he and I disliked displayed photographs, but I found having him with the three dogs on my chimney-piece was a comfort.

Next day another Frenchman arrived, said to have recently made a great success. Binkie pointed out that it had been in a highly unpleasant part, but Peter was sure that, in a sympathetic part, his charm would be devastating, especially to women. When I queried this I was told – very gently – that my views on masculine sex-appeal were just a bit dated. This man had everything, experience, good looks (I thought he had a perpetual sneer). The fact that his English was unintelligible was of no importance, could be corrected by a good teacher in a week. Peter was *sure*, so I gave in and Binkie, none too willingly, agreed to pay a large salary.

My Journal now restores one small memory I cherish:

I went to a sale in the great house, shared by Jacqmar and the great dressmaker, Victor Stiebel, once the home of Mrs George Keppel. One feels the presence of Edwardian ladies in the showrooms. Many of the Jacqmar materials were set out on tables in the garden, a charming and somehow un-English idea. I bought some and then wandered around Shepherd Market and Curzon Street, loving it all. I love even the voices of passing strangers. And one stranger did not pass. She stopped and said, in the too-refined voice which used to irritate me in Londoners and now enchants me. 'Excuse me, but you have a caterpillar on your neck.' She then removed the caterpillar and dropped it on the pavement. I thanked her, adding, 'Poor caterpillar, it needs greenery.' She said 'How awful of me not to have thought of that.' We then retrieved the caterpillar and she found – with triumph – geraniums outside a nearby restaurant. The caterpillar was placed in a magnificent home; not, perhaps, such a good deed to geraniums.

That afternoon I was at last allowed to see Oliver's models for my scenery. I was told that, though barely finished, they now had to be rushed to the scene builders and only the smallest change could be made, but Peter was sure I should love them.

They were certainly pretty, but bore little resemblance to what I had expected. The first scene, the studio of a hardworking American artist in Paris of the eighteen-eighties, was extremely elegant and looked as if it might be in the South of France. My script called for a view of Paris rooftops seen from a balcony, which must occupy at least a quarter of the stage and on which important action took place. Oliver had put the balcony at the back, most of it off-stage. There was *no* view of Paris rooftops. Oliver said he had mislaid it but, of course, it would be found. (It never was.) I pointed out that the hero and heroine had to meet on the off-stage balcony and she had to be seen nearly falling over its balustrade. Peter who, as Binkie had warned me, never disagreed with Oliver, said we must use the bit of balcony that could be seen. We next looked at the model of a private sitting-room at the Hotel de l'Universe et de Cheltenham – James's inspired name for it. Owing to clever false perspective it looked, most unsuitably, as large as a ballroom. The library at the Proberts, a dignified American family long resident in Paris, in my script 'an old book-lined room' had become a drawing-room; not a book in sight. Oliver said he might put some in a little alcove four-fifths off-stage.

I praised more than I criticised – and certainly the models were attractive. To me they were also quite unreal, but I knew Binkie had wanted the play to be kept gay and light. I asked if he had seen them. Yes, indeed, and passed them all. So I felt I had better do the same and not be too niggardly about it. Oliver said, 'Darling Dodie, she's *so* sweet', and then we all had a happy tea during which Oliver's manager, Vagn Reiss Hansen, said didn't we all think Brenda Bruce would be a disaster as Francie, and couldn't we persuade Binkie to import an exquisite American girl Peter knew of? Surely, if we all talked to him seriously. . .?

We got the chance to do so a few days later, when I discovered that he had *not* passed the models of the sets and had *not* seen them since they had been painted. He assured me it was not too late to have them altered and we would go and see them at once. So there was another meeting at Oliver's. Binkie insisted that the Paris studio must stop looking like the South of France, that something must be done about the balcony (it never was) and that there should be masses of books in the Probert's library. But what worried him far more was that the sets were far too complicated for a revolving-stage and would delay scene changes. Simplification was necessary. Oliver wriggled madly, then gave in. But the changes he promised were never made.

The discussion had been so heated that it was hardly the moment to bring up the subject of Brenda Bruce but we somehow did. Peter mentioned the exquisite American actress – no, he hadn't actually seen her. Oliver said Mrs Gene Kelly happened to be coming to dinner with him – no, he wasn't sure she had ever acted but. . . At this, Binkie lost his temper and said either Brenda played or the whole production would be called off. I said I thought his tone was unwarranted and I must have said it fairly strongly as, later, Peter told me that was the only time he ever saw any of my celebrated fierceness. I didn't feel fierce; I was now on Binkie's side because Peter and Oliver had no sensible suggestions to make. They instantly gave in and afterwards Binkie apologised to me and said all his anger was directed towards them because they were *utterly* irresponsible. So they were. The truth was that there was no better bet for our leading lady available and I could only hope that her charm and very great talent would see us through.

We still had three important American parts to cast less than a week before rehearsals began. Auditions went on interminably, particularly as Peter believed that the more unsuitable an actor was, the longer he should be allowed to read, so that he could go home with a little hope. An elderly American was flown from Rome to play the heroine's father, Mr Dosson. No good at all. Eventually Binkie agreed that an expensive American should be flown from New York for the brash journalist who persuades the silly heroine to disclose some secrets of her French fiancé's family. No, Peter didn't actually know his work but. . .

Binkie suggested an English character actor, Elliot Makeham, for Mr Dosson and said, 'He can be very disagreeable, but if you ask him to tea at the Ritz it might disarm him.' He didn't need disarming. I liked him as a man and as an actor, even though his American was, by his own admission, crossed with Cockney. Another good English actor was engaged for the American painter, Waterlow. And so, with Scott McKay on his way from New York for the brash journalist, George Flack, it seemed we should start rehearsals with a complete cast.

During the last days before rehearsals I never had a free minute. I had a sad dinner with Murray, but as he refused to do anything about Valerie Hobson for *Esmeralda and The Cloth*, this got him off my conscience a little. Ambrose Heal lunched with me at the Ritz, but said the prices made him nervous. However, he was far more cheerful than he had been a year earlier and was pleased with himself for reaching the age of eighty. But he said he was too old to come to my first night, as he had to all my others. I had supper with Dick Halliday and Mary Martin in their elegant Americanized flat that whisked me back to Beverly Hills. There was a first night at the Globe Theatre where I sat next to my old friend, the critic of the *Daily Telegraph*, Bill Darlington; the party afterwards was in Binkie's back garden. Harold Conway, one of my earliest journalist friends, invited me to lunch and also invited Basil Dean; we enjoyed this and Basil and I spent the rest of the afternoon together. He seemed even more gentle than the previous year, but I was far from sure God had meant him to be gentle. Remembering him in his ungentle heyday, I doubted if there was any greater man in the London theatre now.

Sunday I kept for myself to do my laundry; the Ritz bathroom wall was admirable to dry handkerchiefs on. And of course I wrote to Alec. He managed to get his telephone call through to me extra early, so as not to disturb my night's sleep. He was finding the Wilton summer uncomfortably hot and humid and was plagued by mosquitos. I knew only too well how he must be longing to be at my first rehearsal next day.

XXI

Brighton Opening

Letter from Paris takes place in the eighteen-eighties and is about two American families. The Proberts, a father, two daughters and a son, have been resident in Paris so long that the daughters, married to Frenchmen, speak their native language with a French accent, as does their young brother who was born in France. The Dossons, a father and two daughters, are on holiday from Buffalo. In Henry James's *The Reverberator* they are from Boston but I was told that, in England, Boston stands for refinement and the Dossons are certainly not refined.

Young Gaston Probert and the younger Dosson daughter, Francie, meet at the studio of an American painter, Charles Waterlow, and fall in love. And the Proberts, charmed by her beauty and sweet nature, agree to their engagement. Then Francie innocently discloses some Probert family scandals to George Flack, the Paris correspondent of a cheap New York daily, *The Reverberator*, the weekly edition of which sells in Paris, and the wedding is imperilled.

Five characters should have been played by Americans, but I was told that assumed American accents would be perfectly acceptable in England. Still, I was glad that we should have one authentic American in what was, possibly, the best male part in the play. Scott McKay proved to be tall and broad, confident and amusing. I liked him on sight.

It was particularly pleasant to be rehearsing on the stage of the Globe Theatre, where so many of the staff remembered me. Jock, the property manager, hugged me and said, 'Eh, my darling, the years have flown'. I reminded him of the first rehearsal of *Call It A Day* when he told me he'd heard I was a very savage author and begged me not to hit him. And he also reminded me of how I'd made the management give him a new overcoat when his was stolen during the pre-London tour.

Letter From Paris seemed full of life and I was fascinated by Peter's direction. As well as giving every movement he gave full instructions about interpretation. This meant that progress was slow, also I wondered if the cast could take in so much so early, but everything he said was admirable and showed how fully he had studied the play.

I soon became, however, worried about Scott McKay, our genuine American. He was charming, humorous, sophisticated, with what was known as 'the international accent', and seemed all set to give a performance on New York café-society lines. Anything less like the tough, crude journalist who was more or less the villain of the piece it was impossible to imagine. But at the end of the rehearsal Peter assured me he would 'get him right', but we must at once get rid of the actor playing the artist, Waterlow. 'He's too crude – all wrong for Oliver's scenery.' This meant that a first-rate actor was changed for a more elegant one whom Peter had greatly disliked at auditions, went on disliking during the pre-London tour and eventually replaced.

Peter was callous about getting rid of actors. I had learnt from Basil Dean that one must not play the wrong actor, no matter whose heart breaks. But a little kindness can help to soften the blow. I came to believe that Peter, normally kind-hearted, had to work himself into detesting anyone he wanted to get rid of.

Before rehearsals began we had made a bargain. I undertook not to interrupt him while he was actually directing; he undertook not to ask me to 'ad lib' extra lines at a moment's notice. I kept my bargain better than he did his. Almost from the first he asked for extra lines, to fit in with his complicated movements. I found I could manage quite easily so I never protested, even if I disapproved of unnecessary lines. Later he said the movements were dictated by the exigencies of Oliver's scenery. Anyway, they ended by working smoothly, even if they did look more like choreography than normal stage movements.

After a couple of days he started asking me occasional questions – and told me, later, that this was against his usual practice. He said most authors responded to questions with a very long speech. He would also ask me for exact intonations. I could always hear these in my head, but was none too sure the right noise would come out of my mouth, but it always did. We seemed to be an ideal combination, and I never saw a happier company. What was more, under the stimulus of Peter's direction, they seemed much better than I had expected – except for the young Frenchman, who got steadily worse. His lips seemed incapable of forming English words. And he played his love scenes as if he had the greatest aversion to them. That blunt man, Vagn Reiss Hansen, after watching a rehearsal, remarked to me, 'My dear, he is not only a queer; he is a very queer queer.' By the end of the week Peter had given up saying he would 'get him right'.

Early in the next week, before the afternoon rehearsal, Peter broke the sad news to Binkie that the Frenchman would have to go. Binkie was adamant: the Frenchman had a run of the play contract. Peter came back apparently resigned and got on with the rehearsal.

I went in search of Binkie. He said Peter was responsible for engaging the Frenchman and must get him right by sheer hard work. I said that, even if that were possible, it would mean neglecting the rest of the company. And it would make Peter *ill*. What about his ulcer? Peter never mentioned this ulcer but Binkie frequently did. I had heard him cancel a meal ordered by Peter, saying, 'Dear boy, you must be out of your mind. Waiter, bring the gentleman a plain grilled sole.' I added that Peter was very, very sorry for his mistake – which I doubt if he would ever have said himself. Binkie capitulated. The Frenchman was out.

But getting rid of him was another matter. I was told *I* must complain to him, about both his English and his acting. If the author objected to him, it might strengthen Binkie's position over the contract. So I did my best and, much though I disliked the Frenchman, I was sorry for him. He said he would try harder. Later, I heard he blamed me for all his troubles.

That evening Peter took me to Oliver's for drinks before a theatre party to see Libby Holman, for whom Peter was giving a supper party that night. I remember nothing about her except that I accidentally referred to her as Lizzie Borden (the notorious American axe-wielder). At Oliver's I met Graham Greene who kept asking everyone how he could kill some cats that were keeping him awake at night. I said he must simply offer his annoyance up to God and the Catholic Mr Greene complained loudly that I was talking to him like a Catholic. Peter, soon to direct Mr Greene's first play, looked at me nervously; I gathered I wasn't showing enough reverence, but Mr Greene seemed quite unresentful. (Only later it occurred to me that in several of his books something ghastly happens to an animal.) We sat together at the theatre and got on very well, talking about Henry James and Beatrix Potter. Of James he said, 'The old boy knew all about evil,' – which wasn't the first thought that would have come to me about Henry James. I liked Graham Greene and wished I could know him better. But it troubled me that when we all crammed into a taxi on the way to Peter's supper party, he started a salacious conversation which seemed to me too schoolboyish for such a distinguished writer.

Peter's red-papered drawing-room looked delightful with its tall windows open onto Brompton Square. In a time of food shortages, I was always amazed at the food served at private parties, much better than in restaurants. Peter's party was a great success, but in the small hours a mysterious row blew up in a little room from which I was firmly excluded by Peter and sent home in a taxi. He said the row would go on all night. It had something to do with Vagn Reiss Hansen having come into a rehearsal and reported to friends on the Frenchman in a way which somehow made Binkie's position over the contract more difficult. Vagn was forbidden ever to come to a rehearsal again, so the next time he did, he crawled in on all fours. I feel sure they all enjoyed the row very much.

Binkie's casting director, Daphne Rye, must have worked fast for by the next morning she had rustled up some young actors who might replace the Frenchman – not that he yet knew he was to be replaced. Our rehearsal had been called off so that we could audition them. It seemed ludicrous that we were now considering virtually unknown actors for such an important part, but no well-known ones were available. There was one youngish actor who was merely walking on and playing the lute in John Gielgud's production of *Much Ado About Nothing*. This was Paul Hansard, aged thirty, short, dark, plump, hopelessly wrong in appearance. But he read well and Peter felt sure he had Passion – you could hear the capital P. I didn't think the part needed Passion, I thought it needed a shy charm. Anyway, Daphne begged us to wait until next day when she would have more actors to offer, especially a young man who could come down on the night train, from Sheffield Repertory Company.

So next morning the rehearsal was again cancelled and again we auditioned young men, none of them as good as Paul Hansard, though there was a fair young man named Richard Gale whom Binkie favoured largely because he was under contract to him at twelve pounds a week which would bring the salary list down. Then a man in a hacking jacket strolled onto the stage. He was of middle height, thin, sandy-haired. I took him to be about forty. He read

Gaston superbly – only he made him a witty, middle-aged rake, say, the Gay Lord Quex. We consulted our lists. This, the last applicant, could only be the boy from the Sheffield Repertory Company – except that he was no boy. I said, 'Daphne told me he was only twenty-three.' 'Never see thirty-seven again,' said Binkie. 'I wonder if he could play Kenneth More's part in *The Deep Blue Sea* in America?' But one part he obviously could not play was Gaston Probert.

During this discussion the poor man stood patiently waiting. 'Good God, he's still here,' said Binkie. Peter called, 'Thanks. We'll, er, let you know.' This seemed to me a bit meagre after what must have been a suspenseful wait, so I persuaded Peter to go and say a few kind words. 'And tell him he can have one of our two-year, twelve-pounds-a-week contracts,' said Binkie.

It was Friday and Binkie wanted to go away for the weekend, so he told us to choose, on our own, between Paul Hansard and Richard Gale. Peter said he would hear them both, with the full company, next day. And Daphne Rye demanded that her protégé from Sheffield should be given another chance. He'd had no opportunity to read the script in advance, she'd only had time to tell him he must put on enough weight for a leading man. So he had put on well over twenty years – he *was* twenty-three. Now he must again travel overnight from Sheffield, on Saturday, and read with the company on Sunday.

There was a rehearsal that Friday afternoon at which the unfortunate Frenchman made his last appearance. He was called to the telephone by his agent and did not come back. The company, told what they had already guessed, heaved a collective sigh of relief. They had found him impossible to act with, very conceited and with a tricky habit of upstaging people. They gave all the support they could to Paul Hansard and Richard Gale next day, and to the now quite genuine boy from Sheffield Rep on Sunday, who now appeared to be a bit young for the part – say seventeen. I felt sure he could hit the right age eventually, but he did not have Passion; also he couldn't get away from Sheffield for a week, which would leave him only a week to rehearse. I had a talk to him and found he didn't mind too much not getting the part as he was being given a two-year contract. His name was Peter Barkworth.

So I let Peter Glenville have his way and choose Paul Hansard. He was a very nice person and it was a joy to see anyone as happy as he was. And he was a hard and willing worker. Rehearsals should now have been plain sailing – except that Peter had now decided that Maxine Audley and Marjorie Stewart should change parts. This was fine for Maxine, who would get a much better part, but just the reverse for Marjorie, who was bitterly distressed. She was a particularly pleasant woman and, though I felt the change would be for the good of the play, I hated to hurt her. Contractually she could have refused, but she nobly agreed and I arranged with Peter that he should talk to her after rehearsal and try to console her. He failed to turn up and I had to do what I could on my own. She told Binkie I had been wonderful to her, but I doubt if she ever forgave Peter. Once again he had shown the callous side of his nature. Binkie simply described it as 'cruel'.

In spite of such worries I was extremely happy from the moment when I was wakened at the Ritz in the morning. While I had my bath in the outsize porcelain bath the maid did my sitting room. Then my favourite floor waiter brought my breakfast, just toast and butter and marmalade, though he often brought me double portions. (A French waiter once said to me, 'Ritz in Paris – everything. Ritz in London – no food at all.' It wasn't quite as bad as that.) Over breakfast I read the *Daily Telegraph*, always listening for the slight swish on the carpet which indicated that a letter from Alec had been slipped under the door. And almost always Laurence Fitch telephoned me to make sure I was cheerful. Then I would be off along the red-carpeted corridor to the lift. While waiting for it, I would chat to the floor waiters whose kitchen, where they cooked breakfasts and sometimes suppers, was nearby. All the lift men were friendly (on my London first night I got a telegram signed, 'The Ritz Lift'). So were the hall porters and the commissionaire. For me, it was the staff that made the Ritz.

Unless it rained (and how seldom it did that hot, hot summer) I walked to rehearsal, along Piccadilly and Shaftesbury Avenue, telling myself, 'I am here, in London, on my way to rehearsal after fourteen years of longing to be.' Then there was a particularly likeable company to talk to and the pleasure of seeing the play coming more and more to life – which it did, in spite of all the miscasting. I don't think one member of the company or the stage management had the slightest doubt of our ultimate success. I felt the James story was stronger than any I had ever invented myself, and Peter thought the situations, on their own, would pull the acting through.

He and I usually lunched together which was apt to be an

occupational hazard, as he would wander out of the stage door so intent on conversation that he had no idea where he was going. Often by the time I interrupted him to remind him we must eat, we had reached some dim back street when he would dive into the nearest eating-place – frequently a café dominated by steaming urns of strong tea. We were often faced by food which I feared was more than capable of waking his dormant ulcer. He seemed oblivious of what he was eating and, if sitting at a table not yet cleared, would polish off food left by previous occupants.

After rehearsal he often came back to the Ritz for tea and sometimes stayed for dinner; otherwise I skipped dinner as, when served in my suite, it was vastly complicated. Two waiters and two clanging trollies, with an oven to keep food hot (and didn't) seemed too much for my modest order. I preferred to wait until after ten o'clock, when my floor-waiter was allowed to cook bacon and egg and sausage, which he brought in with some encouraging remark such as, 'If any of this is left, madam, I shall write to your husband'. All the Ritz staff I met had a gift for being familiar in a highly respectful way. (By now, my favourite lift-man was bringing his Sunday paintings to me to advise him on.)

Peter had been determined to have music composed to cover our scene changes. As I expected our revolving stage to revolve in half-a-minute – as it had done in my *Call It A Day* – this seemed to me unnecessary and Binkie was heavily against it but, as so often, Peter got his way. He commissioned a friend, Ronald Emanuel, and his music when played on the piano was charming. I took it that the theatre orchestra would play it. But I learned there were now few theatre orchestras left. Our music must be recorded and played on a panatrope. A ten-piece orchestra was engaged – which made Ronnie's music sound delightful. This was recorded on the panatrope – which made it sound like hell. That afternoon's work cost Binkie three hundred pounds. He wasn't pleased.

During our fourth week of rehearsals I went to Oliver's to see his large oil-painting of Brenda Bruce which was important to the play. She should have been painted watering flowers on the balcony and there was dialogue about this. Oliver had shown me a sketch which was exactly right. Now, he had simply done a straight portrait – he had conveniently lost the sketch. It was too late to make any change, so I had to cut the dialogue. But Brenda, in the beautiful dress Oliver had designed for her, looked charming and by now I was hoping she would make a great success.

With our Brighton first night less than a week away, life was getting more and more exciting. In spite of our cast changes we were well advanced. So far, Binkie had not attended one rehearsal – I gathered he usually left matters to the director until the last minute. Now he announced he would come on the Friday evening, with John Perry. There was to be an uninterrupted run through.

It was quite unlike any earlier rehearsal; the atmosphere was strictly formal. I had made it a rule never to join Peter uninvited, but for weeks he had invariably sat with me. Tonight he settled down at some distance, with the great friend who shared his house with him, Bill Smith, a particularly nice American, always helpful. Binkie and John Perry also settled some distance from me. The panatrope clanged through the theatre, playing the overture comprising theme music for the two families in the play: cheerful music for the plebeian Dossons, elegant music for the aristocratic Proberts, and there was a charming waltz, all delightful tunes but. . . What *does* a panatrope do to music? To me it suggested an orchestra of quacking ducks; clever ducks who really quacked quite musically, but definitely ducks.

Perhaps it was the contrast of that very loud panatrope – which was heard again after every scene – that made the acting seem so muted, but it was also due to the gloom of Binkie and John Perry. They might have been watching a tragedy. After the panatrope brought the curtain down on Act I, I went over and asked Binkie what he thought of the music. He said, '*Pretty* music', and managed to convey that he didn't want to say anything else. Anyway, the panatrope was now quacking the curtain-up on Act II.

The performance got worse and worse. Brenda told me later that the whole company felt waves of disapproval washing over them. Almost before the panatrope had got the curtain down on the last act, Binkie and John rose and walked towards the exit, beckoning Peter and me to follow; we had been invited to have supper with them afterwards. I said, 'Aren't you going to say a word to the company?' The curtain had risen to show the whole cast waiting. Peter called loudly, 'We'll do the notes tomorrow,' and then we followed Binkie. There was nothing I could do to help, especially as I didn't yet know what was the matter with Binkie and John.

Neither of them spoke until we were in Binkie's house; then they let fly. The pace was awful, most of the acting was awful. Only Brenda won praise. Worst of all was Scott McKay. How dare Peter insist in importing an expensive American actor and then allow him to give a sophisticated performance when he should be brash and crude? Peter could only say he would work harder on Scott. I knew this would be a case of trying to make a sow's ear out of a silk purse, and the silk purse wasn't going to oblige. Scott would remain his own charming self and I was too thankful for his full-size personality to mind.

Surprisingly, Binkie seemed to have no doubts about the play's ultimate success and as his drastic criticisms were quite good tempered, the tension gradually relaxed. I suggested someone should telephone Brenda, who was always dithering with nerves. Binkie agreed at once. Peter, callous as usual, had to be nagged into it. She told me next day that she had been in floods of tears when he rang up.

Over supper Binkie made a suggestion that, for me, offset the depression of the rehearsal. I had persuaded him to engage Peter to direct *I Capture The Castle*. Now, with the utmost casualness, Binkie said, 'What about Vivien Leigh for Cassandra?'

My heroine was seventeen; Vivien Leigh was thirty-nine. But I had recently seen her, across the Ivy Restaurant, looking like a really young woman. And I knew she was better when she assumed a character than when she gave a straight performance. I had a flash of certainty that Binkie's idea was brilliant. Peter was as excited as I was. Binkie, one of her greatest friends, said he would discuss the matter with her.

Next morning an utterly dispirited company were treated to all the adverse criticisms. Made earlier, they might have done good: now they merely lowered morale. I could only hope it might rise again at the Brighton dress rehearsal. I spent the afternoon packing all my luggage, most of which the Ritz would kindly store for me. The manager had offered to let me keep the suite on at half price but, as I expected to be away on tour for a month, this seemed too extravagant. So he said he would let me have it back when I wanted it. During my two months I had grown very fond of it, as I had of all my friends on the Ritz staff.

On the Sunday afternoon train-call I met Arthur Macrae coming down for my first night – as, the previous year, I had gone up to Manchester for his. He laughed when he saw my typewriter, saying it was the badge of an author on the way to an out-of-town opening. I was merely intending to type letters to Alec; *never* had I done any re-writing during a try out. But I refrained from saying this – which was just as well.

At Brighton most of us stayed at the Royal Crescent, a pleasant hotel in a great Regency house. From now on, the management would pay all my expenses. Binkie had provided me with a large first-floor sitting room, overlooking the sea. The windows, on two sides, were so large that one felt almost drowned in light. I loved that room.

When I got down to the theatre, early in the evening, I found an enormous staff wrestling with the sets and the revolving stage. In the past I had often been disconcerted by my first glimpse of scenery, but I had never experienced such dismay as at Oliver's sets. They were utterly overpowering. Peter, as dismayed as I was, hoped he could tone them down by careful lighting next day. Tonight work on erecting them and on practising the changes would go on till the small hours. So we went back to the hotel where we sat talking to Binkie till two a.m. – God knows what about.

Watching the dress rehearsal next day I suddenly saw with overwhelming clarity that the play had no resemblance to the play I had visualised. The giant, overbright scenery, the handsome but overpowering dresses, the ludicrous wigs, the quacking panatrope . . . all were larger than life, whereas the cast did not even seem life-size and got smaller and smaller as the rehearsal proceded. As for the play . . . I said to Peter's friend, Bill Smith, 'It's like something the head girl of a finishing school wrote for the girls to do on Speech Day.'

All Peter's attention was focussed on the lighting. He was trying to stop the scenery killing the actors – but when he did, the actors weren't lit adequately. I reminded myself of other dress rehearsals of my plays which had been followed by triumphant first nights. But those plays had not been overpowered by a decor more suitable for Offenbach; one rather expected a troupe of can-can dancers to come on.

The next morning I did the usual first night jobs: flowers for the women, telegrams for everyone. There was a second dress rehearsal in the afternoon, which must have left the cast deadly tired. Then the first night was upon us.

I sat in the stalls with Ronnie Emanuel who must, I think, have been delegated to look after me; I saw nothing of Binkie or Peter all evening. The theatre was packed, friendly, attentive. I had been warned that Brighton audiences rarely laughed, but there was from the first a constant ripple of laughter. The first scene ended and the panatrope let fly.

I knew that the inter-act scene changes were liable to take longer than the half-minute that was my ideal, and Ronnie had composed enough music to last for two minutes, at the end of which there was silence and I waited for the curtain to rise. Nothing happened – until the music started again and played for another two minutes, then for another two. Then, at last, the curtain rose. During the evening there had to be six inter-act changes during which the stage revolved. None of them took less than four minutes and one of them took seven. All around me were people sitting in the pitch dark, complaining of the delays. Still, the climax of the second act went well and the last act held. The applause at the end was good and there were numerous curtains.

Laurence Fitch and Phyllis had come down from London. He, like a kind agent, expressed optimism. She found the scenery utterly distracting and said she had not taken in the first twenty minutes because she couldn't disentangle the cast from the set. That studio was a complete disaster. The false perspective *looked* false. Scott McKay said the door was obviously meant for a man born on a hill; it was a foot too low for him to get through without obvious ducking. There was still no view of Paris which was represented by a turquoise sky full of creases.

Back at the hotel Binkie entertained friends and avoided talking to me. And dear Arthur Macrae skipped supper and went to bed. I learned later that he had been too horrified by some of the acting to face the cast.

I had been told that Derek Grainger, the *Sussex Daily News* critic, was a brilliant young man who wrote better than many London critics (which was true) and I must pay much attention to what he said. So early next morning I settled down with his review. It began with some mild fun about initial discussions between the ghost of Henry James and Miss Dodie Smith's muse. It was polite to me as a dramatist, but it built up an impression of a dim, dull play. I had been too tentative, too respectful of James. I had used too much of his dialogue – and James's anecdote was too unimportant. Still, the 'little story' sprang into life at the end of the second act. And he praised the direction, the decor (God forgive him) and the acting, though he did think Brenda Bruce unlike the Francie described by James as 'exceedingly, extraordinarily pretty' and, unless she was, the story didn't make sense.

Other notices were even politer to me as a playwright, but less polite to the play. It was said to be dull, snobbish, trivial; and why had I, 'one of the playwrights whose name is a household word, one of the most well-loved of our playwrights chosen to come back with an adaptation?' (Why, indeed, when *Esmeralda and The Cloth* was still shelved? Whatever its merits or de-merits it was typical of my work, and its story combined three highly box-office subjects: religion, love and fashion.)

Binkie now implored me to cast out Henry James and turn the play into 'one of your lovely comedies with lots of lovely jokes'. I doubt if I have ever thought of one funny line to order. I could only offer to tighten, improve, write a brisker opening scene (it wasn't a question of cutting; it was the shortest play I had ever written.) And as there was a large and appreciative second-night audience, the discussion after it was cheerful. I had unearthed from the stage-management that on the first night the curtain had been down for fifty-two minutes. Nobody believed me until I produced the stage-management's time sheets. (Why hadn't Peter Glenville investigated them? Alec had, long ago, trained me to do so.) The intervals between the acts had been normal. It was inter-act scene changes with the audience sitting in the dark that were to blame. Here was something Binkie would get his teeth into. Oliver's heavy, over-elaborate scenery must be massacred and a larger revolving stage should be ordered. Lots of improvements could be made.

I now felt capable of a cheering cable to Alec. My worst job that morning had been sending one which combined truth with optimism.

I did my bits of rewriting. We rehearsed. Business proved to be far better than the Brighton business of that other Henry James's adaptation, *The Innocents*, now a hit in London. I watched my show from every part of the house and invariably heard praise of it. One night Oliver watched it with me and shed real, wet tears at the end, murmuring, 'It's so beautiful'. Of course he meant his scenery and he was hoping to get me on his side about it, Binkie having decreed that the hotel walls must be sprayed a darker shade and the enormous and hideous pictures must be replaced by some which didn't overpower the cast. Oliver said they were a joke, which his friends adored, and he only designed sets to please sophisticated people. (And he never did change the pictures.)

We were to remain in Brighton for two weeks. Near the end of the first one, Binkie went abroad for a fortnight's holiday, having arranged that Peter should spend the weekend with Vivien Leigh at her country home, Notley Abbey, to find out what she thought of *I*

Capture The Castle. With typical scattiness he fell asleep on the train and failed to get out at Aylesbury where he was to be met, waking to find the train racing through the Midlands. By the time it stopped, the guard had arranged for a south-bound train to wait and pick Peter up. He reached Aylesbury after midnight, instead of in time to have dinner with Vivien.

He found her nervous and depressed and she hadn't read a line of the script. With great difficulty he got her to read the first act. She said she liked it but could she really look young enough? He assured her she could, and really meant it; but he felt pretty sure she would refuse in the end. She asked him to lunch with her in London on the following Thursday and said she would give him her decision then.

On Thursday night I was watching the play from one of the end seats in the dress circle. Peter, just back from London, sat down beside me and whispered, 'We're in!' Luckily the curtain fell a moment later and we could talk. Vivien, after again being assured she could look young enough, had now definitely accepted. They had sent a joint telegram to Binkie in which she said how excited she was and how much she looked forward to discussions on his return.

I had told Alec that she was considering the part and warned him, in the same letter, that this was to be treated as a secret. I said that, if I wanted to send news by cable, I would refer to Vivien Leigh as 'The lady'. Now at last I could cable unqualified good news: 'The lady has said yes.'

XXII

The Lady

On the Sunday at the end of our Brighton fortnight, the B.B.C. was
to televise *Autumn Crocus*. I had been invited to watch the
transmission so I decided to stay at the Ritz for the night. The
B.B.C. had been particularly pleasant, sending someone to
Brighton to interview me and asking me to appear on television. As
a hold-over from my early over-publicised days, I always tried to
avoid personal publicity, had never yet spoken on radio and, as a
matter of course, refused the television appearance. I have always
regretted this as it was taken for sheer contrariness. I had yet to
learn that personal publicity was of great value and one must grab
all one can of it.

The taxi-driver who took me to the Shepherds Bush studio told
me (without knowing who I was) that he hoped to get home in time
to watch *Autumn Crocus*. He said he watched all plays televised on
Sunday evenings, which gave me a hint of how wide English interest
in television already was. I told him I was tonight's author and he
wished me luck as he set me down, then drove off to his T.V. in
Putney.

I was shown round the sets and then watched the live
performance on a small television screen. The adaptation was
excellent and the acting was good, with Margaret Johnston as
Fanny. Phyllis played the Muriel Aked part. The play, now twenty-
two years old, brought back memories and saddened me – perhaps
because the thought of past success came at a moment when I was
scared by the thought of possible present failure. My latest anxiety
was that we had no certainty of getting a London theatre. Binkie
had counted on getting the New Theatre from Bronson Albery but,
according to Peter, 'Bronnie' (to many, but not to me; we had not
got on well when my play, *Service*, was at his Wyndhams Theatre)
had said that we needed a star actress who could suggest great
beauty.

Peter and I had arranged to travel together to Birmingham, our next touring date. Just before the train left he realised he had left three scripts in the taxi. Bill Smith, who was seeing us off, would have to go to Scotland Yard for these. Barely a day passed without Peter doing something like this. Now, as he had nothing to read on the train, I lent him a copy of the novel of *I Capture The Castle* (his own copy, unfinished, was in London). He left that in a Birmingham hotel telephone box.

I disliked that Birmingham hotel, where my bedroom was like the inside of a brown paper parcel and had no bathroom. My nice chambermaid told me to be sure to warn her when I wanted a bath so she could clean it for me, adding ominously, 'We have actresses here.' But what got her down worse, she said, were 'the blacks'. I took this to be race prejudice and then found she meant the smuts from the nearby railway station.

The Alexandra Theatre was huge and, though carefully 'papered', far from full on Monday night. Yet the show went much better than in Brighton's full houses and three out of the four notices were really good. Peter decided we should send Binkie an enthusiastic telegram. Peter was strong on enthusiastic telegrams and had already organised them between Vivien and me. Certainly the telegram to Binkie was justified as the business went up and up and we did a good week. Still, the local manager told us that our cast wasn't strong enough for first-rate provincial business, and a fan who had come from Cardiff (he reminded me he had come to the Newcastle first night of *Dear Octopus* in 1938) said, 'Listen, dear, you've been fobbed off with repertory actors – I've seen most of them for years. You should get rid of the lot and start again.'

Peter went back to London in the middle of the week and I went to Stratford-upon-Avon where I saw *As You Like It*, *The Tempest* and *Macbeth*. I didn't like any of the productions but I did enjoy being in Stratford and also a day when Maxine Audley drove Brenda Bruce and me round the countryside. I greatly liked them both. And I enjoyed travelling by car to Oxford on the Sunday, trains being impracticable.

I was told that the Oxford Theatre was the largest provincial theatre in England, though there is a school of thought that the Manchester Opera House is larger. Our sets looked far, far away from the audience on the local revolving stage. But the large size of that revolve meant that our changes were much quicker, as so much could go on it that usually had to be moved by hand, and during the

Monday evening performance I realised the play was going better than ever before. There was only one notice and that was a rave for the play and the cast – but not for the scenery. There was a reference to a 'mysterious bamboo portcullis', which was Oliver's idea of a smoking corner of the period and which Binkie and I were determined to scrap. By Tuesday morning there were long queues at the box office and the business went up and up all week.

Peter, telephoning from London, asked me to make careful notes of the performances. This was probably intended just to keep me happy, but I jumped at the chance of criticising without appearing to nag. I found that nice Paul Hansard had got worse and worse. He was now so self-confident that his love scene suggested opera without music, and Brenda found him almost impossible to act with. She asked me if I couldn't get him removed.

I rang Peter and found he already knew Paul must be changed. We needed a real leading man. I had nothing against one, if I could get one but, if not, I had an idea up my sleeve. Peter Barkworth, the boy from Sheffield, had been sent to us as an understudy. I had watched him rehearse, then asked him to lunch and found him charming and intelligent – if not quite so interesting as that middle-aged man he had appeared to be at his first audition. (That character only turned up again in the late nineteen-sixties, by which time he had become a television star.) I knew he would be far better than poor Paul Hansard.

Towards the end of the week Binkie, John Perry and Peter came to Oxford and Binkie broke it to the cast that we still had no London theatre to open in after the next, and last, week of the tour in Manchester. But if everyone would accept a week out he would book two more provincial dates, at Edinburgh and Liverpool, by then some London theatre should be free. This was enthusiastically accepted and I was highly in favour of it myself, as it would give us time to rehearse a new leading man; also Peter now wanted to get rid of the actor who played the American artist, Waterlow.

All this was discussed at a supper party which, in spite of various disagreements, was really one long laugh. Afterwards, Binkie said to me, 'Do you think we should have had a *jolly* discussion like that if Murray was the director, instead of Peter?' It was true. Faced with such worries, Murray would have been grim with anxiety. Binkie too was anxious, also angry with Peter for his mistakes in casting. But somehow anxiety and anger had been dissipated in laughter. Incidentally, Peter did not give one damn about the actors who had to be got rid of. Again Binkie said to me, 'Peter is cruel.'

Yet he could be so kind. On the Saturday, we returned to London together and he asked me to tea. It was so very pleasant sitting by his fire and stroking his dog, a friendly boxer, that I was reluctant to leave. He must have seen this for as I crossed Brompton Square, he and Bill Smith came running after me shouting that they had found out there was plenty of dinner and would I please stay? But I felt sure they would prefer to be on their own; also I needed to unpack all the luggage the Ritz had stored for me, and settle into my suite again. It felt like coming home.

I arranged for all my cousins to see the play in Manchester, but skipped going myself as I needed to be in London. Nicholas Phipps, a most excellent actor, accepted the part of Waterlow, but the semi-star Binkie had had in mind for Gaston wasn't free and another glamorous Frenchman Peter wished to import from Paris (sight unseen as so often) was turned down because Binkie had heard he couldn't act. So we were back at auditions and, at the end of the first one, Binkie surprised me by saying (I had kept my idea to myself) 'Barkworth would be better than anyone we're likely to find.'

Peter said Barkworth would be fatal – intelligent but too cerebral. We must press on with auditions. Binkie agreed, but arranged that Barkworth must be warned that he mustn't go to his Lancashire home for the week out. He must come back to London on Saturday morning – though not told why. No one in the company as yet knew any actors were being replaced. Auditions continued though Binkie was much occupied with the first night of Noel Coward's play, *Quadrille*, on the Friday night.

I went to it and sat between Binkie and John Perry, determined to be appreciative, but it was the worst play by Coward I had ever seen. At the end John Perry said, 'Thank God, I shall never have to see that again.' Still, I liked Alfred Lunt and liked him even better when I talked to him at Binkie's small, but very grand, party. Noel announced to the room in general that he felt certain of success. He didn't think the critics would like it but he didn't care. Which was just as well.

On Saturday morning we had our last audition, made necessary because Peter was convinced he had at last found a superb Gaston and Binkie, in spite of being a bit battered by the bad notices for *Quadrille* (he needn't have been; it ran for over three hundred performances) turned up to hear him. He was an ash-blond

Scandinavian, huge in height and in width, at present studying at RADA. His chief claim to fame was that he had once played Hamlet in Icelandic. Peter, who had already heard him read and rehearsed him, had the highest hopes. This boy must be given a real chance.

He was given it. Peter let him read scene after scene. Few words were audible, let alone intelligible. At the end of the audition Peter said, 'I can get this boy right.' Binkie said, 'Disaster. Barkworth plays.'

Peter said he'd rather keep Paul Hansard. Binkie said, 'Paul is playing tonight in Manchester and after that he is never again going on the stage as Gaston. That's settled.'

I had never before heard Binkie speak so harshly to anyone and he told me afterwards that he had felt horrified by his rudeness to Peter, 'But it seemed necessary to stop him making yet another mistake.'

Iceland's Hamlet was told his English wasn't quite good enough, and Binkie then made plans to have Barkworth's train met that afternoon. 'Dodie had better take him out to dinner and to a theatre; I'll reserve the house seats at *Relative Values*. And she can tell him just how she wants the part played.' Peter looked furious, so I said hastily that he must come to dinner and the theatre, too. He accepted for the dinner, but said nothing would persuade him to sit through *Relative Values* again. He added that whoever met Barkworth must say not one word about his changed fortunes, just bring him to Brompton Square. It was typical of Peter that, though he didn't want Barkworth, he did want to break the good news, which he did.

Dinner at the Ivy was a success – it was the first time Barkworth had been there. Peter found this touching – 'One's first visit to the Ivy!' By now his kind-heartedness was causing him to enjoy Barkworth's slightly dazed pleasure at what had happened to him. Then possessiveness took over and he said Barkworth ought not to go to the theatre; he ought to spend the evening working. I said he was too tired and I intended to carry out Binkie's instructions and take him to *Relative Values*. By now I knew all about dear Peter's possessiveness, and also his jealousy. He had once told me that he had been so jealous of Peter Brook's success as a director that he had felt he must pray about it – he was a fairly ardent Roman Catholic. So he went to church and prayed. 'And then Peter Brook had a flop'.

Noel's *Relative Values* was far better than Noel's *Quadrille*, but hardly a masterpiece. Barkworth was highly critical, particularly of the acting. But I think he had a fairly pleasant evening. Then I took him back to a grim house in South Kensington where he had found a little room on the top floor for thirty-eight shillings a week, 'to include milk and bread'. He was wondering how he could live in London on his contractual twelve pounds a week. And I knew Binkie, with three run-of-the-play contracts on his hands, for actors who had been pushed out, wasn't going to pay him a penny more.

Barkworth – he was always called that, to avoid confusion with Peter – had a cold when he arrived from Manchester and by the Monday rehearsal it was worse; still he got on well and I was glad to see how popular he was with the whole company. He'd had few rehearsals as an understudy and, though he was word perfect, he was going to take some time to be at ease in the part. And I thought Peter was overloading him with detailed instructions. Still, I had high hopes for him and was certain that Nick Phipps as Waterlow would be good. I had to skip the Tueday morning rehearsal as Vivien Leigh was coming to see me. I had now heard from Binkie that she was far from sure she *would* play in *I Capture The Castle*. Still, she wanted to talk to me. I had offered to come to her but she'd said, 'No, no, there's never any peace in my house. I'll come to the Ritz.'

I had met her, the previous year, at a very grand party she and Laurence Olivier had given, also occasionally back in the nineteen thirties; but I did not really know her at all. She arrived wearing a neat black suit, a black velvet pill-box hat, one beautiful ruby-and-aquamarine brooch and aquamarine earrings. This elegance focussed one's attention on her dark blue eyes. These gave the impression of being large, but (as Binkie once pointed out to me) they were really quite small. The impression of size was due to their brilliance, plus the fact that she kept them very wide open. Peter Glenville once said to her, 'Your eyes are too large for this part. We must somehow clip them together.' For a moment she took him seriously and said, 'No! Nothing must be done to my eyes.'

I found her easy to talk to. She never interrupted – a rare virtue in the theatre world – and in every way her manners were unusually good; indeed, I discounted some of her praise for the play and for the novel as being just courtesy. Still, I think she did like them and her only worry seemed to be as to whether she could look young enough. I tried not to be too gushing about this and inspected her face and throat from various angles before reassuring her. She did, indeed, look wonderfully young.

There was a scene where she had to wear a schoolgirl swim suit. She said she couldn't do that; her figure wasn't young enough. I said she could wear an old-fashioned bathing dress, once her mother's, a family joke. She loved that idea. Oh, there was a scene in my novel where a girl wearing a long, fur, coachman's coat was mistaken for a bear. Couldn't I put that in the play? Well, hardly, seeing that it took place on a dark night out in the depths of the country. But couldn't the coat be hanging somewhere and she could just put it on? 'Oh, please, please, do let me dress up as a bear!' I said I would think about it.

She then said that some of the lines could be funnier. For instance, speaking of her father's dress suit, Cassandra had to say, 'Oh, Topaz will have kept the moths out of it.' 'Kept' wasn't a funny word. Couldn't I improve it? I offered 'chivvied'. She laughed appreciatively, 'Oh, *yes*! Chivvied would be perfect.' I had a swift memory of John van Druten's exhaustion when Irene Selznick insisted that, in a comedy, every line spoken by the leading man needed some touch of humour. But 'chivvied' *was* an improvement.

One of Vivien's worries was that she had not yet found a voice that was right. I said why not use her own? She looked shocked – 'How could I? My voice is deep.' (It wasn't, except when she pushed it down for Shakespeare.) She now felt she needed a voice that was both young and funny. If she could hear anyone speak with such a voice, she would get a recording made and listen and listen until she could sustain it right through the play. That was how she'd acquired her Southern accent for *Gone With The Wind* – though all you really needed for a Southern accent was to say, over and over again, 'Clahm into ma foah doah sedaan'.

It seemed to me that acquiring any accent was very different from acquiring the voice of a seventeen-year-old girl. I feared it might come out like a child impersonation, but of course I didn't say so.

Another of her worries was that she particularly wanted to be acting with her husband during the Coronation season next year. Suppose some wonderful play turned up while she was waiting for *Castle*? It wasn't, she said, as if we could start rehearsals soon. I said we could start them the minute *Letter From Paris* opened in London which would be in three weeks (we now had a theatre, the Aldwych) barely time to get *Castle* cast. It was she who'd wanted to wait till next year. But didn't Peter want a long holiday? And she'd been told I wanted to go back to America. I said both Peter and I would change our plans. But she still wasn't *sure*.

We talked of other things – she stayed over an hour-and-a-half – and I came to the conclusion that, though she had a strong will (Binkie thought her the most determined woman he knew), she had very little *mind* of her own; and that though she considered herself a highbrow she had little intellectual capacity and merely picked up highbrow ideas from others. But throughout I liked her and particularly liked her occasional flashes of humour, which seemed just right for the part I wanted her to play. And I was influenced by Binkie's assessment of her drawing capacity. Quite apart from the talent she might or might not have, she was, he said, a *star*, with more drawing power than Olivier. Her presence in the cast would mean that a long pre-London tour could be sold out in advance.

The more we talked the more I liked her and I felt that she liked me. But when she left I thought we had less than a fifty-fifty chance of getting her.

At the afternoon rehearsal Barkworth's cold was no better and he was obviously flustered by too much direction. And after the Wednesday morning rehearsal he astonished me by protesting. He said he didn't see how he could be ready to open in Edinburgh unless he could stick to his own conception of the part. And could he please cut out some of the movements? How could he express deep feeling while inching between two pieces of furniture for no reason whatever? Peter took this well. I had never before seen an unimportant actor oppose an ace director; but I think now it may have indicated a coming tendency in the theatre. In America, a young actor to whom John van Druten was to give an important piece of direction was to reply, 'Well, I'll think about it over the weekend and then let you know if I can use it.'

There was no afternoon rehearsal as Peter had an appointment with his dentist. He lunched with me at the Ritz during which he said, 'Do you know, I've begun to find Barkworth attractive? He has the charm of sheer goodness.' I doubted if that would be particularly helpful in the theatre world.

During the afternoon Barkworth rang me up. That morning he had told me he couldn't stand another evening alone in his attic and I'd offered to arrange a theatre. He now told me he wasn't well enough. His cold had become much worse and he felt he must go to bed. I asked if he had enough food and he said he had two cakes, some milk and a bottle of 'tonic wine'. Anyway, he felt too ill to eat and he'd begun to fear he might not be able to open in Edinburgh.

I'd learned when he'd lunched with me in Oxford that he had been brought up as a Christian Scientist. But he'd added that he could no longer 'make it work', so I felt he'd better have a doctor. He said yes, if I could get him one, so I cheerfully said, 'Of course,' and he must go to bed till one arrived. He said he couldn't do that as he was alone in the house and wouldn't hear the doorbell up in his attic. So he would sit in the hall until the doctor arrived. I said I'd be as quick as I could.

How could I get a doctor quickly? I felt sure Peter would expect to be in charge of matters so I rang his house, hoping to get his dentist's telephone number. All I got was an Italian maid saying, 'Not speak English. Everyone out,' which she repeated again and again. I rang Binkie. He was out. I then remembered that Oliver Messel, who suffered from arthritis, had often talked of his doctor. I was no longer on particularly good terms with Oliver, but I thought of poor Barkworth waiting in a cold hall.

Vagn Reise Hansen answered the telephone. Yes, indeed, he would get a doctor, but first he would go and see Barkworth; he would be there in minutes. And so he was, in Oliver's black Rolls Royce. Barkworth was whisked away to Pelham Place. Vagn, reporting to me surprisingly soon, said the doctor believed he would be quite well enough to open in Edinburgh provided he stayed in bed for at least two days, though there was just the possibility that he might have jaundice. 'Anyway, he's in bed now and we're giving him a good meal. It's my belief that he's half starved.'

During the evening Barkworth himself rang up, from his bedside telephone. He said he was much better, but was worried because he had been given drugs and there had been so much medical talk. He believed I had a copy of *Science and Health*. Could I lend it to him? It had been my mother's copy and I had come to think of it almost as a relic, so I greatly disliked lending it. Still, I took it round at once. I found Barkworth sitting up in pale blue sheets. There was a gold sunburst-clock over the bed. I wondered what Mrs Eddy would make of such surroundings – though I seem to remember that she went in for gold bath taps.

Both Oliver and Vagn were in attendance and Peter Glenville shortly arrived. I left then, feeling four round the invalid's bed was too much. Oliver, showing me to the front door said, 'Darling Dodie, do ask Binkie to let me do the sets for your lovely new play, *I Capture The Castle*. (Not that he'd read it.) He then begged me to come to tea next day, which I did – bringing a new copy of *Science and Health* and rescuing my relic.

The kindness of Vagn and Oliver over Barkworth was so extreme (only with the greatest difficulty did I get the doctor's bill out of them), that I did eventually ask Binkie if Oliver could do the *Castle* scenery. Binkie made use of one of his favourite expressions, 'Now you've gone *too* far.'

Barkworth didn't have jaundice and was able to turn up for one last rehearsal on Saturday morning, heavily bodyguarded by Vagn. Peter rehearsed until after three o'clock, to the fury of his stage management who had a lot of work ahead of them. Much as they liked Peter, they made no secret of the fact that they thought him erratic and inconsiderate. Vagn, too, was annoyed as by three o'clock Barkworth was tottering. Peter dashed off to see some play at Brighton, so I took Vagn and Barkworth to the Ivy which obliged us with a very late lunch. I was slightly astonished to see Vagn press two double brandies on Barkworth, who naively said he 'liked the taste'. Vagn then took him to buy a hot-water-bottle as he was being sent to Edinburgh in a first-class sleeper that night; this had been arranged by Peter, that mixture of consideration and complete lack of it. The rest of the company went next day and Peter and I went by sleeper and talked till the small hours.

Binkie was unable to come to Edinburgh, but his very nice production manager installed the enlarged revolving stage which greatly helped with the changes of scenery. Oliver still hadn't sent a back-cloth of Paris, but had supplied an enchanting little cut-out of Paris roof tops with washing drying between chimney pots. He sent a message that he knew it couldn't be visible to the audience, but he hoped it might amuse the cast. However, Binkie finally won the battle of the back-cloth by sending a view of Paris which had been used in *Figure of Fun*.

Peter had wakened on the train that morning feeling ill and suspected he was starting 'flu. Still, he held a long rehearsal and that night the company gave about their best performance, to an appreciative audience. Peter was now complaining of difficulty in breathing and stabbing pains in his lungs, so it must have been irritating to him when the doctor who was called said there was nothing much wrong and he wasn't even running a temperature. I took him back to our hotel and assisted him to bed. He had forgotten his pyjamas and had left his dressing gown on the train, so I lent him one of the pre-war cashmere rugs I had been hoarding for years and had only just taken into use. 'Lovely things, aren't they?' said Peter, stepping heavily on the fringe before rolling himself up in the rug.

Next morning all the notices were good, the one in *The Scotsman* was the best the play ever received and particularly good for Barkworth. Peter was delighted, all his opposition to Barkworth now forgotten; and he now said he felt much better but would stay in bed all day. Would I please buy him some pyjamas? No, he didn't know what size and he had hardly any money with him. Fortunately I had plenty. It was a wild wet day, too windy to keep an umbrella up, taxis were scarce and I had great difficulty in finding pyjamas I could imagine any man wearing. However, I did at last locate some and bore them back to the hotel where I found Peter up and in the lounge with Brenda Bruce. He said he had decided to stay only two days in Edinburgh and it wasn't worthwhile buying pyjamas, so would I please take them back? Brenda took to calling me Master Peter's nanny.

The play was going better and better. Peter and I saw the Wednesday night performance together and then I hurried back to the hotel as I was expecting a telephone call from Alec. I decided to have supper in my room. Peter wanted to give a supper party to those members of the company who were staying in the hotel, before he flew back to London very early in the morning. He said he feared he had been neglecting them through spending so much time with me.

I had barely begun my supper when the telephone rang, but it wasn't Alec. It was Binkie with the news that Vivien had at last agreed to do *Castle*. She had given her word which, Binkie said, was as good as a signed contract. Rehearsals must start as soon as *Letter* had opened in London and, Binkie pointed out, I could only spend two more months in England without becoming liable for English income tax on top of American income tax. Two months wouldn't get me through the production and tour of *Castle*. Perhaps I could stay in France during the tour, perhaps Alec could bring the dogs there, where there was no quarantine, and we could both come over for the London opening. Binkie was full of ideas. With Vivien in the cast we could count on a long tour and he could spend unlimited money on the scenery, and the music – no more panatrope; a string orchestra would tour with us. I must come back to London next day, travelling overnight, as a lunch party with Vivien was arranged for Friday. I must have a full discussion with Peter tonight and he must ring Binkie as soon as he reached London, 'Otherwise he'll dash away without telling me where he's gone.' Never had I heard Binkie so excited.

I had only just finished talking to him when Alec's trans-Atlantic telephone call came through and was instantly cut off. I now felt I must get Binkie's news to Peter so I rang the dining room and asked that he should telephone me. He sent back a message that he would be up to see me soon. While waiting for him – and for Alec's call – I fell asleep and only wakened in the small hours – to learn, from the reception desk, that Peter had long since gone to bed. I arranged to be called in time to telephone him before he left to catch his very early plane.

When I did so, I found he had overslept. Would I come along and talk while he dressed? There was only time to give him the news about Vivien, impress on him that he must contact Binkie, and hurry him off. Then I rescued my mangled cashmere rug and went back to bed – until Alec's call at last came through.

Poor Alec, for him the good news about *Castle* was minimised by the fact that we should be separated so much longer than he had expected. I said we must work out some way to avoid that, and I spent the morning writing him an enormous letter outlining my plans. What with that, packing, arranging for my sleeper on the train, returning Peter's plaguey pyjamas and seeing the first half of the play that night, I was thankful when I was at last on my way back to London.

I have always liked sleeping on trains and particularly liked being wakened occasionally when passing through stations, seeing lights, wondering where I am. And that night I had the added pleasure of feeling optimistic about the future.

The lunch party next day was at the Ritz, though it was Binkie's party, not mine. Everyone was in high spirits and, though Vivien still seemed nervous about her own performance, she was full of enthusiasm and excited about the casting, much of which Binkie hoped to get done before *Letter From Paris* opened in London in less than two weeks. We sat on and on in the beautiful Ritz dining room, drinking cup after cup of coffee, until any hotel less well-mannered would have hinted that we ought to leave.

Binkie's typewriting office worked all weekend turning out three dozen copies of the *Castle* script. He had already booked a long tour. I wished he and Peter and I hadn't to go to Liverpool for one last look at *Letter*. Binkie hadn't yet seen the changes in the cast. He sent his car to the Ritz for me on the Wednesday and then we stood on the station wondering if Peter would miss the train or, at least, have lost his ticket. It had become obvious to Binkie that Peter must not, during the production of *Castle*, have all his own way and it was equally obvious to me that interference on my part would be resented by Peter. Binkie intended to cope with this by means of the best stage manager in London, who would relay all my opinions so that he, Binkie, could deal with them without appearing to involve me. It would all, Binkie said, be a matter of careful blue-printing; we must have a very long blue-printing discussion. I wondered if he would have another blue-printing discussion with Peter on how to cope with me, and another with Vivien on how to cope with both of us. But there was no doubt that, for the moment, Binkie and I saw eye-to-eye and he wanted me, either directly or indirectly, to interfere far more than during the rehearsals for *Letter*.

Of our four-hour conversation on the train I remember only three passages. The first at lunch, when I told Binkie not to waste his money on sherry for me as it cost so much and gave me so little pleasure. He asked, 'Does it give you even a pennyworth of pleasure?' I said, 'Yes, just about that.' To which he replied, 'Well, even a pennyworth of pleasure is worth having,' and ordered the sherry.

Soon after that he said something which seemed to me profound. I had happened to say that, as I grew older, I got on better with men than with women. 'At RADA, on tour and at the Three Arts Club I made scores of women friends. Now I never seem to make a new one.' Binkie said, 'Isn't that because you've stopped hunting?' and I instantly knew what he meant. Young women, on the look-out for men, love each other's company, love to compare notes, call on each other for sympathy. I told Binkie how exactly right he was, girls at the Club would call to a girl going out with a man, 'Good hunting!' I often found Binkie surprisingly intuitive.

Perhaps mention of my youthful days at the Club may have led Binkie into suggesting that my old friend, Madge Compton, should play a small part in *Castle*. He had liked her in *Dear Octopus* and had employed her several times since. He also suggested that Phyllis might play the little school-mistress, Miss Marcy. Peter said, 'Utterly out of the question, both of them,' I didn't think either of my friends would be ideal casting, still I asked him, later, why he was so much against them. What had he seen them play? He said he'd never seen them play in his life and he didn't even know what they looked like. 'Then why were you so down on them?' He said he hadn't the faintest idea.

I had. A direct suggestion from Binkie which Peter thought might appeal to me was doomed from the start. I was at last fully cognizant of that irritating flaw in Master Peter's character.

The Liverpool theatre was enormous and, that night, far from full. And the acoustics were so bad that when a laugh did come, it came in the middle of the next speech. Also, Brenda had a shocking cold. Still, Binkie was pleased with the performance on the whole and went round to congratulate Nick Phipps and Barkworth. I had warned Barkworth that he mustn't be as informal with Binkie, whom he had not met before, as Peter and I liked the whole company to be with us. I added that Binkie was enormously powerful in the theatre. Barkworth naively said, 'But is that *good* for him?'

Binkie's only criticism was that the clothes chosen for Barkworth (by Peter) were hopeless and he must have new ones for London. I was tickled, when the company was back in town, to receive an official notice to be at the Aldwych Theatre for 'Mr Peter Barkworth. Dress Parade'.

I shall always remember with pleasure our lunch on the return train journey to London next day. After Liverpool, our hopes for *Letter* were a bit dimmed, but we lifted our minds right off it to talk of *Castle*. Auditions would start next day. Various well-known players would come to see me at the Ritz over the weekend; I knew most of them, but Binkie felt I'd better see what the years had done to them. He then talked of my future plans saying I was the most extravagant woman he had ever met in spite of the fact that I didn't drink, gamble, throw parties, spend masses of money on clothes, jewellery or, in fact, have anything to show for my extravagance.

'Take all your voyages across the Atlantic. You came over – and went back – last year. You've come over this year and now, I gather, you intend Alec to bring the dogs to France for the production of *Castle*. Then, during the tour, you and Alec and the dogs will go back to America, then return for the London opening. Then you'll both go back to America. That makes ten Atlantic trips, all first class, all costing a fortune – and all because you won't quarantine the dogs. And then there's your delightful suite at the Ritz. . .'

Sharing our table on the train was a dignified business man trying to give the impression that he wasn't listening to the conversation, but not quite managing it. Eventually Peter told a story that was famous in the company. At Oxford, he had stayed at an inexpensive hotel where several of the cast were also staying. Returning after midnight, he found there was no water in his bedroom so, knowing that other members of the company were on the same corridor, he wandered along whispering loudly, 'Maxine, Maxine', hoping Maxine Audley would have a carafe of water. The only person who heard him was Scott McKay who said to his wife, 'I'd no idea things were like that between Maxine and Peter.' Failing to get any answer, Peter went to bed thirsty. Next day he got up very early to catch a train for London and, wanting to give Maxine a note about her performance, he again wandered along whispering for her. Again the only person who heard him was Scott McKay who said to his wife, 'Good God, he hasn't found her yet.'

At this, our dignified lunch companion laughed outright and from then on felt free to join in our conversation. Later, when Peter and I had gone off to wash before reaching London, he asked Binkie to tell him who we were. 'Of course he was most interested,' said Binkie. 'And did you tell him who *you* were?' I asked. 'Good heavens, no,' said Binkie. 'The public aren't interested in managers.'

Early next morning I rang Binkie about several things and started by telling him I had worked out how to fit in two more Atlantic crossings. Instead of laughing he said grimly, 'Hasn't Vivien telephoned you yet?' He then broke it to me that she had utterly and irrevocably backed out of doing *Castle*.

She had just rung him to tell him so, stating as her reason that she was too old for the part. He had reminded her that she had given her word, that he had booked a long tour, that the theatre world knew she was to be in the play and so did the newspapers, who were only holding up the announcement until *Letter* had opened. Finally he asked if she knew what she was doing to me. She said she was very sorry, would telephone me at once and come and see me.

'And when she telephones,' said Binkie, 'you mustn't know anything about it or she may get it all over by telephone. Just agree to see her and then do what you can. Our best chance is to get her to meet us and Peter tonight, make her read the part to us and then show enormous enthusiasm. But I haven't much hope really. She has a will of iron.'

She rang soon after I hung up, simply asking to see me, and arrived very quickly. She answered my welcoming smile with a prolonged shaking of her head, then sat down and said, 'I can't do it.'

We talked for just on two hours during which she showed no

inclination to leave. It was almost as if she *wanted* me to persuade her. And yet she stone-walled my every attempt. No, she would not read the part to us. She had read some of it to Peter only the previous evening and he had said she would be perfect once she lived her way into it. That wouldn't do for her. She wanted to come to the first rehearsal knowing exactly what she was going to do with every line. Couldn't he give her a complete conception of the character? He'd said it was too early. And he couldn't tell her what voice to use.

I wondered if someone had put her off the play and asked if her husband had been against it. She said no, Larry had been all for it, but he had warned her that he wouldn't be able to help her as he was working on a film. And that, I came to believe, was the real trouble. She had hoped Peter would stand in for Larry, create the character for her, teach her every line. Peter, as yet, hadn't studied the play or even finished reading the novel, but even if he had he couldn't have done what she wished. I remembered Basil Dean telling Valerie Taylor during rehearsals of my *Call It A Day* that she'd never get the kind of direction she hankered for unless she married her director.

We sat side by side, perfectly friendly, arguing gently and getting nowhere at all, except that I did gradually learn something about her character. She was a woman of great intelligence, but it was an acquisitive intelligence, in no way creative. I knew from Binkie how acquisitive she was as a collector, she bought and bought and bought. And she was just as acquisitive about new arts and skills; singing, tap dancing, flower arrangement, interior decoration . . . she would work and work. But she always had to be *taught*; nothing came from within. And I felt she was an unhappy woman – which was, perhaps, why I said to her, 'Vivien, have you any religion?' She said, 'No, and I sometimes think I ought to get one.' Something new to acquire, no doubt.

I had no desire to hurry her away, but after nearly two hours I felt I must warn her that Margaret Rawlings, a possibility for Topaz in *Castle*, would soon be arriving. Vivien, naturally, had no desire to meet her at the moment and yet she still hung on. At last I said, 'Well, if you don't mind running into Margaret Rawlings. . .' She rose then and I escorted her to the lift, but she still went on talking and it was I who eventually rang for it. As we heard it coming up she said, 'You do forgive me, don't you?' I said – but smiling – 'Oh, no. I shall go on liking and admiring you, but I shall never *forgive* you. Because you could have been perfect as Cassandra.'

She shook her head sadly and got into the lift.

My remark had been one last attempt to persuade her. She *wouldn't* have been perfect, but she might have achieved an interesting *tour de force*.

Margaret Rawlings soon arrived, shortly followed by Peter who was to interview her with me. He obviously didn't know the news about Vivien's refusal (he had been out all morning) and only after Miss Rawlings had gone could I break it to him. He was convinced it was just a scare. We rang Binkie and found Vivien was with him, but he had no hope of persuading her. He asked us to come to him after that afternoon's audition – there had been no time to cancel it.

Binkie had asked us to say not one word about Vivien's defection, so there was nothing for it but to let everyone read. And Peter let them go on and on. It was a couple of hours before we were free to go up to Binkie's office.

He said he had taken Vivien out to lunch and then managed to get her to read the part to him. He had praised her highly and gone on trying to persuade her until she said she felt sick. (She did indeed spend three days in bed.) Now we must simply think of some other actress. But she *must* be a star. And we all knew no suitable star was available.

Peter shortly left and Binkie then said that I must obviously stop pouring out money and get back to America. He had already found I could get a passage four days after *Letter* opened. I asked him to book it for me and told him that, unless *Letter* surprised me by succeeding, Alec and I would have to come back to England for good. Most of the R.K.O. money for an option on *Castle* was now used up (they hadn't taken up the option). I had always said I would never quarantine the dogs unless forced to. Well, now it had come to that, as the only place we could now afford to live was at our Finchingfield cottage. Though I hated the idea of asking him to leave after having had it for fourteen years.

Binkie now surprised me by saying he would be glad to, as he had given up hope that electricity would ever become available there, and he could now well afford to buy a country home of his own. Of course I assured him I would give him plenty of notice of our return.

While waiting to see him, I had overheard him say to John Perry, 'I can't talk any more now; I've had a hell of a day. I've had to cancel the whole tour and I'm utterly bushed.' Yet he made no attempt to get rid of me; he had obviously decided I must be allowed to talk as long as I liked. And indeed I should have liked to go on and on; I had no desire to return to the Ritz all alone. But seeing how tired he was, I ended the conversation. He saw me to that absurd little Globe Theatre lift and, before closing the door on me, said, 'The worst thing of all is that I gave you my word you could trust her.' And what with tiredness and distress he looked very near tears.

I went back to the Ritz and telephoned Laurence, knowing the news would be a bitter blow to him, too. Then I had the fiendish job of wording a cable to Alec. Phyllis was on tour with a new play so I could not pour out my troubles to her. I wonder what I did with the rest of that miserable evening.

XXIII

The Woodspurge

Next morning I got a cable from Alec saying that the thought of seeing me so soon made up for everything. I spent most of the day writing to him, at last having time on my hands as all the weekend auditions and interviews had been cancelled.

That night I went to see *South Pacific*. Binkie had had the wild idea that Mary Martin could play Cassandra. He said, 'Go round and tell her about Vivien's shocking behaviour. She might ask to read the script.' She was, of course, superb in *South Pacific*, but I knew she would never dream of playing an English girl of seventeen. Still, it was pleasant to talk to her and Dick Halliday again and they were deeply sympathetic. I hadn't been back-stage at Drury Lane since the night I tried to persuade Victoria Hopper not to break off her engagement to Basil Dean. She had not achieved the great success she deserved, Basil now spoke of himself as a back number, and my own prospects looked none too rosy. Lots of fun for the whirligig of time.

Next day the Sunday Express came out with the news that Vivien Leigh was going to play in *Castle*, thus bringing me a flood of letters asking for work. Answering them was a dreary job; also by Monday I had started one of my heavy colds. For months I had been surrounded by people with colds and had begun to feel sure I shouldn't catch one. Now I felt sure of nothing.

Preparations for the first night of *Letter From Paris* were now in full swing. I had to arrange about seats for my friends and presents for the company. Apart from flowers for the women, food cheques (bought with American dollars) seemed the best idea as rationing was still strict. Now I was in touch with the company again I firmly registered optimism, but it became a bit shaky after my first visit to the Aldwych Theatre on Tuesday. It was so large, so lacking in intimacy, the sight lines were so bad, the stage so high that, with our revolve on top of it, the first five rows of the stalls would scarcely see

the actors below their knees. And though the theatre was supposed
to have been recently done up, the carpets were worn and there was
a general air of dilapidation. No wonder Peter had felt that getting
the Aldwych was a death knell.

The first dress rehearsal was on Wednesday night. The theatre
was icy cold and Peter said it always would be. In spite of a fur cape
I felt frozen and my cold, which had seemed rather better, got
steadily worse. By the end of the evening I couldn't speak without
coughing.

But my cough was a poor weak thing compared with Brenda's.
(She had been 'off' for two performances in Liverpool.) Twice Peter
Barkworth had to leave the stage and get her a glass of water. Twice
she called to Peter that she couldn't continue. At last, in the middle
of the third act, he called the rehearsal off and told her to skip the
second dress rehearsal, next day, and stay in bed.

The atmosphere was utterly gloomy. Peter had gone back to
thinking that Barkworth was 'disastrous'. Certainly his appearance
was; Peter had insisted on his having a bright pink make-up and a
mop of golden curls on his forehead (a hair style much favoured by
young Covent Garden porters, I'd noticed.) His acting seemed to
me much as usual except that he couldn't play love scenes with a
coughing *vis-a-vis*. What with worry and the icy cold of the theatre I
went home with a raging temperature and spent a sleepless night
being nursed by the night floor-waiter. He brought me tea twice,
re-filled my hot-water bottle and came in every hour just to say
something comforting. I shall always remember myself, sitting up
against the square Ritz pillows (which were filled with something
that felt like soft stones) staring at the knobs of the brass bedstead
and being mothered by that kind young Frenchman.

Mercifully, I was a little better next morning and, even more
mercifully, the second dress rehearsal went well, probably because
the whole company was trying to help Brenda's understudy, Mairhri
Russell; this was her chance to play a star part in front of Binkie.
She hadn't Brenda's subtlety as an actress, but was simple and
young and pretty, and brought to the play a touch of romance. But
the weighty sets sat on the cast as heavily as ever. No breath of Paris
in the spring broke through. The lighting of the daylight scenes
indicated late autumn and it never appeared to come through
windows, but from the front of the dress circle, a rich orange glow.
Peter said that nothing could be done to improve this as he still had
to 'try to kill the sets'. He didn't manage this. They were killers, not
killable.

Everyone acted well at that rehearsal and Peter now found Barkworth 'exciting'. He at least looked human again, Binkie having ousted the bright pink make-up and the mop of golden curls.

Next day, on the afternoon of our first night, Binkie came to see me. He would be away for the weekend so this was our last chance for a quiet talk before I sailed on the Monday. He brought with him a Balmain shawl and an exquisite bouquet of white heather which I said I would carry. (I omitted to mention that for years I had considered white heather unlucky.) He had chosen to have food cheques as a first night present from me as he had to do so much entertaining. Incidentally, he said coping with first night presents was a nightmare to him, particularly in the case of American stars. He never knew if they would give some amusing little joke-present or an antique costing several hundred pounds. We sat drinking cup after cup of tea – there seemed no limit to what Binkie could drink in the way of tea or coffee – until I suddenly realised I ought to start dressing.

It was the oddest feeling, getting ready for that first night. No Alec, no secretary rushing round making lists of the donors of flowers. The little Ritz sitting-room was full of them. No Phyllis, no Ambrose Heal – though a loyal contingent of my old friends was coming from Heal's; so only Laurence Fitch escorted me. He arrived bringing a tiny silver box made to simulate a letter addressed to me with a minute Parisian postmark; I have used it for saxin for over thirty years and I doubt if I ever open it without a flash of memory of that night of October 10th, 1952.

At the theatre I had a job I always disliked: going round dressing rooms to wish the company luck. There is much kissing of grease-painted faces and the men are so often embarrassed because they are half-undressed. And though one knows people would be hurt if one didn't turn up, one really adds to the general nervousness. Brenda had been given something for her cough which she described as 'a bomb'; it would explode and spread a protective film over her throat. Would I like a bomb for *my* cold? I would not. I only coughed if I talked.

I went into my box only after the house lights had dimmed and that far too loud panatrope was suggesting an evening of jollity. The moment before curtain-rise still held a trace of magic for me, heightened by memories of my other London first nights. And the first scene went unusually well, in spite of being the dullest scene in the play. All was well with the second scene, too, and I then counted on Scene 3 to lift the act as it always had on tour. Not so tonight.

The opening comedy went badly. At first I blamed Oliver's hotel set, which seemed to me more stupefying than usual. But I gradually realised that Brenda, though not coughing, was not at her best and on her so much of the comedy depended. Still, applause at the end of the act was solid.

Everyone who visited me in the interval seemed genuinely hopeful and I am good at detecting simulated enjoyment. I began to allow myself a little optimism. We had come safely through our weakest act.

The second act opened well and the moonlit love scene had some charm. It was only in the second scene that the rot really began. This had always been the funniest scene in the play, with Brenda getting laugh after laugh. She missed so many tonight that I began to wonder if she was being heard. I was thankful when we reached Scene 3, the one really dramatic scene, which had never failed to hold. It failed tonight for a totally unexpected reason.

The actor playing the French husband of one of the daughters of the stately Probert family had bad laryngitis and could barely get a word out. In order to make up for this he started to overact with gestures and expression, rolling his eyes and behaving like a *comic* Frenchman. Within seconds the whole atmosphere was wrecked. It was as if he were providing a comment on the scene. Good heavens, what did it matter if a girl had told the scandals of her future husband's family to a journalist who had printed everything? *Why* make such a fuss? And when the poor young man with laryngitis managed to say one line loudly and his voice cracked, there was a loud laugh. All this time Brenda was playing most movingly, but she had allowed herself to dissolve into genuine tears. Again and again, at rehearsals, Peter had warned her against this (and how well I remembered Basil Dean warning Fay Compton in *Autumn Crocus*, 'No real tears from you, dear, or the audience's eyes will be dry as a bone.') And Brenda's exit, which had never before failed to win a round of applause, went for nothing. It was followed by Gascon Probert's return from America just too late to save his fiancée from his family's wrath; and the fact that Peter Barkworth restored some tension was little short of miraculous. Still, the curtain fell to merely perfunctory applause, on a scene which on tour had always received a long ovation.

After that I never had the slightest hope of success. The last act didn't deserve to succeed. Brenda was still weeping real tears – and in a scene which should have been treated as comedy. And now she was coughing; perhaps her tears had neutralised the cough 'bomb'. So she not only failed to get her own laughs; she coughed through other people's. The last scene was particularly well acted by Maxine, Nick Phipps and Barkworth, and Brenda, her tears now under control, played the final love scene beautifully. The curtain fell to much louder applause than I expected, quite solid applause but lacking in real enthusiasm. With real first night success the audience *demands* more and more curtains; on half-baked success it is as if more curtains are being squeezed out of the audience.

Up and down went that curtain, five of its rises being well justified. Then Brenda's solo call got a slight increase of applause, so up went the curtain again – and again and again and again. I learned later that Binkie dashed back-stage to stop any more curtains, so he did not hear the few boos from the gallery which greeted the final one – our eleventh. Laurence insisted he didn't hear them and, like a loyal agent, assured me we should have a six months run at least (which happy news he later cabled to Alec.)

I told Laurence he was out of his mind, but to no one else did I express pessimism, and back-stage I praised everyone heartily. Then I had to face Binkie's party to which Laurence was to escort me – it was bliss now to have an agent whom managements invariably liked. We had first to take my flowers back to the Ritz and Peter said he, too, was coming with me. But he kept vanishing to have a last chat with someone and, when I said I must go without him, he called to Laurence, 'Get a taxi, I'm coming.' We sat in that ticking taxi twenty minutes before he came.

Back at the Ritz, he began to open his first night telegrams. He had a superstition that it was bad luck to open them before a first night and, as he now expected to meet people at the party who had sent them, he insisted on finishing the job. We ended by arriving insultingly late. Binkie had collected some genuine Henry James fans and their praise seemed to me sincere. Otherwise I remember nothing until I was back at the Ritz where the bath and basin were full of flowers. I was reminded of the first night of *Autumn Crocus* when Alec and Phyllis spent hours unwiring my flowers. That play had been booed, too, but everything had come right. Did I tell myself this would again be the case? I did not.

I woke next morning while my nice Viennese maid was tip-toeing round the sitting-room. As soon as she left, I got up and found the morning papers neatly laid out. I read the *Telegraph* first. There was a kind headline, 'Dodie Smith's Skill Unimpaired', and the whole tone of Darlington's notice was kind: memories of my past successes, skilful adaptation, good acting – though Brenda Bruce was 'an odd choice'. Special praise for Barkworth, Scott McKay and Maxine Audley. But all the skilful preservation of James's atmosphere was unable to disguise 'a tenuous story about people who do not greatly matter to us.' No mention of Peter's direction or Oliver's sets.

The Times critic thought the play charming and shapely while it preserved James's international situation, but went all wrong when Francie confronted the Proberts because I did not show that they had been 'delicately schooled in depravity'. (Neither does Henry James.) 'The miscasting of Miss Brenda Bruce works against the play.' Hannen was colourless, the rest of the cast adequate, Maxine Audley and Jessie Evans rather more than that. Nicholas Phipps was pleasant, Peter Barkworth an agreeable hero. Peter and Oliver were again omitted.

The *Daily Express* cheered me by a heavy headline: 'Dodie Smith Unerringly On Target Again.' But the critic had written that I had struck unerringly at the teacup matinée trade and said how dull I could.be when the plot started creaking through the platitudes. There was a reference to Oliver Messel's 'fussy decor', the skilful playing of Brenda and Scott McKay, no mention of the rest of the cast or of Peter's direction.

The *Daily Mail*'s two-inch notice was headed 'An Ordeal To Be There'. And only Brenda Bruce came alive. 'Perhaps the real star is Oliver Messel who smothers the inadequate action with his astonishing sets'.

After that Alan Dent in the *News Chronicle* was at least civil. He said I'd been away a long time, but 'not so long that we cannot remember her as a playwright always perfectly well able to think up her own plots and characters. Why, then, does she bother with Henry James at his stuffiest? . . . everybody strives hard, particularly Brenda Bruce as the naive little heroine . . . and Oliver Messel with luscious clothes and settings. But almost from the start the whole thing – as James himself would say – 'quite beautifully collapses'.

The short notice in the *Daily Graphic* was the kindest. It praised almost everything, then concluded, 'It was apparently too slow for the audience, but for all its faults I found it charming and I recommend it to all with patience and a respect for talent.'

There were still the evening papers, the Sunday papers, the

weeklies, provincial papers, etc. to come, but the pattern was set. And though on the whole the dailies had been kinder than I expected, I knew that *Letter From Paris* would be a dead failure.

I remember standing at my bedroom window looking along Berkeley Street to the trees in Berkeley Square which I had seen turn from June's green to October's yellow. In the net window curtain there was a neat darn, about one inch square. I now find my most vivid memory of that gloomy morning is of that darn, and am reminded of some lines by that favourite of my girlhood, Dante Gabriel Rossetti, in which he remembers gazing, in almost mindless grief, at a group of weeds:

> From perfect grief there need not be
> Wisdom or even memory:
> One thing then learnt remains to me,
> The woodspurge has a cup of three.

That small, neat darn has become my woodspurge.

No doubt 'perfect grief' is piling on the agony, but I must have felt pretty miserable, seeing that this failure was the culmination of two visits to England, would kill my chances of an American production of *Letter* and damage the prospects of *I Capture The Castle*, already damaged by Vivien's defection. And *Esmeralda and The Cloth* – no adaptation, but a play typical of me – would now be up on an even higher shelf.

Some vague memories: My floor-waiter, who had read all the notices when he brought my breakfast, saying critics were getting stupider and stupider and the public would have more sense. Then various people rang up: Binkie, Peter, Brenda, Barkworth . . . and, of course, Laurence. I can't remember what cheering things they managed to say about those notices. I waited for the evening papers, which came around lunch time, before cabling Alec. The three critics, two of them old friends of mine, obviously meant to be kind. They welcomed my return, praised past work, found various things to admire: humour, charm, skill . . . but all wasted on a job not worth doing. A.E. Wilson found the story too slight to stand the weight of Oliver Messel's sets and dear Harold Conway thought them 'fulsomely rewarding to the eye' (whatever that might mean). Stephen Williams considered I had done all that theatrical skill could do with an undramatic novel, and made the play sound dull.

I put in a lot of work on my flowers that morning; never in my heyday had I had more. The most perfect were from Mary Martin and Dick Halliday: dozens of golden roses which arrived in bud and proceeded to open all at the same time, a miracle of efficiency in flowers typical of the great efficiency with which Dick ran Mary's triumphant career. Murray thoughtfully sent his flowers in their own vase, to the relief of my harassed chambermaid who had run out of vases. The most typical of all were Vivien's, accompanied by a note beginning 'Dear, *dear* Dodie'. She had sent a vast welter ranging from giant spider dahlias down to bunch after bunch of exquisite tiny flowers, the stalks of some of them only two inches long; they could barely raise their heads out of egg cups. Vivien, in her aspect of collector and flower arranger, had chosen them to please herself.

In the afternoon Dorothy Tutin came to tea with me. This had been arranged by Binkie, probably to make me feel that *Castle* was still alive. She had been one of my earliest suggestions though I did not then know much of her work and Binkie had always said she was not enough of a star. Now she was engaged to play in the new Graham Greene play, *The Living Room*.

I was not at first impressed by her. She looked nondescript, untidy, rather an ordinary little thing. But five minutes after she sat down I knew she was the perfect Cassandra and a person of great intelligence with a loveable character. She stayed for nearly two hours and didn't seem to want to go even then – nor did I want to let her. I would have asked her to dinner had I not had to go to the theatre.

She talked of Cassandra as a living person, wanted to know which scenes from the novel were in the play, not because of the chances they would give her, but because she loved so many of them. I told her Vivien had objected to the skimpy bathing suit and she said, 'Oh, but I love that, it must be shrunken, it's Cassandra's old school suit. And it must be dripping wet and so must her hair.' She was anxious about the end of the play. 'It *mustn't* be happy. The novel's ending is perfect. She must be just growing up – you must feel life is before her. She must still be in love, but the audience must know she might grow out of it. You must feel the sad ending is really a happy one'.

At the moment she was playing in the film of *The Beggar's Opera* and had to be wakened at 4.30 every morning. 'The telephone operator who calls me is so kind. He tries to wake me *gently* because he's sorry for me'. She was looking forward to playing in the Graham Greene play because it would give her the chance of an emotional part – 'But it needn't run too long, need it? I'd like it to run two months and then I could do *Castle*'.

All we could do was to enjoy a might-have-been, may-yet-be-talk during which I felt shocked that, tempted by Vivien's box office pull, I had agreed to offer her a part for which she was both too old and temperamentally unsuited. Incidentally, Dorothy, from simply reading the novel, had formed a complete conception of Cassandra's character, something Vivien had, in vain, asked Peter to provide her with.

We talked until nearly seven o'clock and, even then, Dorothy turned back for a few last words. I no longer thought her ordinary, she had a most unusual personality. And I remember with particular pleasure her beautiful, delicate hands.

I got to the Aldwych as the audience for the second Saturday performance was waiting for the first house to come out. I knew there would be only a short interval between the two shows, so I rushed around saying my farewells, not wanting to wait until the end as I still had much packing to do. Everyone was putting on a brave face, hoping for the best. A nicer company I never had – nor a weaker cast.

I saw a few minutes of the play, very sure I should never again see it played, and then said goodbye to the box-office and to the commissionaire who told me he hadn't before realised I was the author – 'Thought you were an understudy.' He then escorted me to my taxi with a fatherly arm round my shoulders. As the taxi swung into the Strand I looked through the back window at my name in lights – in solitary splendour as we had no stars in the show – and wondered if I should ever again see my name outside a London theatre.

The Sunday papers did nothing to cheer me though Harold Hobson did find the play extremely subtle and said the booing would hardly worry me in view of the first night booing of *Autumn Crocus*. He wrote at length about the miscasting of Brenda Bruce, praised Barkworth, Scott McKay and Maxine but found much of the acting 'uncomfortable'. Ivor Brown held his notice over for a week (and when it came it was poor) and the notices in the popular papers were bad and tiny except the *News of the World* which was civil and tiny. I wondered if Binkie would run the play for even a week.

On the Sunday evening I went to a concert in the Festival Hall for which Vaughan Williams had sent me seats. I had exchanged occasional letters with him ever since he had admired my novel, *I*

Capture The Castle, and had offered him seats for the first night of *Letter*; he had chosen to go to a later performance. I took Peter Barkworth with me to the concert; he was knowledgeable about music, played the piano well and (I rather regret to say) the organ in church. Knowing him had been something on the credit side of my visit to England for, as well as liking him, I was relieved to find I could get on so well with someone so young. I had made no young friends since I had been young myself and greatly valued a renewed link with youth. (I had felt the same during my two hours' talk with Dorothy Tutin.) It's pleasant to think that my play gave him his start in the West End.

I had planned to spend most of Monday shopping, but my old friend Cyril Hogg who, as head of Samuel French, had watched over the amateur fortunes of all my plays, insisted on lunching with me – or rather, having asked me to lunch and been told I was too busy, said I must eat somewhere and he would entertain me at the Ritz. Alas, he had little to say beyond regret that I had returned with an adaptation and allowed it to be miscast. After he left, I had a long farewell telephone talk with Binkie who said he would run *Letter* for as long as the Aldwych Theatre would let him. Even without my royalties, which I at once offered to forego, this would mean a heavy weekly loss, and I knew how expensive the production had been. He brushed all this aside as the fortunes of war, assured me he would paper the house well and send batches of seats to Heal's and to the Ritz. (I made sure all my special friends on the Ritz staff would get a chance of some.) And of course he would go on trying to find a star for *Castle*.

I had always been fond of Binkie but I don't think that, during our shared successes, I had ever liked him as much as during our shared failure now.

Just as I was at last ready to start my shopping, Peter Glenville and his friend Bill Smith arrived to say goodbye. It was kindly meant and, as always, Peter was wonderful company but I did wish they'd leave. Peter was impervious to hints and it was dusk before Bill dragged him away, saying I should miss my boat-train. Late as it was, I dashed over to Bond Street but found the shops closing or closed. I only just managed to get a couple of new books from a closing Hatchards. (How little I had read during the past four months.) Luckily I already had presents for Alec.

Back at the Ritz I found Laurence, who was to see me off, waiting. He helped me close my trunks and, in the end, I had a last minute rush which was just as well as I had begun to feel sentimental about leaving my denuded suite – not quite denuded for it was still full of my first-night flowers. They were to be shared by my chambermaid and my floor waiters. I said goodbye to them and then to my friends, the lift men; and in the hall the hall porter lined up all the pages because I wanted to tip them. And finally there was the handsome commissionaire who, years later, recognised me when I walked past the hotel.

Poor Laurence, seeing me off, must have been a sad man. The play's failure was a financial blow to him as well as to me. I persuaded him to go before the train left as I knew he had a horror of waving anyone goodbye. I had dinner on the train, at last managed to get my enormous amount of luggage safely on to the S.S. America and heaved a sigh of relief – only to find my cabin was crowded with Southampton journalists. Never before had I been interviewed on sailing for America and I imagined this interest must be due to *Letter's* failure. But the journalists hadn't heard of it and barely of me. They had merely been told some writer was on board and had come to see if I rated a few paragraphs in their local papers. One of them was highly sympathetic about my unwillingness to quarantine the dogs as he could never take a Continental holiday because of his own dogs. It was pleasant at last to find a journalist who believed me about the dogs.

During the voyage I wrote over fifty letters thanking people for first-night flowers and telegrams, a difficult job because I could not claim success and did not like to admit failure, with Binkie doing all he could to save the play. I had no time to make up my Journal, as I usually did on Atlantic crossings.

Anyway, I couldn't have faced the job. It would have added to my homesickness which was almost as powerful as when I first left England in 1939. But then I had been homesick for all England (as I had gone on being for fourteen years) and had particularly longed for our cottage. Now what I mainly missed was the ever-exciting world of theatrical London and my expensive none-too-comfortable, but always tenderly remembered, suite at the Ritz.

XXIV

Look Forward

But I did experience great joy on seeing Alec waiting on the New York dock, his silver hair blowing in the breeze. He had brought the De Soto but with a hired driver so that we could talk during the drive. Once we were out of New York the country looked wonderful, at the height of its autumn colouring. Our yellow Wilton house had clean muslin curtains and the dogs, in spite of their mature years, seemed more puppyish than I had remembered. And for some days I took a noticeable pleasure in my really comfortable bed and our good, though simple, food. But all the time I was conscious of a weight of disappointment, both for myself and for Alec. He never showed his and I hope I disguised mine by reasonable cheerfulness. But I must have been an exhausting companion for I talked almost incessantly, reliving my four months in England, explaining, blaming, excusing and, no doubt, repeating much I had said in letters. I don't know how Alec stood it.

Notices from weeklies, provincial papers, etc followed me across the Atlantic, most of them far better than I had expected, probably because a later and better performance had been seen. But they did nothing for the box office and in around three weeks the Aldwych Theatre turned us out. W.A. Darlington, in a long article for the *New York Times*, praised the play's skill and said its subject matter, of little interest in England, might be of great interest in New York. But hopes of a production there were now nil.

I had not been home long before I realised that Esther was no longer an unmixed blessing as, during the summer, her very unsatisfactory husband, Al, had returned from serving in Korea. Alec had given her a really long holiday and invited Al to stay with her in our house at Wilton whenever he could get leave. But Al found Wilton dull and wanted her to come back to Pennsylvania for all weekends. Again and again Alec had let her go, but she never returned when she said she would. Soon after I got back she was off again, officially for three days but she extended it to five. However, she returned promising it should never happen again. It was all due to Al and she now thought that, instead of leaving the Army, he would sign on again and get sent abroad. If we would just be patient. . .

She was obviously having a difficult time with Al and, as we were very fond of her and she seemed fond of us, we decided to hope for the best and also make life as cheerful as possible for her. We bought a good television set and housed it in the comfortable kitchen; this pleased her so much that she swore that, whether or not Al stayed in the Army, she would remain with us till mid-spring. We rarely watched television ourselves, preferring to read; most evenings Alec read to me.

In mid-November John van Druten asked us to drive to New Haven where his latest play, *I've Got Sixpence*, was to have its out-of-town opening. Shortly before I'd left for England, he had telephoned from New York saying he was arranging for an autumn production, would send the script and then come down to discuss it. And he would only tell me it was 'a religious play'.

Both Chris and Alec had long ago warned me that John, who was possessive about religion, would eventually plagiarise *Esmeralda and The Cloth*. Alec now said, 'Here it comes.' It didn't, quite. The setting was New York, the story was both tough and sentimental and, in parts, unpleasant. The characters were in no way like mine. But there was a great deal about prayer and mysticism, as in *Esmeralda*, and I was quite sure John would not have written it if he had not read, and studied, my play.

Well, there was no point in telling him so now. But Alec, who was furious, did say to him, 'Don't you think your play will affect Dodie's chances of a New York production of *Esmeralda*?' (Which Monica McCall still hoped to arrange.) John said, 'Yes, if mine fails.' I felt sure it would.

What annoyed me most was his guiltily defensive attitude during the few hours he spent with us. He kept assuring me that the production was *fixed* (it wasn't) and he couldn't now change anything and didn't want advice. I offered none and managed to find a few things to praise. We came nowhere near to quarrelling and we had exchanged a few letters while I had been in England. And now, when we set off for New Haven to see *I've Got Sixpence* I felt no ill will. We had a friendly lunch with him before the matinée.

The show was far, far worse than I expected. It was badly cast, the scenery was hideous, John's skill as a director seemed to have deserted him. The audience was obviously bored – there was a woman behind us who actually groaned with boredom. I think the trouble was that, after many managements had refused the script, Starke and Gertrude Macy (who had presented *I Am A Camera*) had got the financial backing together and there had been no experienced management to give advice; but the basic trouble was the play itself.

I always feel that on first nights God gives me a dispensation from telling the truth and both Alec and I pulled our punches. I gathered most people hadn't and John was desperately worried. He asked my advice about several things, but took no notice of it and soon asked us to go as he wanted to do some work – metaphysical work. He had a new technique for getting in touch with God. He simply dipped into various devotional books in the hope of getting some hint. (It seemed a bit like picking a race horse with a pin.) At the moment his main problem was whether or not the leading man should be given a new suit and I did so long to know what answer God obliged with.

When the play opened in New York the reviews were utterly disastrous and I rang John with genuine sympathy. He seemed grateful and I took it that we were on our old affectionate terms. But we were not, judging by the coldness of his few letters, and I never knew why. Perhaps he blamed me for writing a religious play which caused him to write one, which was a failure, or perhaps I had shown more resentment than I meant to and he suspected me of ill-wishing him – he was a firm believer that ill-wishing could have an effect. Anyway, it was a long, long time before we were really friendly again.

We gave Esther four days off for Christmas. She stayed away two weeks without even telephoning. Then her brother rang up, said she had been ill and would be back next day. We doubted the illness and on her return told her we thought she'd better leave. She begged to stay on and, with the dogs milling about her ecstatically and we almost as pleased to see her, we said we'd try again.

During her absence we had spent so much time in the kitchen that we had got quite fond of television. Alec liked the ice-hockey and the boxing and I took a nostalgic pleasure in old English films, full of people I knew. We were watching one of these very late on a bitterly cold night when I saw, pressed close to the glass of one of the windows just behind the television, the face of a pretty cat. Thinking it a stray we took out milk and meat. It dashed off on sight of us, then returned and fed; then disappeared into the night.

The next day it came again and brought a friend and a few days later there were three. By the time Esther was back we were feeding five. She was delighted to help with the feeding. The dogs took no notice of cats' faces against the dark window, perhaps taking them for part of the television. They really were very puzzling, seeming too sleek for stray cats, but too wild to be neighbours' cats. Little did we realise what trouble they were going to give us.

With Esther safely back we were able, in January, to go to New York to meet Binkie, there on a visit. He lunched with us and we spent a happy afternoon together, but he was making no headway in casting *I Capture The Castle* and was still insisting on having a star. We told him we planned to return in the spring and he said he was already on the lookout for a new country home. As well as needing electricity, he needed more than the one bathroom there was at The Barretts. As always, we found him wonderfully good company.

Soon after this we had at Wilton a far worse ice-storm than we had been treated to in Pennsylvania. All the power lines were down and we were without light or heat for five days, our central heating being electrically controlled. We were also short of water as it was pumped electrically and we only had what there was in the cistern. We could have no baths and only flushed the lavatories once a day. Luckily we could still cook as we used bottled gas and we had plenty of logs for our three open fireplaces. Our most difficult problem was keeping Alec's tropical fish alive. We managed this by placing hot-water-bottles all along the tank sides and holding them in position with blankets and cushions. We didn't have one casualty.

As Alec had to spend so much of the day splitting wood and carrying it in, I took over the night stoking of the fires essential to keep the temperature bearable. I rather enjoyed this, going round the house with a lighted candle and sitting for a while by each fire feeling the bitter cold pressing against our double windows. I particularly liked my bedroom fire which took me back to my London bed-sitting room days; never since then had I achieved a fire in my bedroom. It was one luxury money had deprived me of.

We were without gramophone, radio or television – except for the wild cats' simulated television at the kitchen window (now there were seven). We lured them into the house by putting their food in the laundry but none of us – Esther tried as patiently as we did – could ever get near them.

Esther had been at her most lovable during those five gruelling days; but soon after life became normal again there was a telephone call for her just as she was serving dinner. She returned from answering it to say she must at once leave for Philadelphia – she had already telephoned for a taxi. Her husband, Al, now out of the Army (the first we had heard about this) had just removed her refrigerator to his mother's and, according to the friend who had telephoned, was now planning to break up Esther's house. 'He'll steal every stick of my furniture if I don't stop him,' said Esther, dashing into her bedroom in a wild rush to catch her train. We could only beg her to telephone us next day, which she did, saying she must now leave us and would come back to pack her clothes. Her quite horrible young husband (much younger than she was) came with her; perhaps he thought we would try to keep her. We knew she had never been happy with Al, but there was nothing we could do to help. I remembered the woman at the employment agency in Beverly Hills telling me how much she liked the coloured women she found work for and how badly they were treated by their men who, made to feel inferior by white America, so often tried to compensate by ill-treatment of their women. Too true, alas.

Two days after Esther finally left (we never heard from her again) she was replaced by Pearl Burghardt, white and white haired; an elderly widow who weighed over two hundred pounds, though she ate very little. We were to remain in touch with her until she died, around twenty years later. I think of her, and our lamented Esther, as my favourite American women and very thankful I was to have Pearl during the next months, which were to prove quite hellishly difficult.

Early in March Alec developed a bad chill on the base of his spine after a long session on the ice-cold leather seat of the De Soto while trying vainly to get it started. He carried on for some days without telling me. Then I realised he was in great pain and I suggested sending for a doctor. When he finally agreed I knew that the pain must be considerable as, though he didn't share my rather vague belief in Christian Science, he was almost as averse to consulting doctors as I was. The only time he had been to one during our many years in America was when he broke a toe on Malibu rocks. (The doctor there said it was not broken; it was our *dentist* who X-rayed it and said that it was.) And my own doctorless record went back nearly twenty years.

Apart from our general anti-doctor attitude, we were convinced that American doctors rushed one into expensive nursing homes, removed any organ that could be spared and never relinquished their hold over one. So we now awaited our local doctor with some terror.

He proved to be a particularly pleasant, reasonable man (never, actually, have I met a doctor I didn't like) whose first suggestion was that a board should be put under Alec's mattress. This took some getting used to but, at first, did help a little and the doctor said time and rest would soon work a cure. The only trouble was that the pain got worse and worse and pain-killers, which Alec particularly disliked taking, did little to help.

The one bright side was that I enjoyed the doctor's visits and I think he enjoyed them, too. He said it was a pleasure to come into a house where husband and wife were on such good terms with each other. He visited many luxurious houses where the atmosphere was thick with hatred, and there was nothing he could do to help. He was sympathetic towards my Christian Science and a believer in psychosomatic illness, but assured me there was nothing psychosomatic about Alec's; he was simply suffering from the after effects of a badly frozen coccyx. And anyway, it was on the mend and he must now come down for meals and move about the house.

Alec dutifully tried all this but felt worse and worse. He lay flat on his bed until lunchtime; after lunch he lay flat on his bed until dinner and after dinner he lay flat on a mattress on the kitchen floor watching television. He could rarely go out of doors. Luckily the dogs were now too old to need long walks. They would follow me round the pond several times a day, but what they really liked was to lie on a second mattress on the kitchen floor beside Alec. They really enjoyed his illness.

My anxiety was increased by a change in his personality because of the pain: he had become withdrawn. There was none of the normal easy give-and-take of our life and what I gradually realised was that what he wanted most was to be left alone – except for the dogs. There seemed little I could do beyond seeing that the food he generally liked was offered to him (he had very little appetite) and supply him with plenty to read. We had a complete file of the literary English magazine, Horizon, which he re-read almost solidly. Just before he became ill we had begun plans for our return to England. He now said he could not face thinking about it until he was better and so definite was he about this that I began to wonder if his illness was due to some conscious, or subconscious, unwillingness to leave America. But when well, he had not only been eager to return but had said it was, from a financial point of view, essential.

In the afternoons I brought my Journal up-to-date. During my four months in England I had kept an expenses notebook which was virtually a diary and, instead of writing a long summing-up I tried to reconstruct my life day by day, avoiding writing with hindsight. I came to see that I was myself largely responsible for the failure of *Letter From Paris*, through not being resident in England. I ought to have *known* that Oliver Messel was not the right scene-designer, that Peter Glenville was not the right director and that some of the casting would be fatal. I finished off with what must have been some churned up optimism.

> And now the spring is here, with lilac, dogwood, violets, windflowers and dazzling woods (also biting flies). Alec at last seems to be getting better. The dogs are well. As always, there are many things to be thankful for. Sometimes I weep with despair and feel that life is finished – and sometimes I find it hard to believe that a woman of my age can feel so young, so hopeful.

I had taken to reading much poetry, with more pleasure than since my youth. Soon I began memorising it, first half-a-dozen poems by Gerard Manley Hopkins. Then I tackled the formidable job of learning Eliot's *Four Quartets* by heart. They have become my nearest approach to a religion. My so-called Christian Science is not a religion, more a kind of philosophy which has little to do with Christianity which I can accept less and less, even in the *Four Quartets*. To me, the mystical experience transcends all religions. I then worked on Dylan Thomas and found him most difficult to memorise, but I did manage over half-a-dozen poems including 'Altarwise by Owl-light', which I understand only in some region of the mind which has nothing to do with common sense. Of all Thomas's poems I like best 'In the White Giant's Thigh'.

I used to practise my repertoire during long lonely walks taken at sunset, while Alec (on his back) and our companionable help, Pearl Burghardt, watched television. (They loved the baseball and the boxing; I didn't.) I rarely saw a car and don't remember ever seeing a pedestrian. I have a vivid memory of declaiming poems to lilac hedges, somehow distilling happiness from a pretty unhappy time.

Our lease of the house was due to finish in the middle of June, but I arranged for us to continue on a monthly basis. Alec, though still in some pain, felt that our return to England was a necessity, so I allowed myself to think that was settled – except for fearing something would prevent it. And almost at once it was threatened.

Charlie Brackett telephoned from Hollywood asking me to do a screenplay. I longed to refuse out of hand, but had I the right to? The job would mean months of work at $2,000 a week, we could save a large sum, postpone quarantine for the dogs. And suppose Alec went on being ill? Anyway, it would have been discourteous to refuse even to read the book Charlie wanted me to adapt. I waited for it despairingly.

Some days later I was sitting by my bedroom window, where I always sat when reading poetry or vainly trying to meditate. I was thinking about Charlie's job (the book had not yet arrived) and I suddenly felt it was up to me to choose *now* whether or not I did it. This choice must not depend on whether I liked the book; I must decide if, however strong the reasons in favour, I had to force myself to stay in America. And I thought, 'I can't and I won't.' And, most fantastic memory, I recalled the time when, as a tiny child, I decided not to drink the hated orange juice which was pressed on me daily. I simply pushed the glass out of my mother's hand – and wondered why I had never done so before. No more orange juice was ever pressed on me.

I had the most vivid mental picture of the delicately cut glass which my mother had thought would appeal to me. I saw it fall – and in that instant I pushed Charlie's job away. *I would not do it.*

The next morning Charlie rang up to say the Studio had now turned against the project. I assured him I was relieved. And I was even more relieved when the book then arrived and I found it was a tear-jerker about mother love (possibly my least favourite subject) but I could, most unwillingly, have adapted it. As things were, that glass of orange juice had been whisked away without my having to push it. (But had it? Had I not somehow pushed the job away mentally?)

Charlie hoped soon to set up another job for me; but by now Alec, who loathed the book, was better and he was against my writing for the movies again. His final recovery had taken place in mid-June when, as pain still lingered, our local doctor sent him to a New York specialist who, after making various tests, said that there was now nothing wrong with his spine except perhaps 'residual pain' (whatever that might mean) and Alec had better set about forgetting it which, no doubt helped by the hot weather, he did. Within a few days he was his normal self, engrossed in plans for our return to England.

From now on these fully occupied us and the only damper on our spirits was the thought of quarantine for the dogs. But I had come to believe it might be better for them in the end. Alec's illness had made me realise how vulnerable they – and we – might be in an emergency. In England we still had many friends who would help. Pongo's wonderful English vet now began hunting for the best possible quarantine kennels.

We should need a new car – the Rolls was hardly suitable as a run-about in present-day England, also it would now need overhauling after its fifteen trouble-free years in America. We could buy a small English estate car paid for with American dollars as that would rank as an export. But Alec's correspondence with Nuffield Exports, amounting to fifty-one pages, went on so long that I christened them 'Nuffink Exports' – and at the last minute we were told that the car wouldn't be ready for us when we arrived.

We had to arrange for somewhere to live until the dogs came out of quarantine; there were no suitable kennels near the cottage. Binkie now said he wanted to buy it, but we longed to have it back, Alec even more than I did, so we could only offer him another six months to find somewhere else, during which we would live in London. Murray Macdonald offered to let us rent his Chelsea house in Cheltenham Terrace, with the services of his housekeeper. By means of letters we were now as friendly as ever. In the theatre world one constantly makes friendships that don't last. Murray was to be a permanent friend.

We had to decide which of our American acquisitions to take, and what we needed to buy new; there were still so many shortages in England. Many of the things we left behind were auctioned after we left for disappointing prices. The only pleasant surprise were the high prices paid for the three much-gnawed, if seldom used, dog-beds.

I look back on those summer months with pleasure. Planning, shopping, writing innumerable letters – always with the goal of England ahead of us. If only the dogs hadn't to face six months' quarantine! And we had a more immediate animal anxiety: what could we do about the cats?

We were now keeping open house – that is, open back-porch – to ten and in high summer I saw one of the prettiest climb the stone wall which separated our front garden (to which the dogs had no access) from the adjacent wood. She had a kitten in her mouth and, having put it down, went back for five more. They followed her to the back door where they all waited for food which Pearl Burghardt instantly offered, and when the kittens drew back from ice-cold milk she warmed it. From then on all cats and all kittens showed they preferred warm milk; and they had tinned meat too. They no longer came only at night. Dear Pearl could be seen carefully moving her two hundred pounds of weight between them pretty well non-stop.

When the kittens were about six weeks old I advertised in a local paper and got homes for them all. With difficulty we captured them, delivered them and the day the last one went seven more were brought over the stone wall. As Dorothy Parker said about Thurber's dogs, reason tottered.

I had, during my many long evening walks, discovered that some of the cats did have homes, most of them on farms as mousers, which meant they were given little food. But at least four, including the mothers of the kittens, were living wild. One neighbour, a schoolmistress, assured me I need not worry as all cats could live off the land. I pointed out this meant destruction of birds. She said sweetly, as if addressing a small child, 'Oh, they don't eat the birds – just the nasty mice.'

Only one tom ever visited us; he was grey, elderly, lame and bad-tempered. If you patted him, he hit you back. One day Alec buffetted him in return, which enchanted him. After that he took to howling at the front door until Alec came out to him – saying, like Dr Johnson, 'I'll have a frisk with you.' And they would then sit on the front lawn buffetting each other contentedly.

Not long before we were due to leave I tracked Sore Paw (so called by us) to his rightful home and called on his owners, who were charming. They said they'd be only too glad if he spent more time at home. I knew old Sore Paw (his lameness was due to an ancient injury) would miss Alec, but never go short of food, and only wished I could be as happy about the other cats and kittens (I wasn't able to get any more kitten-adopters). Well, perhaps cats *could* live off the land, but for many months I harrowed myself by the thought of all the hunger on our back porch which, for so long, had been a super cats' restaurant.

I find it extraordinary that so many animals made claims on us during our American years: the stranded baby sealion at Carmel, the film star's Great Dane in Beverly Hills, the dog with a fish-hook in its mouth at Malibu, the cat up a tree rescued by Alec at considerable risk, my Karma cat, the lame opossum down a hole, the stray canary Charlie gave a home to and the cat he took off our hands, my bat at Las Tunas; and lastly the Connecticut cats.

Actually, fate still had one more animal problem to face us with, but that was over one of our own animals. In mid-September, five days before we were to sail, our liver-spotted Dalmatian, Buzz, had a complete stoppage of his waterworks. Our local vet said this was due to gravel and he hoped to disperse it quickly. So for three wretched days Buzz was given treatment, and drugs to ease his pain. Then the vet said only an instant operation could save our much-loved dog's life and the operation would need to be done by a very well-known vet who lived sixty miles away on Long Island. Alec hurriedly drove off with Buzz (crashing an open door of the De Soto, already sold, against the garage door; the only accident he'd had in over twenty years of driving) and I settled down at the telephone to send cables cancelling our return to England. In all, there were twenty-two cables.

And all the time I felt sure Buzz would die. I had said my goodbye to him that morning when, drugged though he was, he had managed to climb on my bed as usual. Of all the dogs we have ever had, he was the one who loved me best.

The operation was a success, but we were told we mustn't see Buzz for five days. Then, only a couple of days later, we were rung up and told to bring tempting food as Buzz was refusing to eat. We found him pitifully weak and miserable and, though pleased to see us, he still wouldn't eat. However, after a long sleep leaning against Alec, who sat in his pen, he did accept a little tinned chicken. We suggested we should take him home as he was obviously fretting, but were told he must stay another eight days. Next day we spent two hours with him, taking turns to sit in his pen and feed him; and during that time we realised that, though it was a handsome dogs' hospital, and the operation no doubt was expert, the after-care was deadly. The kennel man said he'd no time to coax dogs and all the food we'd left had got lost. Next day we again made the sixty mile journey prepared to bring Buzz back by force, if necessary. It wasn't; the vet had changed his mind. Our poor dog, still too weak to stand, had been given a scented shampoo and we had to wait while his nails were clipped so that he could go out looking a credit to the hospital.

I lay with him on his mattress at the back of the car. He slept peacefully and as soon as he got home he became a different creature. We planned to protect him from the welcome of the other two dogs but he ran, though tottering, towards them. And when Alec gave them their dinner he got into line and ate a full meal.

From seeming to be at death's door, he sprang into seeming almost normal.

But we had to be careful he didn't bite out any more stitches; he had pulled out two while in hospital. So we dared not leave him alone and took it in turns to sit up at night with him. But at last our local vet said we could again plan our departure so again we managed to book a new passage and I despatched innumerable cables. I had a superstitious fear that something would yet frustrate us, but we did at last, on September 30th, 1953, drive off into a glorious autumn morning, leaving Pearl Burghardt to give the cats a last slap-up meal. She had a job waiting for her, but had refused to go to it until after we left. Leaving Pearl was a lasting sadness.

All the way to New York I expected some accident, but fate had stopped fighting me; all went smoothly. On the dock the De Soto was taken away by its purchaser. I gave it a farewell pat. Its stubbornness in refusing to start when cold had been the original cause of Alec's illness, but it had been a comfortable car and the dogs loved it. They behaved surprisingly well when we settled them into the Queen Elizabeth's kennels; perhaps, after all, they wouldn't terribly mind the six-months quarantine. Fond hope! If only they, and we, could have known then that they had happy English years ahead of them in our Essex cottage.

We made sure the Rolls was safely hoisted aboard and then went down to lunch. Alec said his was the best steak he had had for fifteen years.

I have one vivid memory of our last glimpse of the New York skyline, framed in the circle of a porthole. I thought it beautiful . . . and yet I hoped I was seeing it for the last time. I then accused myself of ingratitude; I had so much to thank America for: comfort, much money earned, a vastly enlarged horizon, a knowledge of literature and music which might never have come my way except as consolations for exile, three great friendships with Christopher Isherwood, Charles Brackett and John van Druten. And our dogs were Americans. Yes, I *was* grateful, deeply grateful. But as that perfectly composed picture of New York slid away from the porthole, I knew that the really overwhelming gratitude I was feeling was because I was now on my way home to England, not just on my own for a visit, but with Alec and the dogs and – please God – forever.

Appendix

(A type-written letter to H.B. Marriott Watson from Henry James, given to Dodie Smith by Christopher Isherwood.)

Lamb House,
Rye.
26th August, 1898

Dear Marriott Watson,

Forgive my taking this means, to which I am now constantly reduced, to achieve celerity, in answer to your letter, as well as to express sympathy and enthusiasm. I shall be very happy indeed to do anything I can to help poor Wells, whom I do not know, and whom I haven't even read, but of whose being ill at New Romney, I had happened so mystifyingly to hear that, no longer ago than yesterday, I asked about him there, at the Inn, where I stopped for tea as the reward of a bicycle ride. They were blank, and could give me no news, so that I am cursing myself this morning for not having got your letter a day sooner. However, I shall communicate with him immediately, now that I have from you his address, and will as soon thereafter as possible ride over to see him – if he be able to see one. Meanwhile I will go into the matter of some house for him here – as to which I can immediately put him in relation with a very good and obliging agent. The difficulty won't be in the agent, but in the paucity of houses in so small and simple a place, and in the fact that at present moment – the height of the little Rye golfing and sketching season – almost everything has, I fear, been taken up. But that may change from week to week. At any rate, I am so infatuated with the dear little red-roofed place myself, that anything I can invent to justify to Wells the recommendation made of it shall not be wanting. And I will, with pleasure, let you hear directly of any issue of the business. Please be sure, meanwhile, that I am delighted you have spoken to me. I should like awfully, after a temporary fever of complicated and not always consciously incurred hospitalities has subsided for me, to get you down here for a day, very deliberately and plottingly. We will talk of that a little later.

Your letter drops into a cloud of coincidences, for I am in the very act of sending you "In the Cage." I am very glad you have heard any good of it – but it is, really, and not in the least as one of the fine phrases of blushing authorship, a most unconsidered trifle. I think of you – all three – with a good deal of vividness, such a summer, in your great garden; but I am literally arriving at the point, in my own very small one, of playing with the fancy that I needn't envy you. To be continued. Yours and your wife's always

[Signed] HENRY JAMES

(A hand-written letter to Mrs H. B. Marriott Watson from Henry James, given to Dodie Smith by Christopher Isherwood.)

Lamb House,
Rye, Sussex

Dear Mrs Marriott Watson,

I returned to this place just after last hearing from you, & an irresistible immersion in many local cares & "domestic problems" have delayed my expression to you both, to you all three, of my great regret at having missed you at Chiswick, & by so little alas – and my sorrow is the greater because, restored to this hermitage, on urgent refuge from the London hurly-burly of May-July, I frankly fear that the possibility of a visit to you at Shere may not prove a very manageable matter. Experience has in general taught me to be sceptical of projected pilgrimages – across the bristling dragons of Town – from county to county. I shall have to build on Chiswick again & I shall pray to be able to do so more firmly. Meantime your book of verses is very charming & touching to me. I have an extreme taste for your grey-veiled muse who slips by with bent head & an almost soundless step; she is full of grace, sadness & discretion as muses should be, & twitches the hem of her dusky crape-like garments away, with so white a hand, when one would most seize it. She is like a friend singing in another room.

Goodnight to both of you! I have stupidly, in my migration, mislaid your letter, & must send this to H. Cottage.

Yours most truly,
[Signed] HENRY JAMES.
May 4. '04.

(A letter from Christopher Isherwood to Dodie Smith about her novel, *I Capture the Castle*.)

333, East Rustic Road,
Santa Monica,
California.
26th October [1948.]

Dearest Dodie,

Thank you so much for "I Capture the Castle". I have now read it right through, carefully, not skipping. It's true that I looked at the end first, just as you feared, but I wasn't any wiser for doing so. To say – "I couldn't put it down" is hardly original, but true. I went on and on and kept pleasantly grinning to myself and occasionally laughing out loud. Your tremendous strength is *detail*. It is like really good carving; the more you look at it, the more you see. No wonder it took such a time to do! The obvious objection – that it isn't "about" anything – doesn't hold up at all and I don't think you can have been quite sincere when you raised it. It is full of meanings, but under the surface, not rammed into the reader's face. I suppose you knew I would like the religious part? I think you spoke of it, once. Well – I did. But what really charmed me and moved me most was when they lock up their father in the tower. That's terrific – and somehow only you could have thought of it. I had an uneasy feeling that *I* only just escaped being locked up somewhere, and the barking of your dogs and the roar of the waves would have drowned my yells! Also "Jacob Wrestling" and the "work in progress" are two of the really convincing books in all literature. I know *exactly* what "Jacob Wrestling" was like. I would never have read it right through, but my idea of it would have influenced me a great deal. I'm glad Rose got Neil in the end. I liked him much better than Simon. I hope Cassandra didn't finally marry him? I kept hoping C. would finally take Stephen – but maybe he was a bore, really. I had an awful feeling, right at the end, that he would turn out like Stewart Grainger (spelling uncertain – but you know who I mean?)

I do wonder what the critics will make of it? It is so beautifully written, so worked over, that you even sometimes smile at the artful punctuation – but you say *nothing* about the Atomic Bomb, or the Negro Question, or Israel. At least, nothing directly; by implication you talk about nearly everything.

And how one knows the castle! Did you draw plans? The illustrations are charming. I particularly liked the big kitchen; it reminds me of the Cruickshanks in *"The Tower of London"*.

I think it is a book that will be very much lived in by many people; because you can live inside it, like Dickens.

The funny thing is, how you use your experience of America. I can't imagine the book being written by anyone who didn't know America – which you always said you didn't – deeply. Every little touch of that is very telling, and *right*. Simon and Neil *had* to be American, and you do that beautifully, without the least exaggeration.

No, Dodie, I don't agree with you at all: all the disparaging things you said about it. Can you have meant them all? And I refuse to compare it with Jane Austen – let alone "The Constant Nymph". Austen is *sordid* and bores me, and the Nymph is bogus. Oddly enough, the only part I didn't care for was the London part. I wonder why? It didn't seem to ring so true.

Here, we live in a daze of house-work. Mostly Bill's. He paints and cooks and carpenters like a demon. I have finished with Dostoevsky (and he with me, I'm sure, if we ever meet in heaven) and am now busy on the travel book. The house is very nice, except that the bridge over the creek – our only access – is about to fall down, and then the waterpipe will break with it. . . Well, well – the deluge won't be après nous.

Did I tell you how much I enjoyed "At Mrs Lippincote's"? The other one ["Palladian", also by Elizabeth Taylor – we had sent them for Chris's birthday] I haven't yet read.

Oh, how I wish you were both here! I miss you bitterly, and now we could invite you – because this house really is roomy and would even accommodate dogs. If one could talk – as in the old days. . . There is nobody now. But I talk to you in my mind, all the time. There is so much to tell you, which would be meaningless in a letter. But I know you are happier where you are, and certainly the beach was never more hideous. But I don't know what it is about this place. I love it, and nearly wept when I returned. And the Canyon is still the Canyon.

All my love to you and to Alec,
as always your loving
CHRIS.